SAGE was founded in 1965 by Sara Miller McCune to support the dissemination of usable knowledge by publishing innovative and high-quality research and teaching content. Today, we publish over 900 journals, including those of more than 400 learned societies, more than 800 new books per year, and a growing range of library products including archives, data, case studies, reports, and video. SAGE remains majority-owned by our founder, and after Sara's lifetime will become owned by a charitable trust that secures our continued independence.

Los Angeles | London | New Delhi | Singapore | Washington DC | Melbourne

Advance Praise

'Sports, like music, has the power to break barriers, to unite, to build, to inspire, to go where nobody has gone before. Madhavi Latha's life is a testimony to this and more.

A national para swimming champion empowering sports-persons across the spectrum, Madhavi's legacy is one of strength, grace and perseverance. As founding general secretary of Tamil Nadu's Paralympic Swimming Association, Madhavi has introduced more than 300 individuals with disabilities to swimming—people who've gone on to compete at both the national and international levels. She has even co-founded the Wheelchair Basketball Federation of India (WBFI). Recently, both the Indian men and women's teams from WBFI participated in the Asia Oceania Zone Championships and the Tokyo 2020 Paralympics Qualifiers, levelling the bar for sportspersons across the globe. Madhavi also leads the WBFI's mentorship programme which enables basketball players with disabilities to realize their dreams and ambitions beyond the court. More power to you, Madhavi!'

A. R. Rahman,
Grammy and Academy Award Winning Indian Musician

'Pleasant, positive, passionate and persevering are inadequate to describe Madhavi Latha's unique personality. Her continuing saga of high achievement, despite all odds, is a shining example of determination and dedication towards any cause she takes up, be it in sports or her professional work in the corporate world. While she continues her selfless journey of encouraging and inspiring more people, we must remember and offer our salutations to her fine family, who have helped in her progress. Madhavi Latha has indeed shown the world that true sincerity of purpose and ability count, always. Long may it continue.'

M. M. Murugappan,
Executive Chairman, Murugappa Group

'Madhavi's story is one of perseverance, commitment to a spirit of service and unshakable confidence in her own potential and that of people with physical disabilities across India. Throughout her life, she has defied the odds and the expectations of her society while ensuring that others who face similar obstacles have the opportunity to do the same. Her endeavours in disability sport shine a light on how each of us can find pathways to success, no matter what barriers stand in our way.'

Jess Markt, Disability Sport and Inclusion Advisor,
International Committee of the Red Cross (ICRC)
Boulder, USA

'During my long years of association with Madhavi, I found her to be an exemplary leader—inspirational, encouraging, educative and purposeful. This book, which is a treasure trove of Madhavi's life learnings, is an inspiration for all of us to chase our cherished dreams by focusing on the art of the possible, or should I say, impossible! It is also a loud reminder that infirmities are only in our mind and we should never short human imagination and willpower. Truly unputdownable!'

Ramkumar Ramamoorthy,
Pro Vice-chancellor, Krea University;
former CMD, Cognizant India

'Madhavi Latha's story is one of great courage and an inspiring lesson for many. Having had the privilege of knowing her for many years, I have been fortunate to have seen her determination and great optimism in the face of overwhelming odds. An enthusiasm and zest for life itself and all that it offers has been the feature of all that she is doing, whether it be swimming, wheelchair basketball or indeed all her other efforts to help the persons with disabilities. This book will be a lesson for us on how adversity can be overcome and on how no mountain is too difficult to climb.'

Dr Sumanth C. Raman, *Sports Commentator, TV Anchor and Doctor*

SWIMMING
AGAINST THE TIDE

SWIMMING AGAINST THE TIDE

True Story of Para Swimmer Madhavi Latha

MADHAVI LATHA PRATHIGUDUPU

Los Angeles | London | New Delhi
Singapore | Washington DC | Melbourne

Copyright © Madhavi Latha Prathigudupu, 2021

All rights reserved. No part of this book may be reproduced or utilized in any form or by any means, electronic or mechanical, including photocopying, recording, or by any information storage or retrieval system, without permission in writing from the publisher.

First published in 2021 by

SAGE Publications India Pvt Ltd
B1/I-1 Mohan Cooperative Industrial Area
Mathura Road, New Delhi 110 044, India
www.sagepub.in

SAGE Publications Inc
2455 Teller Road
Thousand Oaks, California 91320, USA

SAGE Publications Ltd
1 Oliver's Yard, 55 City Road
London EC1Y 1SP, United Kingdom

SAGE Publications Asia-Pacific Pte Ltd
18 Cross Street #10-10/11/12
China Square Central
Singapore 048423

Published by Vivek Mehra for SAGE Publications India Pvt Ltd. Typeset in 11/14.5pt Arno Pro by Fidus Design Pvt Ltd, Chandigarh.

Library of Congress Control Number: 2021942189

ISBN: 978-93-91370-52-7 (PB)

SAGE Team: Manisha Mathews, Neena Ganjoo and Rajinder Kaur

Dear Amma and Nanna,
you helped me build an audacious dream, you inspired me to challenge the status quo and you empowered me to go beyond. This book is a result of your love and belief in me. Thank you for everything!

Thank you for choosing a SAGE product!
If you have any comment, observation or feedback,
I would like to personally hear from you.

Please write to me at **contactceo@sagepub.in**

Vivek Mehra, Managing Director and CEO, SAGE India.

Bulk Sales

SAGE India offers special discounts
for purchase of books in bulk.
We also make available special imprints
and excerpts from our books on demand.

For orders and enquiries, write to us at

Marketing Department
SAGE Publications India Pvt Ltd
B1/I-1, Mohan Cooperative Industrial Area
Mathura Road, Post Bag 7
New Delhi 110044, India

E-mail us at **marketing@sagepub.in**

Subscribe to our mailing list
Write to **marketing@sagepub.in**

This book is also available as an e-book.

Contents

Foreword by Viswanathan Anand — ix
Acknowledgements — xi
Prologue — xv

1. The Bundle of Joy and the Blow — 1
2. The Short-lived Hope — 7
3. My Strength: My Family — 15
4. Schooling Life — 37
5. And I Graduated! — 43
6. My Love for Water — 53
7. Small Deeds, Big Lessons — 59
8. Finding a Job Was a Tough Job — 63
9. Banking on My Abilities — 74
10. My Stint with the Bank at My Native Place — 80
11. Prejudice and Pride — 90
12. Lessons Learnt in the Training Period — 95
13. The Hardships in Finding a Rented House — 101
14. The Dream Posting — 104
15. The Struggle to Gain Ownership — 118
16. Holy Places: Obstacles to Access — 124

17	Moving Out of My Comfort Zone	128
18	New City, New Experiences	134
19	A Rude Shock: 365 Days to Live!	141
20	The Lifeline	145
21	Finding Work–Life Balance, Literally!	156
22	The Discovery of an Unknown Talent	165
23	The Dawning of 'Yes, We Too Can!!!'	167
24	The Ventures That Struck Gold: Becoming a National Champion	178
25	The Journey from a Participant to a Host	187
26	Happiness Makes Life Blossom	195
27	Paving the Way for Future Champions	199
28	Year 2013: Can You Play Basketball on a Wheelchair?	208
29	Year 2014: As the Wheels of Change Turned	221
30	Year 2015: Growing My Network, Learning the Ropes from Experts and Chennai Floods	235
31	Year 2016: Honouring of My Mother	253
32	Year 2017: Making History on the Global Stage	268
33	Year 2018: Making India's Voice Heard at the International Level	285
34	Year 2019: The Year of Many Firsts	299
35	Year 2020: Adapting to the New Normal	325

About the Author — 332

Foreword

A champion is someone who puts aside their personal obstacles and strives for excellence. I have always believed that many battles are won in our minds. When we think of ourselves as true champions, we are able to make ourselves to persevere harder. These words resonate highest when I read and learnt about the story of an amazing athlete, Madhavi Latha Prathigudupu.

She has overcome so much trauma, both mentally and physically, to actually climb higher, rather than weigh down. Her achievements and focus are valuable life lessons for all of us who find ourselves finding answers to our everyday life and its routines. In many ways the power is within you and you are the solution and the problem. So choosing which person you want to be can be the difference.

In the story of Madhavi Latha, we see how she trained herself to be a champion swimmer. The moment she chose to excel rather than crumble is definitely the high point of the book.

The story of how a family environment is important in making its members feel loved and cherished is most heartening.

From being just an achiever to an enabler is a very big step. Not all sportspersons make this change easily. In Madhavi's case, she sees it almost as an organic step in her own journey.

The book is truly inspiring with a lot of heartfelt moments. I am sure that a book like this will help motivate people to excel in both sports and life.

Viswanathan Anand
Five-time World Chess Champion

Acknowledgements

Before commencing my acknowledgements, I want to quote the famous words of our great *vaggeyakara* (poet-composer) in Carnatic music Sri Thyagaraja Swamy. He said, '*Endaro Mahanubhavulu, andariki vandanamulu*' (so many great souls, regards to all of them). I too nurture the same feeling.

When I first began to write my autobiography, I didn't realize that it would be a lot more than my own story. By the time I completed it, I understood how people influence our lives throughout. Some people give us a pat on the back and some criticize our actions. While the former make us feel motivated, the latter make us mentally strong and drive us to successfully accomplish our goals.

In this way, most of our acquaintances will have an influence and purpose in furthering our life's journey. If our moral values are strong, these acquaintances will inspire us to work for the betterment of our society.

Writing my autobiography has given me the opportunity to remember such people and express my gratitude to them.

As a child, I was an avid reader. Seeing my passion for reading, my father expected that I would become a writer later in life. Today, by penning this autobiography, I have got an opportunity to fulfil his dream.

I thank all my family members who have constantly persuaded me to write this book and for the encouragement they extended in this effort. I never expected I could write a book, that too in English!

I could complete writing the manuscript just within two months. Besides the professional editor Mr Pranab Jyoti Sarma, who helped to edit it, my family members , namely my dad, sister Mythreyi, niece Pranavi and nephew Sachin, have played a great role in getting it to this shape. My friends Jess Markt and P. Rajasekharan guided me wherever I sought their expert advice. I express my heartfelt thanks to all of them.

In my childhood days, there were not many photos. My siblings Nirmala, Indrajith and Anantham could find a few pictures with a lot of effort. Shanthi V. has drawn a beautiful picture depicting our bullock cart journey at the time of my polio attack. Mr Shashank has drawn my picture in callipers. I thank them wholeheartedly for giving me the opportunity to recollect childhood memories through illustrations.

My heartfelt thanks to Mr Asad Abid, Mr Kedar Sonigra and team 'TheVibe Studios' for taking a nice pic of mine while swimming which was used for cover page. That brought a beautiful look for my book. My special thanks to Mr Anand Daga for taking a classic pic of mine while playing wheelchair basketball for back cover page.

In spite of his hectic schedule, Mr Viswanathan Anand spent his precious time perusing my story and summed up its essence in his stellar foreword. I am very grateful to him for his kind gesture. Also, I would like to thank my dear friend Veeru Murugappan for connecting me with such a legendary player with a great heart.

I would like to express my gratitude to the legendary musician Mr A. R. Rahman for remembering me and for sharing his kind words about my efforts. As promised a few years ago, he is committed to supporting us in spreading the message of the movement 'Yes, We Too Can!!!'

Mr M. M. Murugappan, a tall corporate leader with a busy schedule, always responded positively and with extreme warmth to my short-notice requests for support. My heartfelt thanks to him for being ever-present to accommodate my requests—his caring and friendly words meant a lot to me.

Thanks a million to our well-wishers Jess Markt, Mr Ramkumar and Dr Sumanth C. Raman for their amazing support to my activities and their kind words and best wishes for me to write my experiences.

Thanks a lot to the journalist Mr Steve Goldberg (FIBA Basketball Wheel World columnist) and the authors Mr R. V. Rajan, Mr P. Harimohan, Sundari Sivasubbu and Siddharth Jayakumar for sharing their experiences.

It appears that it is more difficult to prepare a book proposal than writing the book itself. I express my sincere thanks to Rashmi Simon and Saranya Rajagopalan for helping me with this work.

My heartfelt thanks to Colonel Isen Hover, Sharanya Gopinath, Kalyani Rajaraman and Shashaank Awasthi for providing me feedback after going through some chapters of this book.

In these 50 years of my life, I have had so many experiences and well-wishers. Although I could not mention all of them in my book, they are evergreen in my heart. If I unintentionally hurt anyone's feelings in my narration, kindly forgive me.

Although I am a budding writer, SAGE has come forward to publish my book by having great confidence in my story. I am very much grateful to them and to my friend Saundarya Rajesh for connecting me with such reputed publishers. I am grateful to Ms Manisha Mathews, Executive Editor-Commissioning from SAGE, for her amazing support and guidance to me at each and every stage of the book publishing process.

Finally, I would like to thank you, the readers, for picking up my story to read. I earnestly hope that you would enjoy reading my life story comprising unexpected twists and turns. Also, I hope that you would find at least one takeaway from my story which would be useful in your life.

Prologue

Sitting leisurely in our flat's balcony, I have been thinking about the drastic changes COVID19 has brought in our lives. The present generation has never been through this kind of experience, where the entire world is entangled in the clutches of a deadly virus killing an unprecedented number of people. As it is highly contagious, most of the world is following social distancing. People are completely confined to their respective houses to stop—or at least contain—the contagion. I am not able to do my favourite activities such as swimming/aqua yoga and driving. People can go out only for essentials and when they do, wearing a face mask and carrying sanitizers are compulsory.

Generally, my schedule during the pre-COVID era was quite hectic, strewn with multiple activities. Being a former national para swimming champion, I know the benefits that sports bring to a person with disability first-hand. This awareness drove me to take the initiative in founding the 'Yes, We Too Can!!!' movement and forming the Paralympic Swimming Association of Tamil Nadu along with WBFI. But from the time that the COVID-19 was declared a pandemic, all our activities are taking place online. I currently work as an Associate Vice President with an MNC Bank Group, and for the first time in my career, I am working from home.

I give talks at various forums, addressing government and corporate officials, students and educators, NGOs, etc., on topics related to women and disability. Now I receive invites to talk in webinars. In one such talk arranged by Madras Management Association, I was interviewed by a well-wisher, AVIS Viswanathan. After the interview, one of the audiences suggested that I write a book on my experiences to motivate people. Thanks to this person for reminding me at the right time when I have to stay home and take a break from my many outdoor activities in the transition to adjust to the new normal. My siblings and my uncle Jaya Prakasa Raju (JP) had been insisting for a long time that I write a book on my experiences. I had even written a few pages back then but could not keep up due to my hectic schedules. With the time in hand, I was determined to finish what I once started. As I recollected my journey, from where it had begun to where I am today, my mind went back to my childhood days, as if I were on a time machine. I contemplated on how time can make unexpected and unbelievable changes in life.

As a person with disability hailing from a remote village and a family with modest income, I learnt many life lessons through my interactions and in the process of getting in terms with my identity. Through my story, I believe that readers will see life and its challenges through a different lens, and I sincerely hope they will imbibe important messages not only for themselves but also to use those messages to promote an inclusive society.

1

The Bundle of Joy and the Blow

Year 1970: Our family was living in a remote village named Sathupally. It was situated in the outskirts of a dense forest on the highway between Hyderabad and Visakhapatnam—two big cities in the erstwhile composite state of Andhra Pradesh. It was surrounded by minor and medium irrigation reservoirs which provided water to thousands of acres of paddy fields. There were several mango groves in our vicinity, which yielded different varieties of tasty mangoes.

My beloved parents

Politically, our village was well-known in the district owing to its leaders, who worked tirelessly for the upliftment of the region. My father, Mr Pardhasaradhi Raju, worked as a school teacher and my mother, Ms Varalakshmi Devi, is a homemaker. I have four elder siblings, three sisters and a brother.

My mom got married at the age of 16. She first became a mother when she was 18 and gave birth to 4 children by the time she was 24. Being a young mother and with four consecutive deliveries, her primary focus was on nurturing and caring for her children. She could hardly find any leisure time to experience the joys of the motherhood. Although my parents didn't plan to have another child, I was born when my mother was 30. By then, she had gained maturity and knew well to spend some quality time with us, enjoying the pleasures of motherhood.

'I felt immensely happy when I first saw your cute face, bright eyes, nice long fingers and perfectly shaped limbs. I instantly forgot all the resistance and initial dislike to have a new baby. "How beautiful you are, my child!" I said out loudly. Your beauty made me wonder about God's creation of human beings, and I kissed you fondly,' my mom later told me.

She tells me that I was a very active kid in my infancy, and at times, it used to be a true challenge for her to hold me in her arms. My legs were so strong that when she held me to her chest, it was hard for her to withstand my kicks. She thought I would walk at 9 or 10 months of age with those ablest of legs. My siblings were extremely happy to have a little sister and cherished me every bit. Those were the joyful times of our family; everyone treated me like a princess. For my siblings, I was their adored doll to spend time and play with. A cousin of mine used to compete with my eldest sister every day to give me an evening bath. All my siblings loved to carry me in their arms. However, no one can predict the future. At that time, they didn't know that they would need to carry me for so many years of their lives!

My *annaprasana* (feeding rice or solid food for the first time to a child, celebrated on the sixth day of sixth month from the birth) was arranged on a grand scale. My mother, who is an expert in cooking, served many delicious items such as laddus, *payasam* (a sweet dish made with rice, milk and jaggery) and vadas (popular South Indian dishes). Everyone who attended the ceremony praised my mother and blessed me heartily.

After those beautiful initial months, things changed dramatically. A few weeks after the ceremony, I had a severe fever for five days. Medical help was very meagre in our area, and only unqualified traditional medical practitioners were available to provide treatment. My father brought an experienced but unqualified male nurse who ran a clinic in the nearest town, 32 km (~20 mi) away. He lifted my arms and legs, and when he dropped them, they fell down as if they were pieces of cloth. He diagnosed and declared that I was affected by polio. He promised to cure my disease easily if I was taken to his clinic. Unfortunately, there was no bus service at that moment because the drivers had gone on a strike to protest against the horrible condition of the roads. As an alternative, my father managed to arrange a bullock cart, though it was very difficult to travel in it on a metal road with so many potholes. My parents struggled to hold me through the bullock cart jerks due to the damaged road. Finally, after a long journey in the dark, my parents arrived at the clinic at 2:00 am. Our pet dog followed us, walking behind the cart.

The so-called doctor at the clinic gave me half cc penicillin injections twice a day for four days, but with no luck. So my father decided to take me to Guntur (the nearest city) for further treatment. Luckily, the bus strike was called off and we could take the first bus to Guntur. At the time, the Government General Hospital in Guntur was famous for medical treatment. I was admitted as an in-patient, and a notice was fixed to my bed in bold letters, which read 'BULBOSPINAL POLIO–NO INJECTIONS'. It was already too late as I was given many injections by the previous two unqualified medical practitioners in our village and at the clinic. Doctors said that if I were administered a simple paracetamol

Our journey in distress (artist Ms Shanthi V)

syrup in the initial days, my long-term prognosis would have been much better.

My entire body except my left hand was paralysed. I was unable to keep my neck steady, and my cries had no voice. My left abdomen muscles were paralysed; hence, the burden of my stomach shifted to the left side, resulting in scoliosis later in life. Slowly, I regained my voice, steadiness in neck, some movements in my right hand and a little strength in my right leg. But my left leg was still fully paralysed. The senior doctor told my father that it was a miracle to withstand such a massive attack and still be alive.

In poliomyelitis disease, the polio virus causes permanent paralysis. But the main difference between other types of paralysis and polio is that people can feel sensations in the affected parts. It can only be prevented by vaccination but cannot be cured. The disease was a hyper pandemic in India in those days. My parents, who were from a remote village, had little awareness about the impact of polio and the importance of vaccination in preventing it. None of my siblings were vaccinated.

Initially, my parents didn't know that my affected body parts would be permanently paralysed. And when they did, they were in great mental distress and trauma for several months. My mom told me that it was very difficult to even hold me in hands, as my limbs were like pieces of cloth. My maternal grandmother used to bathe me by keeping me on a big flat stool with low height. They used to keep me on a pillow in order to hold me in their arms.

I cannot even imagine the pain my parents had to go through and the strength they had to gather in order to come to terms with the situation, yet offering me tremendous support in every aspect of my life. People used to comment—drawing on popular belief—that disability to a person might be the result of sins they had committed in their previous birth. And they would think that the persons with disabilities are only a burden for the family and the society and this perception continues to prevail. However, owing to the tireless efforts of disability rights activists and the amazing skills exhibited by the persons with disabilities, a marked change in the perception of society towards the persons with disabilities is being noticed now. While there is a lot of progress, it is still a long way to go to ensure equal opportunity for persons with disabilities.[1]

I was a very cheerful child. I used to be very happy spending time with my family. But when new guests visited, they used to spoil the

---

[1] Generally, I don't want to use phrases such as differently abled and specially abled. My intention is not to show that the disabled are having some special qualities. They are like any other person. According to their needs, some adaptations need to be made in the society to enable them to perform all activities, for instance, a universal design, a design which considers all levels of abilities.

atmosphere in our house with their sympathetic looks and endless suggestions about my treatment. They were really nice for showing their concern, but such sympathy bothered me. Gradually, I became accustomed to their looks and suggestions, and my honest reaction was to laugh off, for which my mom would later admonish me, complaining that I was not disciplined.

2

The Short-lived Hope

When I was seven years old, we got to know that a senior orthopaedic surgeon was visiting our district headquarters, Khammam. We went to meet him; he spoke very encouragingly and recommended that I go for a surgery.

With the optimistic words from the doctor, we believed that with the surgery they would fix my legs and I could walk by myself without any external support. My mother frequently told me that as soon as my father saved enough money for my operation, he would take me to Hyderabad for surgery. In her words, 'You will become NORMAL after the surgery.' Although I didn't have any particular complaint about my physical condition at the time, I very much liked the idea that after my surgery I would no longer get the sympathetic looks and unsolicited advice from guests.

To arrange the money for the surgery, my father borrowed from his friends and subsequently minimized the needs of the family to save money so that he could repay the loan. With the required amount for the surgery, my parents and I went to Hyderabad to meet the doctor and pick the surgery dates.

It was the first time in my life to see a city like Hyderabad. Everything was a wonder, the double-decker buses, big buildings and their rich architecture. In those days, anyone visiting this city wouldn't miss taking a ride in a double-decker bus. We did not miss it either. We sat in the top deck of the bus and got a really good view of the city. It was an unforgettable experience for me.

In those days, staying in hotels while travelling was not a common practice. Particularly when women accompanied men, going to hotels was treated as a disrespectful thing. People tended to stay with their extended families/acquaintances. We stayed at my uncle's (dad's eldest brother) friend's house. There were many women in their house, and all of them were employed. The mornings of their house were similar to that of everyone's house nowadays; they would rush to catch their respective buses. For me, observing them was an amazing experience.

We met the doctor. He was not as friendly as he was in Khammam and advised us to pay the fee. After paying the fee, dates were informed to us.

After completing the work for which we came, we explored the city. We saw the Salar Jung Museum, Nehru Zoological Park, Charminar, etc. For me, it was a whole new world. When we were at Charminar, my parents struggled a lot to carry me, as the stairs were too high. My parents got extremely fatigued, and we managed to go only up a few floors.

One of those days of my stay at Hyderabad, I saw a lady gracefully sitting on a scooter with one leg on the ground and waiting for the green signal light. The sun was setting, and the yellow-coloured sunlight added brightness to her face. She wore sunglasses. With her left hand, she was trying to hold her hair which was falling on her face due to the cool breeze. I still remember that scene, though I don't exactly remember her face. That was the first time I had seen a lady riding a scooter. In my village, I saw girls riding bicycles but not a scooter.

At that moment, I made a resolution to get a job in Hyderabad and ride a scooter. Almost after two decades, my dream came true.

We went to my friend's house. Her father, who formerly worked as a bank manager in my village, was then working in Hyderabad city. I saw a black and white TV for the first time there. We watched a famous play of Sri Gurajada Appa Rao, 'Puthadibomma Purnamma'. It is a very touching story about the ill practice of child marriages. Until then, I only knew watching movies in theatres. To watch a programme while sitting at home was a new experience for me, and it filled me with excitement.

Our Ignorance about the Rights of the Disabled

On the way back home, we took a bus which was fully occupied by other passengers. In those days, there was no advance seat reservation system. It was an overnight journey, and no one was willing to offer a seat to us. So my parents had to stand for a long time, carrying me. After a while, tired of standing, my mom sat on the stairs with me on her lap, getting on and off of the bus at every stop to give way to the passengers. Although one seat was reserved for the persons with disabilities, my parents didn't know about it. Neither the driver nor the conductor guided them on that. I was unaware at that time, but later when my parents narrated their struggles, I felt bad about the inhuman behaviour of the co-passengers. Even if government orders (GOs) existed, ignorant and innocent people were not able to enjoy their rights.

Hope to Become Normal

We went back to Hyderabad for surgery and met the surgeon at the NIMS Hospital. The surgery was to be performed on my right leg to straighten it. Polio had caused muscle imbalance in my legs.[1] To use

---

[1] Generally, muscle strength will be 0 (dead) to 5 (with full strength). When polio affects the body, some muscles strength will be 0, and some may be anything from 1 to 5. It means that polio creates muscle imbalance. In that case, due to powerful muscles, contractures (bending) will happen. In case all the muscles are affected

the callipers, surgery (to correct the contractures) was required. Finally, the surgery day arrived. My parents were stressed out but to everyone's surprise, I was fearless to face it, as my mother's words that I would become 'normal' with the surgery consistently echoed in my mind. I wasn't worried about the pain and was looking forward to getting cured. The surgery was successful. My father brought me many storybooks as I loved reading. I spent most of my time reading them so much that the people at the hospital soon recognized me as a bookworm. Our ward was shared by many patients; there were two rows facing each other, each treated by a different doctor. The doctor treating the patients in the other row was very friendly and sympathetic and offered soothing words to his patients—unlike my doctor, who was a man of few words. I thought if I were in the other row, the soothing words of the doctor would have given me great solace. My parents rented a room near the hospital. My paternal grandmother and my cousin (maternal uncle's daughter) Sampoorna helped us a lot during that time.

When I was in the hospital, a nurse named Raghavamma showed a lot of love and affection towards me. She worked with great patience and empathy for the patients. She spoke with a tender smile on her face and regularly checked if patients were taking their medicines and food on time. I liked her very much and used to observe her even at the cost of my sleep during her night duty. She admonished me many times for not sleeping. Nevertheless, I continued to do so as I loved to watch her style of working. I pretended to be asleep when she came around my bed. It was like a play for me.

One of those days, a young girl who occupied the bed next to me succumbed to her disease. The situation was depressing. I felt very low and was upset. So my mom and my grandma decided to cheer me up; they went to the market and bought me a toy for ₹10 (a substantial

---

by polio, then there won't be any bending. Only when some groups of muscles are affected, bends will be there.
A surgery is done to correct those contractures in the legs which are caused due to muscle imbalance, so that we can use callipers.

amount back then). It was a bike (which moved with a key) with a person and a kid sitting on it. I enjoyed playing with it very much, and it was the one and only toy my parents ever bought for any of their children. I treasured it for many years and safely passed it onto the next generation.

After a month, I underwent a second surgery; this time on my left leg. My parents were in a relatively relaxed state because of the earlier experience. But the surgery was unsuccessful, and we didn't even know what went wrong. I was in severe pain for days after the surgery. After the scars healed, we went to the engineering section; where they took measurements and made callipers for me.

Due to the scoliosis and the paralysed muscles of my stomach, I should wear the callipers from my shoulders to toes and also use crutches to stand and walk on my own. The callipers frame was made of iron rods which stood alongside the body, with multiple leather straps. They were very heavy and painful. The calliper boot would make sure my ankles were in proper position. As something went wrong during the second surgery, my left ankle and fingers were misaligned. Due to that, it was immensely painful even to wear just the calliper boot. The straps were all around my body to hold the frame tight against it, pressing my skin very hard. To sit or bend, I had to unlock the joints at my knees and hips every time. Also, my shoulders and arms would hurt a lot as I had to lift my body and callipers with each step. I was very weak and felt severe pain in my entire body. When I complained about the pain, the engineers assured me that it was temporary and would eventually go away. But the pain in my left ankle never did.

The Bitter Truth

One day, I asked the doctor, 'How long will I have to wear the callipers?' expecting him to say a few days or a couple of months and that thereafter I would become 'normal', as my mother had always told me. But the response he gave me was heartbreaking. He said, 'Till your last breath.' I was in a bitter shock, and my mind went blank. Until then, the only thing that kept me going through this painful process was the thought that it would all end soon and I would be free from the cage that was tied to my body. But the moment I heard him, I lost hope. I became very adamant about not to wear it again. I was happy with my life—reading books, going to school and playing with my friends. I didn't want anything more.

Instead of empathizing with my pain, many people advised me to just tolerate it so that I could move around on my own. I saw them as my enemies and just hated listening to them. They didn't know the pain I suffered and the time and effort my family had to put to get me into that cage every day. The process of wearing the callipers was so exhausting that everyone would be tired by the time it was done. My body was too weak to carry the heavy weight. I used to cry a lot in pain—so much that often my lips turned blue. And sometimes I would intentionally cry very hard with two aims: one to make my family members vexed and give up and other to avoid the painful process altogether.

I used to feel like a free bird after removing the callipers.

Disgust towards Callipers

My family tried very hard to convince me, but it was almost always a futile exercise. My eldest sister, Nirmala, would just not give up, and she even convinced me a few times to wear the callipers. For us, our eldest sister is like a second mother. In the beginning, she could make me walk for some distance, and later, all the way till my school. Although it was very painful and tiresome for me to walk that distance, I felt happy going to school on my own. But I didn't express my happiness for the fear that my family would take it as an opportunity to make me practise walking with callipers. After her marriage, my eldest sister moved out of our village, and I happily escaped from this routine. Tired of my adamant nature, my parents left it to my choice. I heaved a sigh of relief as they stopped bothering me.

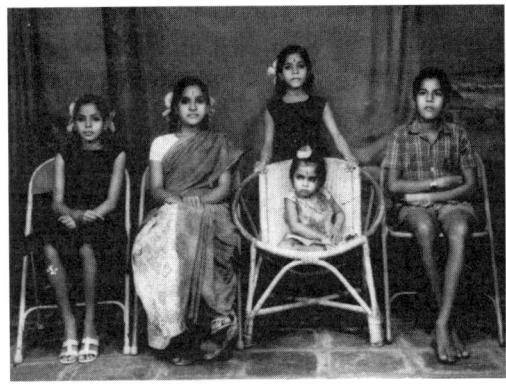 

Left: With my sweet siblings. Right: In cage like calipers (artist Mr Shashank tried his level best without having the model of the calipers I used)

But when my aunts and uncles visited, they brought up the topic. I used to feel embarrassed until they changed the topic. A few years later, when I was in my 8th grade, my family tried to convince me to get new calipers, but I did not let them. I now realize their concern and feel sorry for troubling them. But still, I do not regret not wearing the calipers, considering the difficulties and pain they caused.

Fifteen years later, after I started working, my father came across an article about Mr Pancham Kumar Das, who was administering Ayurvedic medicine for polio. He was from Araria district in the erstwhile state of Bihar. My father wanted to take me to him, but there were many widespread frightening stories about the indecent behaviour of anti-social elements with the passengers during the train journey to Patna. My father didn't dare to travel to Patna with two women, but was in contact with the doctor, who once informed us about his upcoming trip to Chennai. My parents were very happy and arranged our trip to Chennai. I had no interest in any treatment for polio as the doctor in my childhood told me that no treatment would result in any reasonable positive changes. But I didn't mind going along as there were no callipers involved.

My parents gathered a few more friends who had children with disabilities and we all went to Chennai together. The doctor first gave us some medicine. It was fine, but the treatment followed with diet restrictions. I was and am a picky person with a very particular taste in food. I only eat very few varieties of food, and almost everything I like was on the restricted list. Eventually, I started to hate this treatment.

One day, I was able to stand without any support for a whole minute (a progress due to the treatment in my family's view). My sister Mythreyi was the first one to observe this; with great excitement she ran to my mother and other siblings and brought them to me. All of them felt immensely happy to see this development. But the doctor's words from my childhood were so deeply ingrained in me that I neither felt any excitement nor believed that it may actually work. But these medicines left a few unwanted side effects in my body and, hence, could successfully convince my parents to stop the treatment.

One of the boys who came to Chennai with us greatly benefited from the treatment. He could walk with crutches alone. I felt that it could be because he was young. The doctor did say that the medicine was more effective for children below 20 years of age and might not help me much, considering my age (27 years). My parents realized that any further treatment for me would only be a waste of time and energy as I was very stubborn. I was happy that I could bring them to that conclusion. Later I was lucky enough to find an alternative source for my walking—the walker—by the time I got a job.

3

My Strength: My Family

By the time I grew up and started to comprehend things around me, we were living in our own house. Till then, our family lived in rented houses in various villages due to my father's transfers. Owning a house was a dream for my mother. She felt immensely happy for getting her long-cherished desire fulfilled. Our house had a huge backyard. The roof of our house was very high and laid with forest grass. Because of the ceiling height, the house used to be cool inside even during the hot summer months. There was a *pandiri* (a shed covered by palm leaves to give shade) in front of our house. A thick, green creeper with violet-coloured flowers added beauty to it. There were many plants in our house blooming with a variety of flowers. Our house was a feast to the eyes. No passers-by could move forward without glancing at our house, enchanted by its beauty. Our well was always full with sweet water, like a perennial river. Although thatched, its grandeur and elegance would be forever heartening for us. My eldest sister, Nirmala, drew rangolis (an art form in which patterns are created on the ground using materials like dry flour) beautifully, and my second sister Anantham also learnt to draw beautiful rangolis.

Among the siblings, my brother, Indrajith, is the only male child. In those days, girls were not sent to the market. So to fulfil the needs of us four sisters, my brother had to run all the errands such as buying bindi, kajal, etc. We siblings never had any quarrels. My third sister, Mythreyi, enjoyed the status of the youngest child till my birth—being pampered by everyone in the family. I felt surprised to see her love and affection towards me without any disappointment for losing that status because of me. I love them all and am very grateful for being part of this loving family.

For all our birthdays, my mother gave us head baths and prepared *payasam*. She kept aside one dress for each of us for our birthdays. There was no practice of buying new clothes for festivals in our house. It could be either due to financial stringencies or my father's lack of interest in celebrations. Immediately after celebrating my *annaprasanna* on a grand scale, I was affected by polio, and that incident might have led him to not give importance to any kind of celebrations. However, my birthday celebration was, and still is, an exception. It is celebrated as a festival in my family. Once, my mother hand-stitched my birthday dress and, due to overstrain, she fainted. We arranged a drip for her to regain strength. Such was the special affection of my mother for me. She invited all my friends for my birthday and served them a variety of sweets. Wearing a new dress and savouring handmade delicacies by my mom, I celebrated my birthday very happily every year.

My father was working as the headmaster of a school in our village, Sathupally. He earned name and fame not only in our village but also across many villages in our area. People who wanted to submit any application or representation to political leaders or to the government in either Telugu or English approached my father, because they strongly felt that he would present the facts with their feelings resonating in the memorandums. My father never declined a request, even if they came at odd hours. He used to complete their work sitting up into the wee hours. He wrote several welcome addresses for many high-profile dignitaries whenever they visited our area.

As a teacher, my father taught lessons in such an impressive manner that often students mentioned that there was no need for them to revise at home. As an administrator, wherever he worked, he used to give more importance to providing better facilities and safety of the students. During his entire service, he worked in villages only. From the moment of taking charge, he used to arrange for cleaning the premises of the school, erecting fences for the compound, building additional classrooms and maintaining strict discipline in the school. As there were no funds to do these activities, he used to approach local leaders and his friends for support. Whenever he was transferred, students and villagers bid farewell to him with heavy hearts. The deep reverence shown by old students towards my father even today shows his exemplary performance as a teacher. A postcard which contained only his name and village name was promptly delivered at our home safely—such was his popularity in our area. Only upon seeing my father did I develop boundless respect for the profession of teaching.

At the request of some parents, my father performed *aksharabhyasam* (a religious function to start the formal education of the child) to their children. It was their belief that the golden hands of my father would make their children shine in their education. Some people got their applications for jobs filled by my father, for they believed that the golden touch of my father would bring them success.

I could distinctly remember one particular incident where the headman of a village, about 30 km away from our village, sent his vehicle to take my father to their house just to fill up the medical entrance application form of his elder son, who is now a famous doctor in Eluru. That gentleman sincerely believed that our home was the abode of Goddess Saraswathi. As a proof of his belief, all our siblings acquired higher qualifications. My eldest sister, Nirmala, did a double postgraduation in English and Hindi, along with BEd; my brother, Indrajith, did MSc (Chemistry) and an MA in English along with a Master of Education; my second sister, Anantham, did MSc (Botany) and an MA in Telugu, along with Master of Education; and my third sister, Mythreyi, did MSc (Zoology) and an MPhil, along with a BEd.

My father always believed that all girls should pursue education with determination, acquire higher academic and professional qualifications and achieve financial independence. In conformity with that cherished opinion, he provided education to all his daughters and supported them in getting suitable jobs. He helped his elder sister in getting a job as a Telugu pundit. He followed the same principle while choosing a daughter-in-law. He took every opportunity to preach those ideas to his students and our friends.

In those days, child marriages for girls were very common in villages. And many parents believed that the duty of a girl was solely to take care of her in-law's family after marriage. Hence, they didn't give much importance to providing education for their daughters. Some of my sisters' friends who were very intelligent got married when they were still in primary school and discontinued their studies. But we are very fortunate as our parents were progressive in this regard.

My father has some firm convictions. He always tries to be true to his word. By nature, he is social, amicable, kind-hearted and service-minded. He is ever-ready to help people who are in distress to his maximum capability. He is a good counsellor and patiently listens for hours when people share their agonies.

We fully experienced the respect which was showered on us, as the children of parents who were famous for their discipline, righteousness, moral values and responsiveness. We used to observe a positive change in the way people treated us when they found out who our parents are. We could notice these differences because we grew up in villages with strong social solidarity and comparatively smaller communities. I could never expect such relations in cities where people are not even aware who their neighbours are. My favourite identity is 'Rajugari Chinnammayi' (the youngest daughter of Mr Raju).

My father also took the responsibility of his parents and siblings after getting a job. He did his best in helping his siblings, as the financial condition of his family was not very sound. He faced many challenges with his meagre income, yet he tried to support his entire family including his children and siblings' education. By the time I started to understand these things, all his siblings were settled in life. From then onwards to till my sisters got married, our financial position was much better and slowly we could afford many things which improved our lifestyle. Until then there was no electricity. Every evening, my mother cleaned the lantern glass, poured oil and made it ready for use. That was the only source of light for our night-time reading. After some days, we got an electricity connection. Oh, how joyous we were! We could now read in proper light even at night. We didn't need to sit around the lantern; we could sit wherever we felt like. As there were so many poisonous snakes and insects in our area, we would earlier be scared to go out in the night to use toilets. We felt as if we came out of darkness and went into the world of light!

When we could buy certain things for the first time, the happiness we felt was indescribable. The delight we experienced when we bought a Humber bicycle cannot be equated with the happiness we derive if we buy a BMW now. My brother was very happy when we bought a bicycle. I, too, felt happy because it was very easy for my father or brother to take me to places while sitting on it rather than carrying me physically. Likewise, we felt very happy when we bought Rally table fan for the first time.

I am out of words to aptly describe how industrious my mother is. She never takes rest. Despite the support from my sisters, she was always busy doing some work. It was very difficult to look after five children and guests who frequented our home. As already mentioned, the roof of our house was very high. So to clean the roof and the walls, she joined two sticks to make it longer and tied a broom at the end. The following day, she would suffer from shoulder pains. For every festival, she used to paste the floor with cow dung, draw rangolis and prepare sweet items.

During those days, my father was very busy in his profession and teachers' union activities. Whenever he brought his colleagues to our house at odd times, my mother prepared food and served them with respect. Generally, we used to have two or three guests every day. At that time, there was no gas supply, so mom used to cook with firewood. If I were in my mother's position then, I would have not shown that much patience.

My grandmother used to pamper my mom as she was the only girl-child in the family. I always wonder how she managed to handle all the work and responsibilities after her marriage. Mom had three brothers. But she lost her second brother long ago due to a snake bite. I remember my mom telling me so many good stories about her late brother. My eldest uncle was a farmer, and the younger one worked in government service. Her brothers and their families shower same love and affection on her.

Celebration of Festivals

There was always a lot of activity and excitement in our family while celebrating major festivals. For Sankranthi, my sisters decorated the premises of our house with beautiful rangolis and *gobbemmalu* (hand-pressed piles of cow dung decorated with marigold flowers, turmeric and kumkum). I used to be their critic. Sitting on a high platform and having an aerial view, I would offer suggestions to make rangolis more beautiful and appreciate their good work. For Deepavali, we'd burst many crackers. My brother used to make his own crackers from scratch and burst them. My sisters would assist my mother in decorating our home with diyas (small earthen plates used for lighting). I also used to assist them in pouring oil and in lighting diyas. It was a wonderful sight to see.

We used to celebrate Vinayaka Chavithi festival with utmost reverence. The way my father used to perform the puja and his melodious chanting of mantras were feasts for our eyes and ears. All of us used to sit in prayers along with him. We kept our books at the feet of the deity and prayed. For Dussehra, we used to go to the temples, where girls played *bathukamma* (a floral festival worshipping Goddesses celebrated predominantly by women in Telangana region). My sisters used to carry me in their arms and go around those *bathukammas* along with other girls. On all these festival days, my mother used to prepare delicious dishes and serve them to us. We cherished every moment of those festivals. When I think about those days, I wonder how affectionately my family included me in all those celebrations. There was no single incident where I felt being left out.

Entertainment

There was Sundaralakshmi touring talkies[1] behind our house, at a distance of 90 m (~300 feet), built with tin sheets and bamboo mesh walls. If we lay down on our cots in our backyard, we could hear the dialogues and songs from the movie very clearly. We would recite the next dialogue in advance as we had learnt them by heart. When relatives came to visit us, they would be surprised at how we managed to continue studying through all that movie sounds. But we never considered it a disturbance and were very well accustomed to that atmosphere. We enjoyed listening to those melodious songs in the movies but whenever horror movies were screened, we used to get frightened to listen those horrifying sounds. There were no mosquitoes in those days. So during summers, we slept outdoors. We enjoyed moonlight on full-moon nights and observed the bright stars on new-moon days. During holidays, when I used to go to my maternal uncle's house, I used to sleep outdoors along with his children, each one telling many stories until we fell asleep. I used to wonder how the moon follows us everywhere we went!

In summers, when we used to sleep out in the open, the sound of moving leaves of the coconut trees in our yard was like the soothing sound of music to my ears. I liked watching the moon through those

---

[1] Touring talkies are usually temporary screens to play movies. But this one was a temporary structure with a screen and operated for many years at the same place.

coconut leaves. Creating stories around the shapes of clouds was my favourite pastime. When all my family members were asleep, the same beautiful trees began to frighten me like ghosts in that darkness. I was also afraid that the sky might fall on us. Every now and then I used to uncover the blanket from my face to observe how far the sky had come down. Like every kid, I also believed that an old woman lived on the moon and she would tell me beautiful stories. I enjoyed the feeling that the moon was a very pleasant place to be. Later, when I learned in science classes that the moon was only a natural satellite of the earth and there was no life on it, I was heartbroken and my dreams were shattered. It took a few days to regain my composure.

We made dolls out of coconut leaves. My mother stitched dresses for my dolls and also fixed their plaits with pieces of cloth. I decorated them with flowers and played with them, telling them many stories. If I couldn't sleep, I would wake my sister Anantham up and play with her.

The only available entertainment in our area in those days was the movie and cultural programmes at temples during festivals. I liked watching films very much. We were allowed to go to the cinema only once a month. Assuming that I had close affinity with my father, my siblings pressed me to seek permission from him. We never had to pay for my entry ticket to the cinema halls; they allowed me free of cost. This might have been either due to sympathy for my disability or mistaking me to be a young child as I was carried by my siblings. Even if we insisted, they wouldn't charge me for a ticket. Whoever went to the cinema in our house, they invariably took me with them.

Radio

In my childhood, radio was an important medium of entertainment and news. I assumed that some small men and women were inside the radio. One day, when my brother opened the radio to repair it, I was eagerly waiting to see the people inside. To my surprise, there was no one in there. My siblings laughed at my ignorance. It was a great disappointment for me to know that no one was inside a radio. I found it difficult to understand how we could hear voices without people inside.

Television

When I was studying intermediate, we bought a black and white Philips TV. It was a great enhancement in our lives. In those days, Doordarshan was the only channel available. They had great quality programmes. Every Sunday afternoon, one regional language film was telecasted with English subtitles. We made it a point to watch that movie. It gave me an idea about the culture of different states in our country. I watched many Hindi movies. Chitrahaar on Friday was our favourite programme. I used to watch news in sign language on Sundays. It was a wonder for me, and I would often try and practise sign language.

After I got a job, we bought a Grundig colour TV. I now wonder how we celebrated the entry of a colour TV in our house. Until then, we were watching all the beautiful scenes of nature in black and white. On a colour TV, all those scenes looked so beautiful in their natural colours. We loved it very much. After several years, when we gave that TV for repair, the repairman deceived us. It stopped working as he had stolen the vital parts. We all felt sad, as if a beloved person had left us forever.

Reading Habit

From the age of seven I am an avid reader. My father bought many story books for me. I loved reading. I didn't even spare the pieces of paper in which groceries were packed. My father encouraged me a lot in cultivating the habit of reading.

My father had a friend named Mr Babu Rao. He was a teacher, and his wife was a bank employee. They spent a substantial amount on buying books every month. It was a noteworthy habit. There were a lot of books in his house. I remember the exhilaration I felt when I saw so many books at one place when I visited their house along with my dad. I read every book there. It was like a feast for me.

I read a novel titled *Hamsa Dweepam* (I hope I remembered the name correctly!) in *Chathura* monthly magazine. In that novel, I read about Lilliputians and gigantic people for the first time. I don't remember how many times I read that novel and the many dreams I had, as if I had met those Lilliputians. It is a sweet memory for me.

Starting from Chandamama, Balamitra, detective novels and romantic novels, I read books on communism, feminism, spirituality and whatnot. There were two libraries in our village, and I read most of the books in them. The characters in the books I read would have a short sway over me and I would imagine playing their roles in real life as well, more so for professions such as a detective or a scientist. If I read detective books, I wanted to become a detective. I even wanted to become a librarian, thinking that I would get the opportunity to read more and more books. I read Telugu translations of some of the great literary works in the world. In those days, I read *Mother* by Maxim Gorky. I read them all when I was just 13 or 14 years old. I don't know how far I have assimilated them, but they helped me understand the feelings of others, empathize with them and also offer counselling to others using examples from the books I read. I don't know why but elder people came to seek my advice despite knowing that I was just a teenager. Even my dad sought my advice before taking any major decisions. That gave me more happiness as I felt empowered.

My father would take me to the literary, religious and political meetings. One of my dad's friends was a Muslim religious preacher. He was a great scholar. Once he came to our area to deliver a talk, and my dad took me along with him to that meeting. People gathered in hundreds. During the talk, when I looked around, I found that I was the only woman present. I was puzzled. When I enquired about female participants, they took me to them. They were all sitting behind a screen. I sat there for some time. But because of my active nature,

I didn't like to stay behind a screen. I joined my dad again. From my participation in these diverse meetings and extensive readings, I learnt to respect different cultural views and opinions, even if I don't agree with some of them.

A few years ago, I read a novel[2] and in its story a couple gave birth to a lovely child. Their friends greeted them profusely. But after a few months, the parents noticed some abnormality in the child's behaviour. Doctors confirmed that she was a person with intellectual disability. With that revelation, the sympathy expressed by relatives and friends, the advice offered by other people, and the innocent acts of the child multiplied the mental agony of the parents. When I put my parents in their position, I could not control my tears.

I read this novel when I was 41. Even though I was present in every situation and I witnessed my parents' struggles, I could never really understand it from their angle. The realization hit me only when I read this story from her parents' perspective. It is no wonder that I could not realize how patiently my parents overcame the torturous mental agony caused by my physical disability. Till today, my parents pay utmost attention to my needs with so much love, affection and care. They never gave me a reason to feel that they were mentally suffering due to my physical condition. Therein lies their greatness!

I remember another poem[3] in which a person said to God, 'Oh, Father! When I was in happiness, I found two sets of footprints in the path I was treading. But when I was in suffering, I found only one set of footprints which I thought were mine. Where were you then?' God replied with a smile, 'My son, it was then that I was carrying you in my arms to help you overcome the suffering. That is why you could see my footprints only.' Similarly, the discomfort and inconvenience caused due to my disability was borne by my parents to make me feel comfortable.

....
[2] It was published in *Chatura*, a telugu monthly magazine. It is for women and family, with general interest, cartoons and a novel a month.
[3] From the 'Footprints in the Sand' poem—author unknown.

Fire Accident and the Devastating Cyclone

Time was passing by peacefully. Suddenly, a great calamity befell on us in 1975. It was summertime. A fire broke out somewhere in the village. The wind was blowing at a galloping speed, and a chunk of fire fell on our house and soon began to engulf the entire house. There was no time to grab our belongings. We could only carry a box which contained our certificates. In no time, our beautiful house turned into a heap of ashes. Our lovely dream had shattered right in front of our eyes. My mother was absolutely devastated with that incident and took a considerable amount of time to regain her composure. Our neighbours, Mr Pratapa Reddy, a lecturer, and his wife, Mrs Suryakumary, came to our help in that difficult time. They lived across the street. We resided in a vacant portion of their house for three months without paying rent. Overwhelmed by grief, whenever my mother didn't eat, Suryakumary aunty consoled her and made her eat. Their support in those tragic times is unforgettable to this day. It was a rude shock for us. We lost everything we had earned till then.

Slowly, my father began to construct a new house on the same land after clearing the debris. He could not mobilize enough money to complete the work all at once; it became a five-year plan. The construction work became a continuous process. Gathering brick by brick, he constructed a tiled house. It took nearly 10 years to give complete shape to our house.

There was always a heap of sand in front of our house in my childhood as my father continued the construction work of our house depending on the availability of funds. I used to daily play in the sand with my friends. With sand, there was no fear of getting injured. I could make movements by crawling very actively in the sand.

In 1977, a violent cyclone had struck Diviseema (an island in Andhra Pradesh approximately 240 km [150 mi] from our village) and washed out the entire area. Thousands of people were swept away into the sea. At that time, we started to rebuild our house. After completing some work and making it liveable to some extent, we shifted there. Only outside walls except the front side were raised. The front side was a 5-feet bamboo mesh (used for the wall and doors). The dreadful cyclone also hit our village and caused great damage to our house. As there were no wooden doors, only bamboo mesh was tied to close the doors. The gusting winds vehemently tried to blow away the mesh doors. All our family members except me stood behind the east-side door, pressing it with all their might, as it was crucial for the safety of our house. There were no frames on the windows; only bricks were laid in layers, without cement. By morning, they were all crumbled, leaving big holes in the walls. We could not sleep that night as we fought the winds to safeguard our house. At that time, there were no thefts and even monkeys in our village. Therefore, with only mesh walls and open windows we could live without any fear. Of course, we had no valuables in our house to lose! But we could not forget that horrible experience for many years.

Pickling

During summer months, the biggest project for mom was to prepare pickles. She would start the process as early as in March. She would start with buying good-quality red dry chillies and other ingredients, drying them under hot sun, removing the stem and hand-pounding them with a long wooden pestle. While doing that, she would cough and sneeze intensely due to the strong smell/chilli particles that emanated due to the pounding. I didn't know how she managed to do that back-breaking and suffocating work. My dad and brother were responsible to find and buy good-quality mangoes. When they brought the mangoes, we helped mom in cleaning them with water and a dry cloth. Dad and brother helped mom in cutting those mangoes to the required size. Mom mixed those mango pieces with hot chilli powder, oil, etc., in a basin and later preserved the pickle in jars. Mom mixed the remaining pickle in the basin with rice, made a morsel and offered it to us. That was the tastiest food for us. Apart from mango pickle, mom used to prepare many other pickles—tomatoes, red chillies, gooseberries, etc. With mangoes, she also used to prepare different types of pickles. I love pickles very much.

Seasonal Fruits

In our premises we had many fruit trees/plants such as custard apple, sapota, banana, papaya, guava and coconut. We used papaya leaf petiole as a straw and played a lot with water. We used to make whistles with coconut leaves and played with them. Bananas from our backyard were very tasty. My parents gave them to all our friends when they ripened. We used only natural manure and never any chemical fertilizers. Apart from having home-grown fruits, we used to buy toddy palm, watermelon, jackfruit, tamarind and many other fruits from the sellers who came to our street. Jackfruit is my favourite. Once we found a beehive on one of the trees in our backyard. We drove the bees away and plucked the nest and procured pure honey from it. It was so tasty! Although my father was very strict with regard to spending money, he never said no to food items. He faced many difficulties in having nutritious food in his childhood due to poverty. He wanted to provide his children all seasonal fruits and other items of their choice. He never liked spending money on clothes or other luxury items. He always told us to have only two khadi dresses. Although we are obedient in every other aspect, we couldn't follow this one. We are not interested in leading a luxurious life either, but nowadays, the meaning of luxury has undergone a lot of change.

Pet Animals

In my childhood, my dad bought a buffalo with its calf to have sufficient milk for us to drink. From then on, there was no dearth of milk, curd or ghee. My dad liked his pets very much. He treated them as members of our family. He provided sufficient fodder for them to eat and lie down happily on it. We also had a dog, a cat and hens at our home.

When the buffalo gave birth to a calf, it was winter. My dad brought the calf into our house and put a blanket on it to save it from the cold. By morning, it had spoiled the hall with urine and dung. They were given saline if needed. When my father returned home from work in the night and opened the front gate, the animals in the backyard shed would immediately stand in attention as a mark of their love for him. They recognized his arrival by the very sound of the gate opening. He used to go and spend some time with them before entering the house.

In our area, there were many snakes and other poisonous creatures like scorpions. More often, I spotted them in some corner or under the plants. In those days, snake catchers were treated as heroes. In spite of all these fears, my father used to go to the cattle shed in the dark to greet our pet animals.

Teenage

As I was growing into my teenage years, the guests that visited our house used to ask me and my mom many questions—whether my menstruation cycle had started (they had doubts that due to my disability I might not get them); who would marry me; if nobody comes forward, we should lure the groom by offering excess dowry to compensate for my disability—all inane questions and suggestions. I hated their unnecessary curiosity or inquisitiveness. When they asked such questions, I felt very irritated because I considered those things to be my business and not theirs.

Finally, when that day came, my mother was worried, wondering how I would manage my periods with this severe disability. I managed fairly well.

I was treated like a princess in my family, and in school, I was a bright student. I used to get a lot of appreciation from my teachers, friends and other well-wishers. My parents' siblings also love me and appreciate my intelligence very much. With all this great support, I never felt inferior to anyone.

From the books I read on feminism and from my general understanding in those days, I was in a view that most of the challenges faced by women were due to the underlying male chauvinism in the society. Moreover, people whom I counselled with my limited knowledge from the books I read were also women. I was convinced that their sufferings were due to their husbands or other male members in the family. With this conviction, and also after continuously withstanding the questions and comments from some of the guests, I felt it would be better to avoid marriage. My parents were of the same opinion too. They knew the challenges women were generally facing in those days in getting married and later in their family lives. They thought that it would be difficult for me to manage all those responsibilities. As we all decided this in my early teen years, we never made any attempt in that line. I don't have any regrets for that either. Later, when I interacted with many male colleagues at work, I got the opportunity to listen to their views and perspectives. I slowly realized that I should not judge anyone based on their gender. A person may not behave in the same manner with everyone or with the same person in the same manner every time. Although I came out of the negative feeling about men, I never tried to reconsider my decision. I am comfortable with my present life. I don't want to trouble anyone. I am able to do many things for society beyond filling the standard societal role of a wife, as per the values with which my parents brought me up.

My Siblings' Weddings

My father was strictly against giving/taking dowry and lavish expenditure on weddings. He tried to implement his ideals with true spirits in his life. He performed my eldest sister Nirmala's wedding by getting it registered in 1978 in the Registrar's office in a very simple way with the support of my brother-in-law N. K. Raju and his family. It was sensational news in our area. In those days, no arranged marriage was simply registered without a big fat wedding. Most of the registered marriages happened in the case of love marriages, where the bride and the groom took a decision against their parents' approval. We invited very few people, and even our close friends didn't know about my sister's marriage.

Later, for my second and third sisters' weddings, my father had to oblige to the views of their in-laws as they were particular about conducting the wedding in a traditional way. In most of the movies that I watched since my childhood, right at the time of tying the knot (a key moment in Indian weddings), someone would come and shout 'stop!' With this cinematic imagination ingrained in me, I was worried that a similar event would happen during my sisters' weddings. But fortunately, their weddings were performed peacefully.

At the time of my brother's wedding, my father could implement his ideals again. My sister-in-law lost her father in her childhood. My father took the responsibility of her father. He made arrangements for the wedding at our house. That was also a simple register marriage. But this time, the Registrar came to our house as we could request in advance. We invited friends and relatives for lunch.

Mom and Me

After graduating from 10th grade, I continued my education from home and applied for a degree privately. Since I was home most of the time, I got to spend maximum time with my mom. She was very hardworking with the household chores. I wanted to help her, but she doesn't like to see me doing any work as I have to put extra effort. The only opportunity where I got to support her was in helping her in grinding rice/black gram paste and chutneys in a manual grinder, and I liked it.

Initially, there were only three more houses near our house. Our neighbours (Mr Abdullah, Mr Pratapa Reddy and Mr Chenna Rao) and we had a very close friendship among our families. In the afternoon, after lunch, in the absence of male family members, my mom and those aunties along with our tenant aunty used to have huddles discussing various interesting topics. As I was studying privately at that time, most of the time I also used to join them.

Dressing

In my childhood, my mom stitched nice gowns for me. Later, I wore knee-length skirts and a full jacket. I could not wear long skirts (*lehenga*), as I was crawling on the ground at that time. But I had a great desire to wear it, nonetheless. After seeing my interest, mom stitched me two *lehengas*—one in blue and the other in honey colour. I loved them very much. If I wore them, I could not move around and had to sit in one place. Since I always like to be free, I decided not to wear them again. I gave them to a friend. Although I wanted to wear half-sarees like my friends, knowing the challenges, I let that desire go. I had to seriously think about what I'd wear when I would get a job and go to work. After I started walking with the help of a walker, we decided to opt for Punjabi attire. From then on, I began wearing salwar–kameez. I love to wear sarees. There have been some three occasions when I wore a saree with the help of my sister-in-law and sisters.

Even today, I can't buy readymade dresses due to the hump on my back and short height due to compression in my spine. Mom buys cloth material and stitches clothes for me.

Theft at Our Home

During summers, we used to sleep in the open yard. In one of the summer seasons, our tenant Krishna Kumari aunty's relatives visited them. We knew their relatives, and they also knew our relatives very well as they resided in that portion of the house for a long time. We were chatting till 12:00 am and laughed a lot. Our front yard was filled with cots. Mom joined our conversation quite late as she had to attend to the household chores first. Her cot was close to the main gate. We all slept. At around 2:00 am, I woke up to a sound and saw a person. I could not understand what was happening.

Then my sister Anantham woke up. By the time we realized that he was a thief, he started running and reached the entrance. Later on, we realized that there were two of them. Before escaping, one thief snatched the gold chain from my mother's neck. My sister Anantham who was eight months pregnant jumped over the gate and ran after the thieves (four bamboo sticks were kept horizontally as a gate; the thieves had removed two sticks). But they vanished in a jiffy. Even in that tense situation, everyone was surprised how my sister jumped over the gate eight months into her pregnancy. And while coming back, as she opened the gate and came inside, everyone laughed. My dad and brother went till the end of the street but couldn't catch them. It was a shock for all of us. Theft was not common in our area. Later, we came to know from public talks that those thieves were from Stuartpuram, a notorious place for thieves. We never slept outside after that incident.

As the stolen chain was the *mangalsutra* (an auspicious thread uniting the souls; the groom ties the auspicious thread around the bride's neck on the day of their holy nuptial), my parents felt very bad for losing it. Next day, when our maid was sweeping the front yard, she found the sutra which was tied at the time of their wedding. Although we lost the gold chain, my parents felt happy for getting the *mangalsutra* back.

After a few years, another thief broke into our house. At that time, our front wall was not fully up. There was a gap on the top. It was of considerable height, and we thought that no one could enter. But with the help of the motorcycle parked in the veranda, the thief could enter easily. He stole some money from our tenant's room. After this incident, dad arranged for grills in the veranda.

Two thefts brought two changes. The first one made us sleep indoors. I felt very bad for missing the wonderful opportunity to be with nature. And because of the second one, I lost the opportunity to sit on the half walls in our veranda and to have the aerial view of our front yard.

Opportunity to Go Upstairs

Many a time, when I attended a function, the main event would be on the ground floor and meals would be served on the rooftop. Sometimes, the entire event would be on the rooftop. As I could not go upstairs, they used to bring me food to the ground floor. I didn't like to eat separately; I did not attend just to have food. Food prepared by mom is the best one for me. I went there to greet my friends and to meet others, not to eat alone. Later, whenever we got any invitation, unless it was on the ground floor, I stopped attending. As I could not climb the stairs, my enthusiasm to spend time on the terrace multiplied manifold. I wanted to see the outside world from the top. Once, when I went to my aunt's house in Guntur, I got the opportunity to go upstairs. We all slept on the terrace. I liked that experience very much. Until then, I only saw the sky, moon and stars from ground level. I felt so happy to watch them from the top floor. I felt as if I was closer to them. I always feel very grateful to the person who invented the elevator, as it made our wish to reach the top floors possible.

My First Train Journey

My uncle informed us that a senior acupuncture specialist was visiting Repalle in Guntur district. Dad and I went to Vijayawada. From there, we had to go by train. For the first time, I travelled on a train. My uncle's friend and his daughter accompanied us. That girl and I became good friends. Dad bought fried groundnuts for us. Munching on those ground nuts and watching the scenery sitting by the window seat was a great experience. Although I love train journeys, due to accessibility issues, nowadays I don't travel in trains.

Curiosity on Death

In my childhood, whenever I heard any news related to death, I wanted to know more about it. What is death? What would happen to a person after death? So many doubts in my tiny brain. But mom used to get angry if I asked anything about death. From the books and after speaking to my brother, I understood that the body of the person is either buried or burnt, according to their custom. I could see some problems in each case. If they bury me, how would I breathe? And if I tried to breathe, sand might go into my nostrils. And if they burn my body, how would I tolerate that pain? Little me, but not so little doubts. Although I had those fears, I didn't share them with any of my family members—as I knew very well what their reaction would be.

My Two Aims in Life

After listening to my parents' words since my childhood, I wanted to become independent, without giving much trouble to others. After observing my parents' supportive nature towards the people around, in spite of having their own challenges, I decided to do something for the society. These two aims remain unchanged, and I am sincerely committed to them.

My Nieces and Nephews

When my elder sister gave birth to a girl child, Sunanda, we were all overly excited to see the first kid of the next generation. My father's aunt used to tease me saying that with Sunanda's entry, no one in the family would pay attention to me and treat me like a small kid any more. Even then I enjoyed my niece's company without feeling jealous. After giving a bath to her, when my mom and sister brought her out, I used to be with her only. Applying powder, dressing her up—I used to do these small things with utmost care and love. A year later, her brother and my first nephew, Sudhir, was born. I still remember how naughty Sunanda was in avoiding going to school. As the age gap between them and me was just 10–11 years, they started calling me Bujjakka (Bujji [my nickname] added to *akka* [sister]), instead of aunty. My brother Indrajith's children, Pavani, Prasanth and Pranavi; my sister Anantham's children, Vindhyasri and Padmasri; and my sister Mythreyi's children, Sahithi and Sachin—all of them continued addressing me Bujjakka.

Left: Sister Nirmala's registered marriage. Right: Darling nieces and nephews

When they were in primary classes, all of them used to come to our place in the summers. My parents and I used to wait for the summer, and other vacation time, to have all of them in our midst. As my birthday falls during the summer vacation, all of them used to come by at that time. We would have a great time. As they are all in different locations/countries now, we hardly meet at one place. However, due to advancements in technology, we can have conference calls. For my last birthday, all of them greeted me on a videoconference call. I remembered their childhood days when we all met in person.

Funny thing is that even their children call me Bujjakka! It is not just a name; it is an emotion for me.

4

Schooling Life

As mentioned earlier, I developed a strong interest for studies before going to school due to my mother's words and by observing the kind of dedication my siblings showed towards their studies. Before joining school, I used to cry because I wanted to go to school with my siblings. To pacify me, sometimes my brother used to carry me for a walk around the school. One day, my sisters took me along with them to the school. I sat along with my sister Anantham in her class. There, I saw my father in the role of a headmaster. Everyone in the classroom was addressing my dad as 'Sir', including my sister. Then I innocently asked my sister why she was addressing him as 'Sir' instead of dad. Everyone laughed at my innocence. That was the first time I went to school as a guest.

Our school was Panchayat Samithi Upper Primary School, Sathupally.

Later, at the age of five, I joined the school. My entire family felt very happy, and my own joy knew no bounds. My mother was the first teacher for all our siblings. She taught us Telugu alphabet even before we joined school.

As my father was the headmaster and my siblings were in senior classes, I didn't feel any inconvenience. But I never got a chance to attend my father's lecture in school as he used to only teach senior classes. I felt bad for missing out on an opportunity which every student of his class cherished.

Beside our house, a lorry driver called Mr Satyam lived with his family. His daughter Shyamala and I were good friends. She studied in the same school as mine; she was many years older than me but started her studies late. At times, she carried me in her arms to help me go to school. She used to tell me so many things, including the changes that take place in the body of girls when puberty hits them.

From the first standard onwards, I started securing the first rank in my school. I used to play a lot with my friends Anitha, Shehnaz, Swarupa Rani and Ananda Kumari. Anitha and Shehnaz used to come to my house to play in the sand with me in the evenings. Anitha's house was just across the street from school. During lunchtime, she would quickly finish her lunch at home and come back to the class to play with me. While coming, she would also bring some food which her mother had prepared.

Although I was consistently getting first rank in the class, I used to spend relatively lesser time studying. I spent most of my time either playing with my friends or reading books other than the class books. No one could complain as I was always the topper of my class. Everyone thought that the level of my class was not commensurate with my ability and sharpness. Hence, I skipped 6th standard and appeared privately for 7th standard directly. During that summer season, I completed studying my 6th standard books in two months. Even though I didn't stop reading other books, I stood first in the district-level common exam for seventh class.

When I was in primary school, as everyone appreciated me for my brilliant performance in studies, I thought that doing well in studies was the only great thing. I used to wonder why some of my classmates were not giving importance to studies and not getting good marks. Although I clarified their doubts when they approached me with regard to our lessons, I didn't value them enough in my heart due to their poor performance in studies. One day, I had to go to the toilet urgently. No one was available to help me except for one classmate who used to get very poor marks in exams. On that day, the way she supported me in going to the toilet with a lot of love for me and with great patience, I was humbled and realized that everyone has their own great qualities. Getting good marks in studies alone should not be the yardstick to judge one's personality or place in the world.

In those days, I used to get eye infections frequently. My family thought that it might be because of constant reading. I used to read thick books in a short time. If I start reading a book, I generally don't stop till I finish it. Due to the frequent eye infections, I consulted an ophthalmologist, Dr Jupally Sitharama Rao, in my village and asked him about my family members' theory. He told me that it was not the case. He also told me that eyes are meant for reading and advised me to continue my habit without any fears. I developed great regards for him because of that advice. He told other people that I was his friend, which made me feel very happy.

As I skipped one standard, in the 7th standard I got new classmates—Vasista, Sunitha, Sudha, Alivelu, Vasantha Sobha, Vidya Latha, Jhansi, Rama, Hima, Prasad and many others. All my friends are still in touch with me. In the 7th standard, mathematics was taught by Mr Mallikharjuna Rao, a great teacher. I think mathematics became my favourite subject because of his teaching. He used to encourage us to prepare problems ourselves and solve them, apart from working on the problems in the textbooks. Although all my siblings left our school for higher studies and my father got transferred later, I didn't face any problems as all my friends were very cooperative.

I loved playing with my friends very much. But slowly, when I was growing, I realized it was difficult to play with my friends as those sports were not adaptive. In the initial days, my friends used to carry me in their arms and tried to play as they didn't want to leave me out. But it became very strenuous for them to carry an equal-age person and play. I started to keep myself away from sports. My parents also suggested that I stay away from the playground because players might fall on me by mistake and cause injuries to me. At that time, I thought sports and Madhavi were two different worlds.

After 7th standard, I joined SBS Government Junior College for my high school studies. For that year alone, the school's administration had allowed female students who opted for composite mathematics to study there, as Girls High School was started separately from that year onwards. Ours was the last batch with girls in the high school sections attached to Junior College. I started going to school by a rickshaw. My father or brother would drop me at college whenever the driver didn't show up. I always wanted to go to class on time. My father or brother used to start only a few minutes before the class timing, calculating the time required for the ride to college. But I wanted to go a little earlier to avoid any unexpected delays. I used to be stressed every day because of this. I didn't want to be even a minute late and miss a single word of the teacher. One day, it was raining heavily. In spite of that, I made my brother drop me at college. My class teacher scolded me for coming in that heavy rain. Finally, they cancelled the classes for that day. Any day if classes were cancelled or let off early, I had to wait either for my rickshaw driver or call another rickshaw driver if we could find one on the road. Someone from my friends would always stay with me to give me company.

When I was in school, if I needed to use the washroom, my friends used to carry me to the toilet. I didn't have a wheelchair then. As mentioned earlier, I didn't use callipers. With my intention to not trouble others, I used to avoid going to the washroom as much as possible. In those days, many schools and colleges did not have toilet facilities. We had to go to the rear side of the college where many eucalyptus trees grew. I had very loving and caring friends. They were always ready to extend support when I needed them. Even now, some of them are supporting my social activities.

During the College Day function, I used to get prizes in study-related competitions—elocution, essay writing, etc. But none in sports. Every now and then I used to participate in chess competitions and win second or first position. It used to be difficult for me to climb the stage and often my friends used to receive my prizes. Every year, the founder of the college, Sri Bandi Sobhanachalam, used to give out medals to meritorious students. For receiving the gold medal, my father used to carry me onto the stage. Receiving a medal on the stage amid the claps from all the audience was a great experience. My parents used to feel very proud on those occasions.

My Teachers

I respect all my teachers very much. However, among them, I have even more regards for some teachers.

Mr Lakshmana Rao was my English teacher when I was in high school. Whatever English I know today, it's mainly because of the foundation laid by him. When he taught a lesson, we used to feel as if the characters in the lesson were playing those roles in front of us. He possessed such amazing teaching skills.

Mr G. Babu was my Telugu teacher in high school. Apart from explaining the lessons in a lucid way, he used to include his travel experiences too. It was a great inspiration for me. I love travelling very much. I remember enjoying listening to his experiences immensely.

People Who Make Us Feel Empowered

As I used to observe my father's discussions with his friends, I learnt many things on various topics such as politics and literature. All my father's friends knew me well. Similarly, my mom's friends and my sisters' friends are my friends too. My brother had strict instructions from my parents to not bring his friends home, as there were teenage girls at home. Hence, we didn't know his friends except a few family friends.

All my sisters' friends liked me very much, and I also liked them a lot. My sister Mythreyi's friend Sudha was different from others. She never showed me any sympathy. In fact, she used to challenge me to take up some new things, pushing me out of my comfort zone. But I used to feel very comfortable with her, I didn't know why. Later, I came to know that her brother also had a polio attack. He studied well, walked with callipers and played chess very well. His family members were habituated in showing empathy rather than sympathy to him. They encouraged him to do things on his own so that he could be self-reliant and independent. I suppose she wanted to give me the same treatment. She never paid any special attention to me, and I really appreciated that.

5

And I Graduated!

After completing 10th standard, securing first rank, I wanted to join intermediate[1] course with MPC group (mathematics, physics and chemistry) in the same SBS Government Junior College, Sathupally. To secure an admission, we approached the principal. Both intermediate and high school composite mathematics classes were conducted in the same building under the administrative control of the principal.

Till 10th standard, all our classes were conducted in the same room. In intermediate, each subject had a different classroom. As mentioned before, I used to crawl on the ground at home in those days. When we explained my situation and requested the principal to conduct the classes in one room and also make the place accessible for me, he expressed his inability to consider my request. As I was entering teenage, I felt embarrassed to crawl in front of other people. Finally, I decided to continue my studies privately. Our previous principal Sri Gopala Rao felt very bad about this situation. He had a very good opinion of me, considering my track record in studies during his tenure. He expressed his concern that if such a brilliant student didn't get the opportunity to go to college, after

---

[1] Education structure in our area was: kindergarten (Nursery, LKG and UKG), primary school (1st–5th standard), high school (6th–10th standard) and intermediate (1st year and 2nd year).

some time she might stop her education due to the lack of support. I felt that had he been the principal, he definitely would have made some arrangements for me.

I was selected for Prathibha Award, which is given to meritorious students for their brilliant performance in SSC public exams. Scholarship benefits under that award would be for five years if the student pursued his/her higher education in any government college. But due to lack of disabled-friendly infrastructural facilities in colleges, I could not join any college to continue my education as a regular student, and thereby, I was deprived of that benefit.

Homeschooling

To appear for intermediate privately, I had to choose a group. I love mathematics and definitely wanted to have it as one of the subjects in the group. I could not opt for the MPC group as I had no access to labs to perform experiments for the practical classes, because I was appearing privately. I had only two choices left with the combination of mathematics, that is, MEC (mathematics, economics and commerce) and MEL (mathematics, economics and logic). I opted for MEL group since I didn't like commerce then (who would know that I would end up working at a bank for the rest of my life!). But again, there was another obstacle. As per the rules at that time, if the subject was not taught in a college, a student could not write the exam from that college. I had to appear for exams at the college where all those subjects were being taught. In the college in my native place, logic subject was not taught.

I strongly wanted to study mathematics. Hence, my father sent his friend to Hyderabad, representing me, to permit me to write the exam in the college in my native place as an exceptional case. He explained my situation to the concerned official who had also studied the subject of logic. He advised me through my father's friend to not choose logic as it would be very difficult to prepare privately without proper guidance. He also said that he had no problem in granting the permission if I still preferred that subject.

In spite of knowing the challenges very well, I opted for logic as one of my optional subjects. For me, there were two challenges: one, I had to study mathematics without any lecturer's support, and two, I had to study an entirely new subject, logic, which no one in my village had even heard of. Thankfully, God has given me a sharp brain. My friends used to share their English and mathematics class notes with me. I depended fully on textbooks, guide books and my friends' notes. For economics and logic, I had to study all by myself. For mathematics, my cousin Rahul, who was doing his graduation in a local government degree college, taught me whenever he found time.

My second language in intermediate was Hindi. My grandfather, who was a scholar in Sanskrit and Telugu, helped me understand a few Hindi lessons. At that time, he was 80 years old. He lost his memory due to old age and was unable to recognize even his own children. Even then, he taught me Hindi. Surprisingly, he remembered all the *slokas* and poems despite losing memory in other areas. He practised homeopathy and helped many people recover from their health problems, besides curing cattle's and chickens' diseases in our village. He had so many books on homeopathy. He gave all those books to a homeopathy doctor in our area. He not only loved his children and grandchildren but also cared for all the people he came across in his life. We revered him greatly for his pious nature.

Although I was not going to college, my friends used to be in touch with me regularly. I didn't get the feeling that I missed them anytime.

When I was in the first year, new tenants occupied the home across the street. They had two daughters, Jayalakshmi and Saroja. Jayalakshmi was also in the first year. I got a new friend, and our families also became very close friends.

On the day of the logic exam, I was the only examinee in the entire centre. Chief superintendent, invigilator, police and other staff were present at the exam centre just for me! It is an unforgettable memory for me. I completed intermediate in first class and scored good marks particularly in mathematics and logic, which everyone thought was a tough task.

Teaching: My Passion

When I started appearing for intermediate privately at the age of 15, I thought of conducting private tuitions so as to not miss the touch with the external world. I love to mingle with people in general. Initially, my father didn't like the idea as he thought it might be a strain for me. He never likes anything which he thinks might be strenuous for me. But I could finally convince him. Initially, I started conducting tuitions to primary class students from a local English medium school. My father strictly told me that the number of students must not exceed 20. As students were from different classes, we thought that accepting a limited number of students would give me the opportunity to pay individual attention. I followed his advice. I introduced some initiatives apart from covering their syllabus, namely (a) learning one Telugu poem daily from *Vemana Satakam* or *Sumathi Satakam*, which contain character moulding morals. (I strongly feel that everyone should love and learn their mother tongue and yet respect other languages), (b) weekly discussion on any one of the great leaders' stories with the students to motivate and (c) to encourage them to come prepared with important news from the daily newspaper to be up to date with the current affairs.

Slowly, I earned a very good name as a tuition teacher. After some days, there was a great demand among students to join my tutorial. But my father didn't allow me to increase the number, thinking that I would be strained. In spite of parents coming with great recommendations, my father used to decline those requests if the number exceeded 20. After I started conducting tuitions, my friend's sister Vidya Chandana, who was in the 10th standard, joined as my student. From then, I had students who were just one-year junior to me until I stopped conducting tuitions.

When I was in the intermediate second year, my friend Mohini's sister and her friends, who were in first year MPC group, requested me to start mathematics tuition for them. I accepted their request. Now when I look back, I wonder how I had accepted their request without any fear. I studied privately on my own without having the support of any lecturer. Teaching that subject to students just one year junior to me was not an easy task. Those who underwent that challenge would understand my words better. Frankly speaking, I worked hard and studied mathematics in depth to teach students more than when I appeared for my exam. Those students continued attending my tuition till the completion of their second year.

When I was in my degree second year, one day, some first-year degree boys approached me. In those days, there was no regular mathematics lecturer in our local government degree college. They were struggling a lot. They came to know that some of their classmates (girls) were coming to me and so they also wanted to join my tuition. I said 'yes' thinking that teaching to 1 student or 40 would require the same effort, unlike teaching students from different primary classes in the evening.

After they left, my sister came to know that I had accepted their request. My sister told me that I should have taken our father's permission before accepting their request. She also told me that it would be very difficult to manage those hefty, tall and naughty boys. She expressed her concern that those boys might not listen to me. I didn't worry about the height, weight or naughtiness of students. I didn't think that anyone needs to consider those things while accepting a person as a student. But I was worried much about not taking permission from my dad. When they asked, I didn't think about their gender; I just accepted them as I would to any other student. I waited anxiously till my father returned home in the evening. I prepared myself to receive his scolding. But my main concern was if he didn't accept it, how would I inform those students. If I commit to something, I don't like to step back. Fortunately, when I informed this to my father, he took it very lightly and told me that he would bring a small foldable black board, a pointer and a chalk box as the student count increased. As promised, he bought all that stuff and fixed a board on the wall. I heaved a sigh of relief! I was not thrown into an embarrassing situation of breaking my commitment with the students. I conducted classes for degree students in the morning and for primary or middle classes in the evening. I used to prepare a lot to teach degree students. I didn't want to be nescient in front of my students.

In degree mathematics, there were some important theorems, one or two of which would most probably appear in the question paper. By that time, my cousin Rahul moved to another place and he told me that he would visit me during vacations and teach those theorems. But unfortunately, he could not come due to his other commitments. I prepared for all other chapters on my own but for this one alone, I waited for him till the last minute. With him not showing up, we tried to get support from any maths lecturer or any senior students studying their masters. But no one came forward to teach me. Finally, I learned them by rote and reproduced them in the exam in toto out of my memory. But when I had to teach the same chapter to my students, I felt like catching a fever. I studied the textbooks in both Telugu and English languages and also referred to various guide books. I tried to understand the reason and logic for each and every step, and how the final step came about. I took it as a big challenge. Finally, when I explained that chapter to my students, I received a standing ovation from all of them. They told me that no one explained theorems with such great ease to them. All my sincere efforts came to fruition! I was greatly satisfied on that day as a teacher.

In those days, if any of my students expressed their inability to pay the fee to me citing their financial constraints, I waived it off for them. More than earning money, my aim was to prove myself as a successful teacher and to support the people who were in need. Many people without even knowing me personally come forward to help me many times in my life. I have been experiencing this from my childhood. I may not be able to extend help to the same people who helped me, but I took advantage of every opportunity that came my way to help others in ways possible for me. It gives me immense satisfaction that I am able to contribute back for the betterment of the society.

One of my students, Aruna, daughter of a bank manager, had become a dear friend to me later. Earlier, when her parents approached me to join her in my classes, they introduced her saying that though she was a bright student, she was not very serious about her studies. She would avoid tuitions on some pretext or the other. After joining my tuition classes, she liked the way I taught. Even when she suffered from fever, she used to attend the tuition, ignoring the advice of her family to stay back and take rest. She developed a strong interest in studies and liked me very much. Her father used to come to pick her up and waited outside our house under a tree. Although we invited him inside, he never came and just waited outside. At that time, I didn't know that he would become my boss later. Life is full of thrilling and unexpected experiences. And another unusual thing is that when I was doing my MBA (in banking and finance), after many years of my graduation, Aruna became my teacher as she had already completed her CA by that time.

Teachers feel happy to see the growth of their students. It gives them immense satisfaction.

I derived that satisfaction from many of my students. They reached great heights. Many of them are in touch with me till date. Aruna is the founder of an organization which deals in financial accounting; Sudhakar is a doctor in the USA; Tulasi Prasad, Swapna, Sriram, Rajesh, Surendra and some other students are in the software industry; Raghava, Ramesh, Ganesh and Ravi are into business; D. Rajesh is a senior physiotherapist; Vidya Chandana is a district-level government officer—just to name a few.

Aruna and some other students of mine are supporting me in my social activities even today. I am very happy with their growth and concern for fellow beings.

Amla Tree

In our house, we had an amla tree. It gave small amlas that tasted very nice. They were very delicious, especially when we ate them with salt. Even the thought of them makes my mouth water, and I can't describe that taste in words. As the tree was next to our cattle shed, it used to get abundant natural manure. It was one of my favourite fruits in childhood. When I conducted tuitions, all my students used to wait for my green signal to go and grab those amlas after the class. Those students used to try and climb the tree to pick the fruits from the top branches. As its branches were very brittle, they used to get good scolding from my mom. I used to take those fruits to my school and offer them to my friends and teachers. Everyone used to like them very much. It is a fond memory for me.

Graduation Exams

I could write my exams for intermediate in my village itself. But the only undergraduate college in our village was then under the affiliation of Kakatiya University. All my siblings had graduated from Osmania University (OU). I also wanted to graduate from OU, for which I had great respect. Because of this, I had to write exams in Kodad, which comes under OU, and it was the nearest place to my village. I opted for a group with mathematics, history and public administration. I had to write language subjects (Hindi and English) in the second year. My elder sister, who did masters in Hindi, helped me prepare for my exams in Hindi and dad helped me with English. In the second year, mom, dad and I went to Kodad and stayed at one of my father's friend's house for four days.

For the first exam, the invigilator didn't allow my rickshaw till the examination room which was on the ground floor. He stopped the rickshaw at the main gate itself. My father requested him a lot to allow the rickshaw up to the exam hall, but he refused our request. My father carried me from the main gate to my seat in the examination hall. But the same invigilator came to the main gate and allowed my rickshaw till the exam hall on the second day. We wondered about his gesture. We later came to know that he was very impressed with my performance in the first paper, which he observed during his invigilation. Hope the educational institutions would realize the rights of the persons with disability at least by now.

As we had to stay for a greater number of days in the third year, we decided to take a room on rent. Through our family friends, we could get a room for ₹100 for one month in a lower-middle-class area. In those days, we didn't have the financial capacity to stay in a hotel. My mom and dad brought all the necessary items including grocery, brooms and ash to wash utensils from our home. We went there fully prepared. We only bought vegetables. Our landlady expressed her displeasure for not asking any help from them and bringing big luggage for a short stay. After going there, using the toilet was a big challenge for me. They didn't have a proper toilet. They were used to going out in the fields to answer the nature's call. To take a bath, however, there was a temporary enclosed area. Our landlady, Ms Kamalamma, was a very nice lady and very supportive. Finally, she and my parents requested her neighbours (who are also our distant relatives) to allow me to use their toilet. Every morning, my father used to take me there on the house owner's bicycle along with my small plastic stool, as it was an Indian toilet. Being a teenager, I used to feel embarrassed for my daily trip to the toilet in front of all our neighbours. For me, using a toilet was a big event. I used to feel very bad if I had to go more than once, thinking of the trouble it would cause others. Every night, I used to worry about the next morning's ritual. My thoughts were full of toilet requirements and exams. I even started wondering why God bestowed upon us nature's calls altogether.

My parents and I were a wonder for the people of the area. They were all farmers and would generally get their daughters married immediately after they become teenagers. They did not give importance to girls' education. In my case, I was a girl with severe disability, and my parents bringing me all the way to a different place and taking up these challenges to make me write the exams were unbelievable for them. They were very friendly with us. Although I mingle with strangers very easily, I could not speak to them much due to my hectic schedule of preparing for the exam. My examination hall was on the third floor. My father used to carry me in his arms up to that floor. How strenuous it would have been for a 50-year-old person to carry a 19-year-old girl to the third floor!

After my exams, when we were leaving that place, all the people of that area came till the end of that street to bid farewell to us. Such was their love, affection and admiration for us. Even today, I remember that scene very well. That frame is captured in my mind forever. Nowadays, with a smartphone, we can capture all important moments in our lives. But in those days, we could only capture them in our brains. Our landlady didn't take rent from us because she had great respect for my parents and was very impressed with my hard work and brilliance. In spite of being in a financial crisis, she didn't accept any amount from us even when we insisted.

Two months later, our results were announced. I had passed graduation with first class. Madhavi Latha, BA (Mathematics)—a proud feeling for me. I thank my parents, siblings, cousin Rahul, friends and all other well-wishers wholeheartedly for their loving and affectionate support in acquiring my degree.

Later, after many years, we met Ms Kamalamma, our landlady in Kodad, in Hyderabad. At that time, she proudly told us that their daughter did her postgraduation and was working in some organization. She also told us how enthusiastically she was waiting for that very moment when she could share this good news with us.

Now, if I look back and think about this part of my life, I can't understand whether to appreciate myself for my determination to do what I wanted in my life in spite of so many challenges or to scold myself for troubling my parents to fulfil my wishes. But one thing is crystal clear—my parents' unconditional love. A big salute to them for their determination to provide education to me in the way I wanted, and for their vision to make me independent by educating me and making my life more meaningful.

6

My Love for Water

From my childhood, I loved water very much!

At our home in my village, we have a well, in front of which a ground-level cement platform was built for free flow of used water. In my childhood, my mother or sisters drew water from the well to bathe me. The advantage of well water is that when the outside weather is cold, the water inside is warm and when the outside weather is hot, the water inside is cold.

Taking a bath directly with our well water is one of the sweet memories of my life. I loved our well and the tasty water in it.

When I saw any water sources such as ponds and lakes, I felt like jumping into them. Whenever I went to temples in my childhood, I used to request my family members to take me to the pond. But they only showed the pond to me from a distance, thinking that going near it might be dangerous for me. The more they kept me away from water, the more I wanted to go near it.

In my childhood, every now and then, my brother used to take me on a bicycle to Bethupally Medium Irrigation Reservoir in the evenings.

After seeing such a big reservoir, I wondered how big the sea would be to look at. One day, when its bund was breached due to heavy rains and the water overflowed, all the villagers went there to see the gushing water. My brother took me too. After seeing the heavy water flow which submerged hundreds of acres of paddy fields, I felt a bit dizzy.

During my high school days, once I went to my friend Vasista's house along with other friends. Her father was a forest range officer. Behind her house was a mini forest. We sat under trees and played. At that time, someone told us that there was a lotus tank nearby. We all wanted to go there but were afraid of our elders. We decided to go anyway due to our love for water and lotus flowers. As everyone thought it's nearby, they decided to carry me and take me along with them. But even after walking for a long distance, we could not find it. Actually, it was in a far-off place. My friends struggled a lot with carrying me; they carried me in turns. Finally, we reached there. After seeing the tank full of lotus flowers, we felt so incredibly happy. They made me sit at a spot far away from the water. One of our friends ventured into water to bring some flowers. Rest of us were quite tense. As soon as she came back safely, we heaved a sigh of relief. We played with those flowers for some time. Although we didn't want to leave the place, thinking about the scolding we would get at home, we started back. My friends were already too tired. Carrying me again had become a big challenge for them. They started walking slowly. After some time, they could not walk at all; they were far too tired. At that point, we found a cement bench (without backrest). They made me sit on it. We felt so happy and thanked the people who had constructed it. Suddenly, we realized it was a grave. We all got very scared. Even in that scary situation, my friends took me into their arms and started running till we reached Vasista's house. It was a totally thrilling experience with mixed feelings of joy, fear and sadness for troubling my friends. I feel blessed to have such loving and caring friends. Usually, whenever we went to see a dead person, mom would allow us to enter into our house only after taking a head bath, as per the traditions she believed in strongly. So on that day, without telling her about this incident, I took a head bath quietly.

It was a dream of mine to dip my feet in a pond and sit in a relaxed mood, listening to light music. When I shared my dream with my colleagues one day, they humorously suggested that I keep my feet in a bucket full of water, close my eyes, imagine it is a pond and listen to light music from my tape recorder. My desire to enter into water was increasing day by day.

After a few years of joining a public sector bank, I went on leave fare concession (LFC) along with my parents to Chennai, Mahabalipuram, Kanchipuram and Tirupati in 1995. At Mahabalipuram, upon seeing the beach, I wanted to go near the water desperately. But it was so difficult to take me to the shore in that sand. My father could see my disappointment. He was looking for an opportunity to fulfil my wish. He saw the horses taking tourists for a ride on the beach. He could find a place where there was a wall with a low height. If I sat on the wall, I could shift to the back of the horse standing on the other side of the wall. But to reach that wall, my father had to walk in the sand, carrying me. Just then, my father found a person with a bicycle. He requested him to lend him the cycle for a few minutes. That person obliged and gave his bicycle. Finally, my parents made me sit on the wall, and from there to the back of the horse. After sitting on the horse, I feared that the horse might run away. But the jockey holding its reins made the horse walk slowly and very near to the water. Although I didn't get the opportunity to touch the water, I enjoyed the cool breeze and nearness to the sea. It was one of the great moments of my life.

We went to Mahanandi with my brother's family in 2002 when I was working in Hyderabad. Fortunately, there I got the opportunity to dip my legs in the *pushkarini* (temple pond) and keep my hands in the inflow of water to the *pushkarini*. It was my first experience with flowing water. When my niece Pranavi entered into the *pushkarini*, I encouraged her, sitting on the edge of it.

In the latter part of my life, I shifted to Chennai to join a multinational corporation (MNC) bank group. After coming to Chennai, we went to Marina Beach many times. But during all our visits, I only enjoyed the cool breeze, as it was not possible for my father to carry me for such a long distance in the sand to go near the water.

One day, we went to Golden Beach in Chennai. One of my students, Tulasi Prasad, who was working in Chennai, also accompanied us. My father and Tulasi tried to take me in the wheelchair near water as we found a short path to reach the sea. But it became a Herculean task for them. They brought one plastic chair, as its weight would be much less, from a shop owner at the beach. Even with that, they could not carry me in the sand. Suddenly, two people came there to support us. They looked like workers from the nearby shops. They carried me in that chair and took me to the edge of the water. For the first time in my life, I could dip my feet in the sea water! Oh, what an unforgettable moment—my joy knew no bounds.

After some time, the intensity of the waves increased. My father decided to go back, though I still wanted to be there for some more time. We were searching for someone to support us in going back. Again, the same two people came back to help. They might have been observing us as they knew we would require their support while returning. They brought me near our car. I was in a very happy mood. I wanted to give them whatever amount they would demand. When we offered them some money, they got quite hurt because their sole intention was only to help us. They didn't do it for any monetary reward from us.

Whenever a hotel staff or workers at other places help me, I offer money to them. Some people accept it. But others just help me out of their concern for fellow beings without expecting anything in return. I don't want to hurt them in either case and will be in a dilemma in such situations whether to offer or not.

On that day, I felt like God came in their disguise to fulfil my long-cherished wish!

After a few years, destiny sprinkled some magic in my life. I became a national para swimming champion. But more on that later.

We bought a flat in Chennai in 2017. After a lot of search, we bought it mainly because it had a swimming pool. Having a swimming pool in our apartment's complex gives a lot of comfort to a person like me who loves to swim daily.

As a swimmer, I tried swimming only in pools. But I always had a desire to try swimming at least once in a river.

God blessed me by fulfilling that wish too. In 2017, I went to a naturopathy centre which is on the banks of Krishna River. There they built a steel cage-like structure adjacent to the edge in the river where people could swim without any fear of drowning or getting washed away. That was the first time in my life I got the opportunity to swim in a river in a secured arrangement. I felt elated after having swam in running water, enjoying its freshness, unlike swimming in still water in the pool. Spiritually, too, I was greatly satisfied swimming in the sacred river Krishna.

Later in 2019, we took our Indian men and women's teams to participate in Paralympic Qualifiers held in Pattaya, Thailand, in the capacity of the president of Wheelchair Basketball Federation of India (WBFI). The hotel where we stayed was on the beach. I used to swim daily in the 300-m length pool in the mornings. One morning, our team's physiotherapists Ashkar Ali and Ambareesh as well as coach Thayu helped me go to the sea for a swim. Had my father been with me, he would have not allowed me at all due to his concern for my safety. It was a great feeling when I entered the sea for the first time in my life—I was in a euphoric state. I swam for half an hour in the sea. Luckily, on that particular beach in Pattaya, the intensity of waves was less. Closer to the shore, one feels the intensity of waves more. Once we went a bit further into the sea, it was calm. I never even dreamt of

Left: Aqua Yoga Right: Sea swimming

swimming in the sea, but God is very kind for having bestowed such an amazing experience on me.

After coming back from Pattaya, I went to Mussoorie to address the IAS officers who were attending their mid-career development programme at Lal Bahadur Shastri National Academy of Administration (LBSNAA). Immediately after my talk, I went to Dehradun airport to catch my return flight. But due to heavy fog, our flight got cancelled. I had to stay there for one day. I got an opportunity to stay in Rishikesh with the help of LBSNAA officials. My place of accommodation was just beside Mother Ganges, and my room had a great view. By the time I reached the guest house along with my sister Anantham, it was night. I could not sleep that night. I have a great respect for river Ganga; I was sleeping just beside her—that feeling itself excited me to no end. I woke up very early in the morning, at around 4:00 am. I took a bath, got ready, opened the curtain and waited very eagerly for the sunrise to see the river. Finally, the moment came. It was a very delightful experience to see the magnificent river from our room. On that day, with the support of the staff there, I could go near the river through one of the accessible ghats for wheelchair users. I dipped my hands and legs in Mother Ganges. The water was freezing cold though. But being overjoyed, we didn't care about the freezing water. In the evening, I even got the opportunity to give *harathi* (an offering of lit camphor to the deity) to Mother Ganges. What a divine opportunity I had!

7

Small Deeds, Big Lessons

I begin this chapter by asking my reader three simple questions:

Do you think you need to have a lot of money in order to help others?

Do you think you need to wait till you are settled in your life before you start supporting others?

Do you hesitate to appreciate the good work done by unknown people?

If your answer to any of these questions is in the affirmative, then please read these experiences of mine which I am sharing with you here. Each has a story to narrate; each highlights the extraordinary difference a so-called ordinary act can make in our lives.

One day, when I was working in Hyderabad, I was trying to cross the road. I was riding a Kinetic Honda scooter which had been modified according to my needs; an additional two wheels had been attached to balance the vehicle. I was sitting on my scooter, patiently waiting to cross the small lane which connected two main roads. It was always busy with heavy traffic, and there were also many shops on both sides of the road. Suddenly, I saw a boy holding a stand with tea glasses foolishly jumping into the middle of that busy road. Looking at him, I thought he must be delivering tea to some nearby shops. I was worried about his safety but as he was now standing right in the middle of the road, vehicles were compelled to stop as they didn't have any place to overtake that boy. Irritated, the drivers started honking continuously.

To my surprise, the boy gave me a sign with his eyes and hand to cross the road. He had actually done this to enable me to cross the road, which I did. I looked back to thank him but there was no sign of the boy. My heart was filled with gratitude, and I was amazed that he was so helpful and caring at such a young age. Also, like a true yogi, he did not even expect a word of thanks from me. I pray for his well-being even today.

Sometimes when I am driving on traffic-heavy highways, some lorry/truck drivers also stop their vehicles to enable me to cross the road easily. These are the people who enrich my life's journey so magically.

Later in 2004, I bought a Maruti Zen, which was modified as a hand-operated car. In the initial days, when I was driving my car, my concentration would always be on controlling the steering wheel and on the front view of the road only. One day, my father was with me in the car. Suddenly, he told me to slow down as an old couple was waiting to cross the road. I had actually not seen them as they were standing on the side of the road, but I felt really bad for not observing them. I immediately slowed down, and they crossed the road. At that time, my father told me to always support those who are struggling to cross the road while I am driving. My mind turned to those considerate lorry/truck drivers who had helped me on the highways.

This episode was like a huge eye-opener for me. I realized that we do not need to plan great things or events to support our fellow beings. Even a small act goes a long way, and therefore, these acts should become our way of life.

In another incident, one of my ex-colleagues, Rajesh, received an award (a gift coupon) meant for new joiners for his best performance. He had just completed four or five months of service. Rajesh could have got whatever he wanted, say a shirt or a pair of shoes, with the gift amount of the coupon. Instead, he bought rice and sugar and gave them to an orphanage. When I came to know this, I asked him what prompted him to do so. He replied in a humble way that he thought that his contribution would help the organizers of the orphanage to prepare some sweets for the residents as the festive season was approaching.

My next question to him was how he had got that idea as we generally see people doing such activities at a much older age, or after retirement. He replied that as he was not sure of the span of his life, he wanted to do whatever he could without waiting for an ideal time. Rajesh's attitude towards life really impressed me. Indeed, I was learning some great life lessons from youngsters.

On another day, while driving back from office, I stopped at a crossroad, waiting for the green signal. We all have, at some time or the other, got this feeling that someone is staring at us. I experienced a similar feeling, and so, I turned my head and looked towards the left. There was a truck standing just next to my car. Using his eyes and hands, the driver made signs to convey to me that he had been following my car for some distance and that he appreciated my driving skills. All this happened in just a few seconds. I thanked him for this compliment with my facial expressions.

When the lights turned green, he took a left turn and I a right turn. He knew very well that we wouldn't meet again, did not even know me, yet tried to convey his appreciation. He was driving a bigger vehicle than mine and was, in all probability, a better driver. It seems that he had a good heart and wanted to encourage others. It invariably brings a feeling of satisfaction when we are appreciated by an expert in that field. Even today, I look back at that incident with a sense of happiness.

A small act, a single word, a sign of appreciation or a look of encouragement brings so much joy. I strongly believe that we should not hesitate in appreciating others, even if we don't know them. In this wonderful journey we are all connected, and reaching out to someone with kindness, in whatever small way, will only strengthen this circle of life.

8

Finding a Job Was a Tough Job

Since my childhood my parents used to emphasize on the need for becoming financially independent. They told me not to become a burden on anyone in my life. In my parents' view, as we didn't have much property, it would be better to study well and get a job for financial independence. Whenever they got a chance, they used to remind me about this. So I was fully motivated to get a job. I started to think about the awkward situations I would have to face when I join the job. The thought of crawling in the workplace was embarrassing. Till then, as mentioned before, I used to crawl around in home and someone in my family carried me in their arms when I went out. Although I insisted that I should be left at home, they never agreed to it and took me everywhere they went. I used to feel very sorry for troubling them. Also, there was no work from home option back then which I could opt as I did in junior college.

Fortunately, my brother, who was working in Hyderabad, came across people who were using walkers in their rehab. He brought one for me at the right time. It was an aluminium unfoldable walker. It was like a ray of hope. I tried to walk with its help. It was very stressful, but

I didn't complain. It was at least not like the callipers. When I wore callipers, I felt like I was trapped in a cage. But with a walker, I felt relatively relaxed in my movements. I was determined to walk away from this adversity and work independently. Within a few months, I could walk for a few metres on a smooth surface. Years later, when I shared this story with a physiotherapist, he was surprised. He said that it would take a minimum of six months' training to strengthen the shoulder muscles to take up the burden of holding the walker and lifting the body to be able to walk. I could successfully walk with the help of a walker, slowly but independently, without any training.

While doing my final-year graduation, my father suggested that I apply for a Life Insurance Corporation (LIC) assistant's job. Till that time, my father was of the strong opinion that only medical and teaching professions were safe for women. In my case, he felt that it would be difficult for me to go to different classrooms to teach students. That's why he started exploring various options. As there is a branch office of LIC in our place, he thought it might be a better option. In those days, as we were in a remote place, we didn't get any type of career guidance. After checking with a few well-wishers, we could buy some preparation material for the written test for the LIC assistant position. I started preparing seriously even before they released recruitment notification for the posts. As most of the questions would come from arithmetic, I started preparing for it. I found it easy as I was teaching mathematics to primary/middle school students, apart from teaching degree students.

Simultaneously, I paid the fee for my MSc (Mathematics) degree and started preparing for it.

A few months later, LIC notification was released. I applied for it with the support of my father and brother.

As per the policy of LIC, not everyone who applied would receive a hall ticket (a letter with the approval to enter into the exam hall). They would send hall tickets to applicants based on their marks in graduation. I didn't get it. I was worried. When we checked with other applicants whom we knew, we came to know that few people received their hall tickets even when they got less marks than me. Then my father went to Warangal to meet the senior divisional manager to find out the reason for me not receiving the hall ticket. He informed my father that applicants with legs-related disabilities were not eligible for that post. He enquired whether I acquired any typing qualifications. For a typist post, they would consider even the applicants with lower limbs-related disabilities. In those days, when our junior college principal told us that he could not make any accommodation for me to study in college, we came back silently and appeared privately. When the LIC officer told us that I was ineligible due to my disability, we accepted it quietly. We never questioned them as to why they were not providing equal opportunities to me. When my father came back and told me about the senior officer's words, I felt very bad for not getting the opportunity to apply for that exam in spite of me preparing so hard for it. We decided to join the typing classes. In those days, Mr Bhavani Sankar was the only person with a typing institute; it was on the main road very close to our house. My father knew him very well. My brother also learnt typing there. I started going for classes. Sitting on a tall stool and typing on the typewriter was a challenge for me due to its height and my low reach. But I never uttered a word about it. I wanted to get a job at any cost. Hence, I refrained from making any complaint on issues which were inconvenient for me. He was a good teacher. I made some good friends there. I had to go to Tiruvuru, a nearby town, for exams. I practised English and Telugu higher. But with Telugu, I was not so comfortable as it's a bit complicated with requiring multiple keys for each alphabet. So it used to take more time. Finally, we went to Tiruvuru and attended the exam. I cleared English higher type exam in first class. I was eagerly waiting for the LIC notification. Around that time, one day my cousin Murali came to our place. In the conversation, we explained all our trials for the job. Then he suggested that I apply for a bank job; he informed us that he had seen some employees with disabilities in banks. He was also working in a bank. In those days, the big question for us was who would give a job to a person with severe disabilities like me. Taking his advice, we waited for Banking Service Recruitment Board (BSRB) notification. They used to conduct one centralized written test to recruit staff for all public sector banks. Based on merit, they allocated the selected candidates to all public sector banks. Again, I started my preparation rigorously for the BSRB exam. The notification was released. I applied and got a hall ticket. We could cross the first step successfully!

My examination centre was in Vijayawada. As my uncles stayed in Vijayawada, accommodation was not an issue. We went to the exam centre well in advance. Examination hall was on the fifth floor of an engineering college building which didn't have an elevator. When we approached the officials explaining our difficulty in going to the fifth floor, they understood our problem and agreed to arrange my exam in a room on the ground floor. We felt happy, and I was waiting for the exam to begin. Then, as my father was speaking to some officials, he came to know the procedure just 10 minutes before the exam. As per that, the invigilator on the fifth floor would sign my question and answer sheets and then send them to me with someone. There was a specific sequence in which they should distribute the question papers to applicants based on their hall ticket numbers. And the process could not be started earlier as it would reveal the questions to other applicants in advance. So I would lose a few minutes due to the delay in bringing the papers to me. Hence, my father rushed to me and told me that he would carry me to the fifth floor as he didn't want me to miss those valuable few minutes considering the competition involved in those jobs. Had we checked with them about giving me the additional time that I would miss due to that delay, what they would have told us we really didn't know. But my father didn't want to wait. He carried me to the fifth floor without taking any break as we were running out of time. After reaching the fifth floor, he was already gasping. I could not see his strain. After reaching there, they directed us to the farthest room which was allocated to me based on my hall ticket. Somehow, he carried me till the room. Irony was that my seat was on the last bench. But by then, he was fully exhausted that he could not help any further. He asked me to go to the last bench taking support from other desks and benches along the way. I was trying to do the same, but he could not bear to see me struggle either. So he carried me till my seat, even though I asked him not to carry me anymore. But in the hurry, we forgot the hall ticket and exam pad in the ground floor room. So my father toughed it out and rushed down to the ground floor and came back running with my hall ticket and exam pad all over again. By that time, he was beyond exhausted and was struggling to breathe. But he made it right in time. By the time I got my hall ticket and pad, the invigilator came to my bench and gave the papers to me. When I started looking at the question paper, I could not see anything as my eyes were filled with tears. But I controlled myself as I knew very well that all my dad's efforts would be wasted if I sat and cried without writing. After that, I tuned out everything and focused only on my exam. I did well. But what my father did on that day was out of the world. Due to such intense strain, there were even chances of a heart failure. He would not have taken up such a risk, had it not been a matter of my career. I can't express my gratitude for my parents in words. Today, what I am and where I am is only because of their selfless efforts and heaps of love and affection.

On 25 December 1990, BSRB written test results were declared. I was selected. We celebrated that achievement. My interview was going to be held in Warangal. JP uncle (my father's brother) was working there at that time, so we went to his house. He is a very loving and caring person. We greatly respect and love him. Immediately after getting his job, he took the family responsibilities from my dad. His landlords were nice people; they even invited us for dinner. We had dinner under the moonlight; it was a nice experience. I always love to be close to nature, but it was rarely possible for various reasons.

Next day, though my interview was post lunch, my father and uncle took me there very early. When we reached the venue, interviews of the morning batch were going on. My father and uncle are generally overcautious.

The clerk who was scrutinizing the papers and sending candidates into the interview room saw my physical condition. He might have developed a soft corner for me. After the last candidate's interview was over, he went inside and informed the interviewers about me and requested to go for my interview, so that I need not wait till they commenced the interviews after the lunch break. They also accepted and called me in. I went inside. The clerk told my dad that I would come out within five minutes as interviewers would be hungry and would want to finish it fast. But they took 25 minutes. When I was responding to every question confidently, they started asking more and more questions. I could see a great appreciation on their faces. I came out confidently.

As the interview room was on the first floor, my father/uncle carried me. While coming down, when my dad saw the interviewers coming that way, he tried to put me down thinking that if they saw him carrying me, they might not consider me for the post. We were that much ignorant and innocent about the rights of the persons with disabilities on that day. We had so many fears regarding whether anyone would give a job to me after seeing my severe disability.

The interview results were announced, and I was selected for the bank job. Our family's joy knew no bounds! We were all so elated. By that time, almost all my siblings had jobs. However, in my case, as all of us had many doubts, everyone heaved a sigh of relief after seeing the results. We were all of the view that my appointment in a bank was confirmed as I was selected in the interview.

After a few days of the announcement of interview results, I received a letter from the bank to come to Hyderabad for a medical test. We felt very happy upon receiving that letter. We went to Hyderabad to take the medical test. By that time, my brother had shifted to Hyderabad along with his family as he'd got a job in the city. We went to my brother's house and from there to the address given in the letter. The head of the medical board was a paediatrician. He referred me to an ophthalmologist, a general physician and a gynaecologist. All the reports were fine. Finally, when we met the head, he asked us some questions about my condition and my abilities in managing day-to-day chores, etc. At that time, my sixth sense told me something was wrong, but I didn't know what it was. Since my childhood, I have been observing that what my sixth sense indicates becomes a reality.

They told all the candidates to come to Hyderabad to collect their appointment letters on 18 March 1991. We came back and started making arrangements to go again and receive the appointment letter. Suddenly, one day we received a telegram. We got scared. Generally, in those days, people used telegrams for informing serious health conditions of a family member or some other bad news. That's why everyone was scared of telegrams. It was mentioned in the telegram that the head of the medical board declared I was unfit for the post, and so, I need not go to Hyderabad to receive the appointment letter. And it was also mentioned that a detailed letter would follow. It was a bitter shock for all of us. All our hearts were broken. I could not control my tears. Till that time, in case of all other people we saw, the medical test was just a formality. We never saw anyone getting rejected in a medical test. It was very difficult for us to digest the rejection after reaching that level. That news caused great disappointment to my parents who were fully hopeful for me settling into a new life with a secure job. They lost hope that I would get a job. But they were desperate to ensure that I should work and be on my own. At that time, my father developed a strong desire to retire from service under voluntary retirement scheme (VRS) and to request his employers to give an LDC post to me instead. Although I felt bad for the rejection because of my disability, I didn't lose my confidence. It's mainly because of the confidence I gained from conducting tuitions. It helped me in many ways. After teaching degree students, I gained more confidence to face interviews. I started earning at the age of 15. Although it was a very small amount, I felt happy that I was able to support my dad. My dad struggled a lot in life. Without any financial support and any other type of backing, and with a meagre salary (in those days, teachers' salaries were very low), he took care of his parents, siblings, wife and children. No one was there to support him, as all our relatives were also facing their own challenges. Hence, I felt happy that I could be of some help to him. However, my mother used to spend that amount to buy things only for me, like a watch, gold bangles, etc. Because of the good name I earned by conducting tuitions, I was confident of starting a tutorial on a full-fledged basis if I couldn't get any job. Hence, I strongly refused my father's proposal to take VRS.

Later, we received the letter from the bank as mentioned in their telegram. In that letter, they added a sentence at the end saying that in case we felt that there was an element of human error in the doctor's judgement, we could prefer an appeal to the bank. That sentence was a ray of hope for us. We didn't want to lose the opportunity. We wanted to try our luck. At that time, due to holidays, my brother came to our place with his family. We left them at our native place to take care of the house and took their house keys and went to Hyderabad. We prepared for a longer stay in Hyderabad, if required.

After going to Hyderabad, we didn't know whom to approach—whether to go to the bank directly or take the opinion from an expert in this area. My sister-in-law's brother suggested a lawyer. When we met the lawyer, he went through the bank's letter and advised us to prefer an appeal first as mentioned by the bank. As per the lawyer's view, only after exhausting all the available options should we knock the doors of the high court, seeking justice. In those days, bank unions were very strong. Someone suggested that we should meet the employees' union leader. My father went and met him. By that time, the medical board's head might have updated him about my case. Hence, he simply told my father that he heard about my case and came to know that my physical condition was very bad. He suggested that my father should find something for me so that I could do some work while sitting at home. One of the senior officers' union leaders was from my native place. My father approached him as well. But he told dad that he couldn't intervene in this matter as it was related to the employees' union. Thus, we didn't get any support from either of the unions.

We went to the government hospital where I had my surgery to get callipers, which I hated in my childhood tooth to nail. But at that time, I could no longer avoid it as I was desperate to get the job. It was a hot summer and in spite of the hot weather, we travelled almost 10–12 km in an autorickshaw daily to practise with the callipers.

We also decided to meet other orthopaedic doctors to take their opinion about the bank's rejection due to my disability. Every orthopaedic surgeon that we met strongly felt that mine was a genuine case and that I should get the job. At that time, my sister-in-law suggested Dr Vijayakumar, a veteran doctor. We went to him. After seeing my walker which was of an aluminium frame, he suggested that I should use a visco walker which would be foldable and have wheels in the front. He also told us that it would make my movement easier. As there were no wheels for my walker at that time, I had to lift the walker at every step to move forward. Actually, it was a very good suggestion as it lightened my strain. From then on, I used a visco walker for many years. It was more comfortable for me than using the aluminium frame walker.

The doctor also did another great favour to us. He gave a letter to one of his friends, Dr Srinivasa Rao, who was working as the head of the orthopaedic department at Gandhi Medical College. He said that as he was only a private medical practitioner, his certificate would not carry any weight. His friend who was a government doctor could be of much more help to us than him as his opinion would have more value. It turned out to be true. We went to Dr Srinivasa Rao; he was a very friendly person. After examining me, he gave a very good report saying that I was able to sit for long hours and walk with the help of a walker slowly but independently. He also mentioned in that letter that as per his view, I was fit for the bank job. It was really a very supportive document for our representation, considering his designation in a government hospital. As mentioned earlier, my father is very good in preparing representations. He drafted a nice one for me, clearly explaining my intelligence, my marks in various examinations, and my ability to sit on a high stool and typing for hours. He also raised a valid point about rejecting my case without taking the opinion of an orthopaedic surgeon by the previous medical board in spite of mine being an orthopaedic case. We attached Dr Srinivasa Rao's letter and submitted our representation. When we went to the bank, my father ensured that I would walk with my walker in that office to show to those officials that I could walk with the walker on my own. In those days, we innocently felt that if I didn't walk on my own, I wouldn't be eligible for that post.

All the officials in the bank were empathetic and polite with me. The concerned official promised to look into my representation and take necessary action. We did everything we could. We stayed for almost two and a half months in Hyderabad. If my brother's house was not there, we would have struggled a lot. Luckily, we didn't have any issue with regard to the food and accommodation. After a few days, we received a letter from the bank to be present before another medical board constituted by them under the leadership of another doctor. He was a very nice person. This board took the opinion of an orthopaedic surgeon, along with the opinion of all other specialists. Naturally, no orthopaedic surgeon would label me as unfit. Finally, the bank accepted my representation. So my job was confirmed. It was great news for all of us.

Generally, we worry about a job until we get it. And later, we start worrying about the place of posting. In my case, my father was on the verge of retirement. I thought that till his retirement, it would be ideal if I got a posting in my native place; later on, we could go to any place as per the management's instructions. With that intention, we requested the management to give me the first posting in my native place. The management was empathetic, but the union leader objected to it for some other reasons. This time, my father and I went and met the employees' union leader, the same person who told my father earlier to arrange for some work at home for me. Frankly speaking, I didn't like meeting him due to his earlier suggestion to my dad. But as I had to work in the same bank with him and as he was in a powerful position, my father insisted on me meeting him to be on good terms. Dad and I went to him. He congratulated me for getting the appointment. He told us that he could not support me at that point of time in getting a posting at my native place due to some other issues. But he promised to bring me back to my native place within six months. I didn't consider his words to be credible, as my heart was filled with total aversion for him. But I never expressed my feelings to any of my colleagues throughout my service in that bank. To my surprise though, he kept his promise. Later, on the date of my relieving from my first place of posting exactly on the completion of six months, I took the relieving letter from his hands as he came there for some official purpose. At that time, he reminded me about keeping his promise.

We went to the bank's zonal office in Warangal and received our appointment letter after three months of sincere efforts. Finally, we came back to my native place after receiving the appointment letter. It was a great surprise for the people in my native place. Everyone appreciated my parents for their strong determination and sincere efforts to fight for my job in spite of not knowing anyone in Hyderabad. Many people said that they would have given up at the onset as they didn't have the courage and patience to go to that extent. Really, it's a wonderful achievement considering our knowledge, experience and contacts in those days. With that experience, I realized that if the cause is genuine and if our will is strong, God helps us in the guise of many people. Everyone we met supported us in a manner which was possible for them. We must share the credit for that achievement with all those good souls.

9

Banking on My Abilities

My first posting was at Paloncha. My mom and I had to manage living there all by ourselves when dad had to be in Sathupally, as he was still in service. Prior to my joining, my father went to Paloncha and searched for a house near the bank. More than comfort, he searched for a house in a secure place, as he was not going to be with us. Finally, he did find a house. The owner of the house was the proprietor of a transport company. He and his nephews would work day and night. The lights would be on throughout the night, and someone would be moving around. Hence, we had nothing to fear about. With all the required luggage, mom, dad and I went to Paloncha. Mom and dad arranged all the things in the house. It was a three-room house, and the rooms were in a straight line like train bogies. With the support of our house owner, my father arranged for a rickshaw driver to take me to the bank and bring me back in the evening. He looked for an auspicious day to join the job. It was 10 June 1991. My father and I went to the bank. My sister Anantham's friend Sailaja's husband, Mr Ashok, was working there. We met him in the bank. He took us to the manager's cabin and introduced us. The manager, Mr Prasad, verified the papers. I observed that he was chewing paan throughout the time I was in his cabin. Due to that paan or maybe it was his nature, he didn't speak much. He asked for a photocopy of some documents. My father went out and brought all the copies. Thereafter, he completed all the formalities. It was lunchtime by then. The manager came out along with us and introduced me to a senior colleague, Ms Janaki Devi. My father left for home after that. For some time, I felt lonely as all the other staff were busy with their work. But later, I acquainted myself with the staff and they were friendly, nice and courteous. In my initial days, I was praying to get a transfer to my native place as early as possible. But when I received transfer orders from there after six months, I felt very sad to leave my beloved colleagues. Generally due to personal reasons, employees worry about the place of posting. But with regard to a job, wherever we go, I think that after some time we end up feeling comfortable. That's what my opinion and experience have been.

At that time, I thought of continuing my postgraduation after settling in the job. But amid all the tensions and due to the busy schedule, I could not continue my preparation for MSc (Mathematics). My father felt bad. He wanted to see me as a postgraduate in mathematics. I could not fulfil his desire till today.

The following day, my father left us in Paloncha and went back to my native place, as he had some urgent work at the school. Mom and I felt lonely. For the first time in our life, we both were alone in a new place. Dad used to visit us during weekends. If he was busy, we would go to him. But whenever my mother and I went, we had to struggle a lot while boarding the bus. If dad was there with us, he would carry me in his arms and make me sit in the bus comfortably.

In the initial days, my mother used to come behind my rickshaw till my office to confirm if I reached safely. Gradually, after a few days, we got used to staying at our new place. Our landlords were very nice people. Dad told them to take care of us in his absence. They used to enquire if we needed anything. Other neighbours were also very friendly. When dad came, he brought vegetables and groceries. Other than going to work, he made sure that we need not go out for anything.

At the bank, the staff were very friendly. At first, the dispatch section was assigned to me. Although it has its own value, generally people think that it's an inferior job. I thought that my manager might have given me that job with the intention to give me a lighter job considering my disability. I used to read all the correspondence (both inward and outward) thoroughly before taking action on those letters. Other than the confidential matters, every correspondence would come to me. Due to this, I could understand the nature of work which was being carried out in various departments of the branch. Even after reading all the correspondence, I used to complete the work in just two hours. My colleagues told me that I would soon move from that seat if I worked that fast. Their prediction came true. Slowly, some other work was being assigned to me. Within 10 days, I was moved to the drafts counter. My colleague, Mr Rambabu, and accountant, Mr Sugunakar Rao, guided me a lot in writing the drafts. Majority of the customers in that branch were retail customers. One day, a college student came to take a draft. After giving him the counterfoil, I told him to collect the draft after some time. But he didn't understand it properly and went home without collecting the draft. He came to me in the afternoon. By that time, I had called his name many times. When he came to me, he told me that he thought that counterfoil itself was the draft. After he went home, his family scolded him. When he was narrating me the story, I had to control my laughter with great difficulty. After he left, I laughed a lot. I behaved like a kid at times. Actually, I identified with that college boy, as I also didn't know anything about drafts before joining the bank.

I did not receive my first salary in cash. It was credited directly into my account. It was something new for me. My father received his salary only in cash. My monthly salary was around ₹1,750. As I joined on 10 June, I received around ₹1,200 as salary for the month of June. When I withdrew the salary, my colleagues in the cash section gave me brand new currency notes. It was a nice experience. Out of that, we gave ₹500 for rent. I felt bad giving such brand new notes (felt bad not about the amount but about giving away new notes).

At the time of my handling drafts section in our bank, a fraud about misuse of bank drafts in another bank was published in the newspaper. As per that news, a colleague of a drafts section employee cheated that person and took some drafts from the draft book without his knowledge and cashed them. After that, my colleagues used to tease me while asking me to be careful with them when they came near my desk. Even though I knew that they were just pulling my leg, I had my own fears. I was very careful in locking the drawer when I left my seat.

Sometimes I worked in savings bank and current account sections when staff were on leave. As Mr Anjaneyulu sat just beside me, I used to get clarifications from him on my doubts. My senior Mr Rajendra Prasad told me the points that were to be verified after receiving the cheque from the customer (such as date, amount in figures and words, signature, order or bearer, whether the order instrument needs to be checked for endorsement where required, etc.). I was surprised to see them verifying all these points in just a few seconds. They looked like extraordinary people to me. But soon I also picked up speed and started checking all the required points in a few seconds. I felt proud. The ledgers were very heavy, especially Current Account ledgers, in size and in weight. I didn't know how I managed taking out and keeping them inside frequently. The current generation can't even imagine it as they know working simply on lightweight laptops.

In my family, no one had the habit of taking alcohol. Whenever I saw anyone on the road in a drunken state during my childhood, I would get scared. This was mainly because of the influence of movies on me in which they portrayed alcoholics to be abusive and ending up spoiling their lives with the addiction. After joining the bank, when I attended a dinner party for the first time, the male staff tried to send female staff off as early as possible, as they wanted to celebrate with drinks afterwards. Next day, when everyone was so courteous and friendly as usual, I was puzzled as it was not in line with the thoughts I had so far towards people who drank alcohol. I was so innocent until then and had no idea about social drinking.

Mr N. S. Prasad, Mr Rajendra Prasad, Mr Suryanarayana and Ms Padma are also good friends of mine. The first time I saw Mr Rajendra Prasad, I felt as if he were my brother. He is also very affectionate towards me. Our special assistant[1] was Mr B. P. Rao. His family and Mr Rambabu's family became our family friends. I knew Mr Ashok's wife Sailaja anyway, as she is one of my sisters' friends.

When I joined the bank, colleagues and customers called me 'Madam'. I felt like a fully grown-up woman. Till then, I was used to being treated as a kid by everyone. I felt elated when people addressed me in that way. When we are young, we love to be treated as adults, and after growing up, if someone tells us we look young, we feel happy. That is the irony of human nature.

In Paloncha, there is Venugopala Swamy (Lord Krishna) temple. I like that temple very much. We used to go there in the evenings during weekends. It's a very calm and peaceful place. My family members came to Paloncha during Dussehra vacation. They all had a great time. They went to the Kinnerasani project. Due to the presence of a coal-fired thermal power plant, Paloncha was known for pollution in those days. If any vehicle was parked, within minutes we could see ash layers on it. Such was the poor quality of the air.

The time at which I left the bank each evening varied a lot depending on the workload. Generally, there used to be heavy workload in the drafts section. My rickshaw driver often had to wait for a long time for me. That's why he slowly started to come late. Sometimes, even if my work was completed early, I had to wait for him for a long time. Whenever nearby branch manager Mr Madhusudhana Rao visited our branch, he used to observe my long waiting periods for the

---

[1] Special assistant is a post which is in between the clerical cadre and official cadre.

transport. After seeing this struggle, he suggested that I should buy a vehicle to be more independent.

After a few days, we came to know about some relatives who were living there in Paloncha. They visited our house often. By the time we started feeling more comfortable with that place, I got transfer orders to Sathupally. Actually, I felt very sad to leave my colleagues and neighbours, even though I was transferred to my native place—which was what I had wanted in the first place. All my colleagues came to the bus station to bid me farewell. My parents and I were moved very much by their love and affection.

With a heavy heart, we left Paloncha.

10

My Stint with the Bank at My Native Place

I joined the Agriculture Development branch (ADB) of our bank in my native place. Earlier, there were 100 villages under that branch. Later, due to the changes in government policies, that number came down drastically. I felt extremely happy to see Aruna's father, Mr Someswara Rao, as the branch manager. Life gives us many surprises; in my life, that was one of the pleasant surprises. He is a very nice person, a sincere and committed official who is also very humble and down to earth.

After working for almost six months in the Paloncha branch in the drafts section—and sometimes in current and savings bank account sections—I thought I had already become an expert in banking. But at ADB, my entire knowledge in drafts was of no use, as only a few people took demand drafts (DDs). I felt like a fresher all over again. It was an entirely different atmosphere and different type of work. Here, most of the customers were farmers. No customer addressed me as 'Madam'. As I had joined immediately after completing graduation, they treated me like a college girl. The first time a customer called me by my nickname, I was shocked. I could not understand how he knew my nickname, 'Bujji'. Later, I realized that they addressed me like that as it was a common nickname for girls in our area without knowing it as my nickname. As I am also from the village, I could adjust to this addressing within no time. I was the only female staff in that branch. My other colleagues were Mr Rajendra Prasad, Mr Sesha Rao, Mr Peter, Mr Venkateswara Rao, Mr Ram Prasad, Krishnaiah, Nageswara Rao and vehicle driver Dastagir.

The work assigned to me was to take care of deposits and withdrawals of savings bank, current account, fixed deposits, etc. I had to take out the ledgers, post the entries and keep them back again. I had to do this almost all day long and had some difficulty in doing so. But I couldn't realize what the problem exactly was. Our branch manager noticed my inconvenience and asked me how I was feeling. As I had faced many challenges to get this job, I didn't want to express any of my inconveniences. I thought that they might feel bad about recruiting a person with disabilities and take the extra burden of solving my challenges. Hence, I told him I was fine. But he didn't quit, and he understood that the reason for my inconvenience was the insufficient height of my chair. It was a wooden chair. He hired a carpenter and arranged for increasing the height of the chair along with a footrest (to compensate for the new height) and a large writing pad. With those modifications, I felt very comfortable. If all the bosses were that compassionate, how happy would the employees be. Particularly when a person with a disability joins in, I feel that the organization should assign a buddy to them till they adjust to the environment so that they could be comfortable and share their work-related difficulties, if any.

I wanted to learn other skills. Generally, I used to be busy with my desk work during working hours. So I wanted to stay back and learn from my seniors after work. When I told them this, they didn't accept. Our manager gave them strict instructions to not keep me in the office after work hours. They told me that they would teach me only if I got permission from our boss. Then I explained to our boss about my interest in learning new skills and requested him to allow me to stay late. Although he permitted me to do so, he suggested that I complete the learning as early as possible. If I got late on any particular day, he would send one of our colleagues to escort me till my house. That was his level of concern for the safety of his female colleagues. God is great, for he gave me the opportunity to work with such nice and kind bosses throughout my career.

I remember being so overwhelmed with emotions when my boss got transferred. Even today, after having many years of experience and even after knowing that transfers are inevitable for any employee, I become so emotional when I have to bid farewell to my beloved colleagues.

Hampi Visit

I took leave for the first time after getting the job and went to visit my uncle Dr P. V. V. Raju's place, Gangavathi, in Karnataka. He is my father's younger brother. He is the first doctor in our family. With his inspiration, now we have around 30 doctors in our family. Whenever we get any health issues, we call him even today. He treats his patients with a nominal fee from the beginning. From Hyderabad, we went by bus. We travelled via Rayalaseema area. It was my first visit to that place; the landscape was mostly dry and arid. En route, we saw people walking long distances to fetch water. It was for the first time in my life that I stepped on another state.

As usual, I struggled to find an accessible toilet. As most of the places didn't have accessible toilets back then, I would end up holding nature's calls for a long time, many times. We finally reached our uncle's house and had a really nice time there. All the elders recollected old memories, and I enjoyed listening to them a great deal. One day, my uncle and aunt took us to Hampi, the capital city of the erstwhile Vijayanagara Empire ruled by Emperor Sri Krishna Devaraya. What an amazing place it is! Even a thousand pairs of eyes won't be enough to see those sculptures. If one had to see each and every sculpture in detail, they would have to spend some months doing so. I remember seeing some foreigners drawing sketches of those sculptures. I later came to know that they stayed there for months together to complete those drawings. It was difficult for me to walk for a long distance with the walker. I saw a maximum number of sculptures around that place in whatever distance I could manage.

They showed us the place which used to be the court of Sri Krishna Devaraya. I got goosebumps all over my body upon seeing it. I read so many stories about that great emperor. We brought home a small stone from Hampi as a souvenir.

To Counsel

One day, when I came back from the bank, there was a guest at home. He was dad's senior colleague; dad introduced me to him. He always feels proud to introduce me to his friends. During the course of the conversation, I came to know that his daughter had suddenly acquired a disability when she was in the 8th standard. When I enquired about her studies, he told me that she had discontinued after that incident. He wanted to transfer some properties in her name and look for an alliance. But I strongly suggested making her independent first and then thinking about marriage. He requested me to come and meet her once. So one day, dad and I went to his village and met her. She was a very enthusiastic girl, and she promised to study further. I later came to know that she had appeared for graduation examinations. It made me very happy.

Skill Building and Acquiring Professional Qualification

After shifting to my native place from Paloncha, I slowly started supporting some needy people from my salary. It was a very small amount, since my monthly income was meagre in those days. But I never forget my two goals in life: to be independent and to support others to the extent that is possible for me. From that time onwards, I made it a point to spend some amount from my salary either to support known people in need in my circle or to write a cheque to a genuine NGO.

Slowly, with the support of my seniors, I learned many skills in that branch. Later, our branch was shifted to a new bank-owned premises, which was closer to my house. A new manager named Mr Venkata Ratnam joined us. I started learning from the field officers about the loan process. We had to manually apply interest for thousands of accounts. We felt very happy, as we got a machine to calculate interest which was just like a bigger calculator. From one of my seniors I learnt how to operate it. Generally, if we learn more skills, more work will be assigned to us. My senior colleague who knew all these skills also got transferred. But since I had learnt everything from him, I could manage the work in his absence.

When I was in Paloncha, Mr Madhusudhana Rao suggested that I buy a vehicle. One day he called and gave me information about a hand-operated tricycle. I bought one tricycle shortly after. But since it was not motorized, it was tough to ride. One's hands must be very strong to operate it. I tried using it a few times, but eventually I quit as it was really difficult for me. My colleagues then suggested that I buy a scooter.

Dealing with customers in ADB was generally more different than in other branches. Farmers would treat us like their family members; they would tell me all their family issues, like a wife suffering due to her drunkard husband or problems of old parents with their young children, etc. As they didn't know much about the schemes available, I used to suggest schemes suitable for them as per their needs. Even if I shifted to another seat, they would come to me to fill the forms; they had a lot of confidence in me. I used to clear the customers' cheques very fast. However big the queue in front of me, I ensured to clear them all very fast. Appreciation in the eyes of the customers used to motivate me a lot. One day, an elderly person who was the head of a nearby village cleared his gold loan. He requested our manager to arrange for delivering his jewellery through my hands. Such was his affection for me.

As ours was a specialized branch, many officials from across the country used to come to hone their skills in our branch. As I slowly became a senior member in the bank, I got the opportunity to respond to the queries of auditors (both internal and external). It was a great learning experience.

At one point, I decided to appear for Certified Associate of Indian Institute of Bankers (CAIIB; Part I) exams. This qualification is very important for bankers in India. Instead of preparing for MSc (Mathematics), I decided to appear for CAIIB, as it was important for my career. The exam centre was in Khammam, our district headquarters. Exams were held during weekends. When we went to Khammam, our accountant Mr Prabhakar and his wife Ms Premalatha invited us to their house and treated us very well. Both of them showed a lot of affection for me and respect for my father.

As usual, my exam hall was on the top floor and my father carried me there. If I remember correctly, we went to Khammam on three weekends by bus and wrote the exams for five papers. I cleared all the papers. If we completed Part I, we would get one increment.

While preparing for Part I, one of our colleagues in the main branch helped us a lot. He took classes during weekends and even gave us biscuits and fruits. He was a very sincere officer with great patience. He was always very positive, and we never saw him in a negative mood. One day, to get clarity on some doubts, we went to his house in the morning before going to the bank. At his home, we came to know that his wife had some mental health-related issues. He alone was taking care of the entire household work and his two young daughters, on top of taking care of his wife who was like another child. What a marvellous man! Good qualities of patience and nurturing aren't really gender-specific.

Again, a new manager, Mr Balakishan, joined our branch. Our branch business hours started from 11:00 am, as it used to take time for the farmers to come from their villages. Our boss suggested that we close the office after business hours and come early next morning to start work with a fresh mind and complete all the work before customers start coming. My colleagues Mr Anand, Mr Vali, Mr Srinivasa Reddy, Mr Nagaraju and Mr Venkateswara Rao are people with a great sense of humour. Until the customers came, we used to work in a very friendly and jovial mood. Although we had a lot of work to do, without feeling any strain, we used to complete it very fast in such a friendly environment.

Some of my colleagues are also my family friends. I remember that when Mr Vali joined our branch, on the first day, I offered him the special items prepared by my mom for lunch. Later, when his wife came to our village to search for a house, she told how happy Mr Vali was when I offered food on the first day. I wondered for the value they gave for such a small gesture of mine. He treats me like his own sister. His wife became a very good friend of mine. She treats my parents as her own parents. Till date we are in touch. A few years ago, when I went to their son's marriage along with my family, they showered on us similar love and affection.

A man named Suleman had a tea shop in front of our bank. I didn't have the habit of taking tea or coffee, so he would insist me on drinking that energy booster drink (chocolate milk) Boost, whenever he brought tea for others. He also used to join us in our conversations. Recently, when I went to the ADB, I saw him at his shop. With the same affection, he brought Boost for me.

The annual closing day for banks is 31 March. As there were no computers at that time, we had to start very early to close all the work by that date; we had to work overtime. The staff would get overtime allowance, of course. Hence, for the staff, it was like a festival. Managers would also arrange for food for the staff, as we worked till very late, daily, during that phase. Although a lot of work was there, it was great fun to work with all the colleagues, with so many jokes and funny comments filling the air. Although I was the only female staff in the office (except for the sweeper, Kasimbee), I never felt uncomfortable or left out. All my colleagues were gentlemen.

One day, I had an adventure at work. I went to the washroom after lunch. They arranged a stool inside the washroom for me. As I was about to answer nature's call, I saw a snake in a corner; it was a viper. My heart stopped beating for one second due to fear. Although I had encountered many snakes since my childhood, never had I been locked with one in a tiny space. As I had already untied my dress, it was going to be a problem if I stood with the help of my walker. So I decided to tie the dress while keeping an eye on the snake. But it was not moving; it might have eaten a frog and rested in this cool spot due to the hot weather outside. Then slowly, without much sound, I opened the door and came out with my walker. Immediately after coming out, I closed the door and started shouting. All the staff came rushing and our manager called a snake catcher. No harm was caused to anyone. When I narrated this incident to my parents, my mom cried a lot thinking about me in a situation where I could not run to save myself. After this incident, for some days, someone would always verify the safety of the washroom before I went inside.

Mr Balakishan joined our branch as branch manager which was his first posting as head of a branch. I had never met anyone like him before. Before coming to our branch, he took suggestions from his seniors and went through the training material for branch managers. He implemented all that he learnt in letter and spirit in our branch. It was a great experience observing the initiatives he started in the branch. Generally, branch managers start concentrating on improving the business of the branch immediately after taking charge. But he started with housekeeping first. When he took charge, all the old files were in a godown-like place in our branch, kept in a haphazard manner. He got them all arranged in a systematic way. One Monday morning, we were all surprised to see the files arranged properly with an index. He started quality circles in the branch to encourage the staff to get involved in a problem–solution approach. By observing him and by participating in the initiatives he started, I learnt a lot.

Most of the time, I would only think about bank-related work. I am a task-oriented person. I would always think about updating myself with internal guidelines and current affairs related to the banking industry. Either working in the bank or thinking about areas in which I could improve myself to work in a better way, I didn't realize that I had become a workaholic. When I was declared unfit in the medical test by that doctor and rejected for the job, I might have unconsciously decided to prove myself after joining the bank. Initially, I might have worked hard to prove myself, which, later, might have become an obsession. Subsequently, when I got reports saying that I was equivalent to three people and an asset to the branch, my ego might have felt a huge push. It's only now that I am trying to analyse my past behaviour from the viewpoint of an outsider. I didn't do this analysis at that time.

During the tenure of Mr Balakishan, I got to learn the work related to reports and other correspondence too, which I hadn't learnt earlier. When we received a new performance report format for the branches, which was very crucial at the bank level, I found an error in it. Due to that, there would be a problem in getting the exact value of one key parameter at the bank level. I brought that to the notice of my boss. He then notified the head office. For this, I received an appreciation letter from our managing director's (MD) office. I felt extremely happy. Till then, I had gotten appreciation at branch and regional levels. Receiving appreciation from MD's office for an employee who was working in a rural area was an unbelievable feat. All the bosses may not be ready to share the good work of their subordinates with the higher officials. My parents felt very happy after seeing that letter. Dad got that letter framed—that was the extent of their happiness.

In those days, there were no computers; everything was manual. Under our branch, there were about a hundred villages. Naturally, some unrecovered loans were written off. To give a no objection certificate (NOC), we had to check those old records. I took up the task of preparing a list of written-off accounts, village-wise. It was a tedious task. The old registers were very dusty, and I had to wear a mask and gloves. Nevertheless, I verified all those registers and prepared a village-wise list for all the hundred villages. The branch manager and field officers were very happy with that work. After that, the verification process became very easy for the field officers while giving NOCs or giving loans. Whatever amount is recovered from written-off accounts is a direct profit. The document which I prepared was kept in the strongroom very safely, and copies were given to all the field officers. It gave me great satisfaction.

11

Prejudice and Pride

After learning all the necessary work in our branch, I was contemplating on the big 'what next' dilemma. I am not someone who can do stereotypical work. As I had completed CAIIB Part I, I became eligible for a promotion test. The officials who came to our branch from other places for training or auditing would always encourage me to take that test. Till that time, with my bitter experience in joining the bank due to that negative medical report, I never tried applying for senior-level posts either within the bank or outside. I was not sure whether I would be accepted or not. My manager and other well-wishers in the bank encouraged me to write the promotion test. But my well-wishers outside the bank didn't like this idea. They thought that in the present post, I might not be transferred frequently, but if I got a promotion, I would be transferred every three years. Considering my physical condition and my parents' age, they thought that opting for promotion was not a good idea. I discussed this matter with my parents, and they encouraged me to write the exam. They have always supported me in facing life boldly. By that time, my father had retired. So my parents could accompany me wherever I would be posted. From his retirement benefits, my father bought a plot in my name in my native place. Even after making me financially independent, my parents still wanted to buy some property in my name to give me financial security.

Finally, I decided to take the test. I started implementing it immediately and started preparing for the exam seriously. It's a very tough exam. I got the material as suggested by my colleagues. I prepared very well as usual. I wrote the exam and eagerly waited for the results. The results came out, and I was selected in the written test. I was on cloud nine. Our telephone was constantly ringing throughout the day. All my well-wishers and all the officials who came to our branch for various works called me to congratulate me. They had great affection for me. They all felt very happy as if it were their result. I told them there was another step, the interview. But they all took it lightly and told me that with my knowledge and experience, I would get through it very easily. In their view, I had got the promotion already, and the interview was just a formality. After listening to them, I started enjoying the written test results without worrying much about the interview.

I started preparing for the interview. I had to speak with our customers only in Telugu, as most of them didn't know even a single word in English. In case officials came from other states, I spoke to them in Hinglish. I worried whether I would be able to respond fully in English without any difficulty. The interview date was announced, and I went to Hyderabad for it. I entered the interview room. I could communicate in English without much difficulty, as it was easy to speak about official work in English. One thing I observed was that the interview board's chairman didn't ask me a single question. I remember that he didn't show any interest in listening to my responses. My sixth sense told me that something was wrong, but I didn't know what it was. Due to this, I did not feel very happy. On that evening, we went to Birla Mandir in Hyderabad. It's Lord Venkateswara temple, built with white marble—a very nice and peaceful place. The first time I went there, we didn't know the temple had an elevator. So my brother had carried me. Someone saw our struggle and told us about the elevator which was for the elderly and persons with disabilities. From then onwards, we started using it.

When I was enjoying the peaceful atmosphere there, one of our colleagues who came there to visit the temple told me that our interview results were announced and I didn't get the promotion. He also told me that he had heard it was because of my disability. I could not believe it. My mind became blank. Till then, whenever I attended any exam or interview, results were always positive. After some time, my mind slowly started processing the facts. Tears started rolling down my eyes. They didn't stop for almost 30 hours. The more I thought about the results, the more I cried. I felt pain in my heart and throat due to extreme sorrow. Then I got angry. When I worked with a lot of commitment and sincerity, no one thought about my disability. Everyone appreciated me. Now at the time of recognizing my efforts, how could they simply reject me? That question had overtaken my mind. Generally, if anyone faces a problem while getting a promotion, they may get upset with the boss. But in my case, I knew very well that excellent reports were given about my performance by my boss, and his boss too.

I was confident of my performance in the exam and the interview. I strongly believed that the rejection was only because of my disability. But my manager tried to convince me saying that it might have been because of me not getting good marks in my written test. He advised me to put more effort in preparing for the next test. I was angry at that time. I told him I didn't have any interest in writing the exam again only to face rejection. But my parents and boss tried their level best to prepare me for the next exam without thinking about the previous or future results. Finally, I accepted. I took it as a challenge. I got more material for preparation. In those days, *The Economic Times* was not delivered in our area. I subscribed to get it by post. I think that due to my vigorous preparation, fumes were emanating from my body. As a result of intensive preparation, after the exam I compiled a book to support the people who prepare for that exam with 390 rationales. That was the level of intensity of my preparation. I didn't want to give anyone the smallest chance to comment on my performance in the exam. But how much ever I tried not to think about the previous result, it haunted my mind frequently. With that, my motivation levels used to come down, making me feel that all my efforts might go waste. No words can describe the mental agony I had gone through in those days. But then, I would pick myself up and motivate myself somehow to carry on.

I wrote the exam. As usual, I was selected in the written test. This time, no one ventured to congratulate me. I started preparing for the interview. After I went to Hyderabad, just before the interview, I came to know that the chairman for the interview board was the same person. Even before entering the room, I had lost all hope. But after coming to that level, I didn't want to go back. I entered the room with a lot of reluctance.

To my surprise, this time, the entire interview was taken by the chairman. Most of the questions started with 'if you get promotion, would you be fine for transfers, if you get promotion, would you be…', etc. I was surprised. I felt very positive after the interview. And soon I came to know that I was selected.

Later, I came to know through some well-wishers that the chairman had initially thought that it would be difficult for me to manage the staff and other matters as a senior officer, which is why he hadn't selected me earlier. But he later came to know through many people about my performance and started feeling bad, it seems, for not selecting me in spite of my excellent performance in all aspects. It seems that I stood first both the times in written test/performance reports/interview. I came to know about this through reliable higher officials; I don't have any proof of it though.

But if it's true, think about how much mental agony I had to go through because of one senior official's perspective on a female employee with disabilities. He could be a nice person, but he must have thought that out of overenthusiasm or high ambition of becoming an officer, I had not thought about the challenges involved in managing the staff and other matters. Many a time, some of us may try to take decisions on behalf of others out of love and affection for them, thinking that we are doing them good. But perspectives of all the people in this world may not be the same. Hence, ultimately it may give a bitter experience to both the parties.

Later on, in a meeting, while introducing me to a customer, the chairman of the interview board had said that the bank needed officials like me.

12

Lessons Learnt in the Training Period

After getting the promotion, selected candidates had to undergo a one-year training programme in Hyderabad.

All my batchmates were very active, sharp and enthusiastic. In my batch, there were three female colleagues—Sarada, Lalitha and Neeraja, apart from me. We all met for the first time at our staff training centre. Within a short time, we all became very close friends. I worked in three branches in Hyderabad during the training period to acquaint myself with various roles. I stayed at my brother's house. Apart from the Industrial Finance branch (IFB), I worked at OU and Nallakunta branches. At Nallakunta, Mr Ganesh Pai was the branch manager. That branch was situated in a residential area. Naturally, retail customers were more, and among them some were retired employees. It was a nice experience to observe the way Mrs Rajeswari handled the retired employees. She used to complete their work immediately. But they were interested more in sharing their health issues and other personal challenges with her than getting their work completed quickly. She used to hear them out very patiently while completing other work and give them suggestions on their health issues. I saw some very senior officials who had retired from the bank waiting like general customers for their turn to get their work done. Although I'd never worked with them earlier, I gave them the same respect out of empathy, as if they were still working with the bank in that position.

Later, all my batchmates were posted at the head office to attend an important project. The entire batch worked for six months on that project. Senior officials in that department, Mr Rajeswara Rao and Mr Ramakrishna Harsha, used to guide us. Due to his friendly nature, Mr Rajeswara Rao became very close to our batch within a short time.

My Independence with Scooter

After going to Hyderabad for training, I faced commuting as a big challenge. Till that time, both in my native place and at Paloncha, the distance between my house and the bank was just a few hundred metres. But in Hyderabad, the minimum distance was 10 km. Initially, I commuted by autorickshaw for a few days. It was too expensive, and I had to wait for the auto for a long time as well. Since my childhood, it was my dream to move everywhere independently. Whenever I went to my friends' places, I could come back only depending on my father's/brother's availability. If I went by rickshaw, I wouldn't know whether I would get a rickshaw while coming back. As long as I sat there, I would be thinking about the availability of a rickshaw only.

Left: Affectionate batchmates in 1st promotion Right: The scooter that gave me wings

Once we went to Birla Mandir. I had a great time there but while coming back, no city bus was available as it was late in the night. We waited for a long time. On that day, my brother walked for a long distance, carrying me. We didn't find any transport. I felt very sorry. Till then, many such incidents in my life had occurred. I might have enjoyed the place I went to but while coming back, due to non-availability of transport, with the struggle my siblings and I faced, my happiness dried up.

We bought a Kinetic Honda scooter. We also found a person who could modify it. After modifying the vehicle by attaching two wheels on both the sides, the mechanic sent the vehicle to our house. His assistant asked us whether we needed his support to take the vehicle to the Regional Transport Authority (RTA) office. My dad and brother confidently told him no, and he left. After that, my brother started the engine and tried to go out. But it was not moving in the direction my brother wanted to. He tried a lot. Dad scolded him for not riding it properly and asked him to leave it. Then dad tried, but it was the same result. I was dying with laughter. Seeing me laugh that hard, they got irritated. They told me to try it instead of sitting and laughing at them.

I was eagerly waiting for the moment. I went there and sat on it. They told me how to start it. I started it, pressing the auto start button. Slowly, I started moving it. My dad and brother encouraged me to go out in our lane; it was a small lane with not much traffic. Successfully, I came outside of the house. It was like a miracle for me. They were not able to ride it, but I could. Later, they realized that because they were keeping their foot on the ground, it became difficult for them to ride. As I could not use my legs, it was easy for me. Then they told me to drive it to the RTA office. They told me to follow them. I got scared. But they convinced me saying that they would go very slow, and that I just had to follow them. Our journey started. They were on the left side of the road, going very slowly, and I was following them. We came to the main road. Suddenly, buses and lorries appeared like elephants to me. I felt like an ant in front of them. For so many years, I was seeing buses and lorries. But I never felt so.

I was following my dad and brother, keeping only a few inches of distance. At one signal, they crossed. When I was trying to cross it, a red signal came on and I had to stop. After crossing that signal, I saw them waiting for me. But I was dying with fear till I reached them. Finally, we reached the RTA office. Along with registration of my vehicle as invalid carriage,[1] they completed my driving test on the same day. That official asked me to go forward, backward and take U-turn, etc. I didn't know how I managed to do all those things. He told me to improve my speed as it would be a challenge if I went slowly on the road. I nodded my head like a good girl.

Later, I would go to OU campus, with dad or mom as my pillion, daily for practice, as it was close to my brother's house. OU campus is a beautiful place. Some places were very quiet. Learning to ride a scooter has been one of the most cherished experiences of my life. While riding my scooter, I could go fast, which I couldn't do while moving with the help of a walker. I could go wherever I wanted. I could stop wherever I wanted and for whatever amount of time. I felt a great sense of independence. No words could express my happiness.

One day, when mom and I were going to the OU campus, my scooter suddenly stopped in the middle of the road. Someone helped us in bringing it to the side of the road. I tried a lot; some passers-by tried too, but it didn't start. Then we saw a person going on his Honda bike. We stopped him and sought his help. He tried to start it manually, but it didn't work. When he saw the petrol level, the tank was empty. I can never forget the expression on his face when he looked at me after seeing the empty tank. Poor guy, after trying so hard to start the scooter, he was sweating a lot. After seeing our situation, he offered to bring petrol in a bottle for us. We paid him for the same. Until he came back, we waited on the side of the road. It was an embarrassing situation. Till that time, I was riding the scooter happily without thinking what it would require to ride a scooter. I got proper scolding from my dad and brother. It was a great lesson for me.

---

[1] Invalid carriage is a vehicle adapted for use for a person with disability.

Later, my father accompanied me to the office. He would come with me to my office in the morning and then take a bus to go back home. In the evenings, he would come to my office taking a city bus and ride back together. After a few days, when he was confident about my driving skills, I could ask him to stop coming with me.

After I had become fully confident, I started taking my brother's three kids on my scooter to OU campus every evening. We used to have great fun and enjoy nature there. Sweet memories!

While riding a scooter on Hyderabad roads to go to my office, I remembered my wish that I had at the age of seven—to have a job and ride a scooter in Hyderabad. After almost two decades, I could finally fulfil my wish.

While going to the head office during my training period, our batchmate Neeraja used to come along with me on my scooter as a pillion rider. Her house was near my brother's house, so I had a very good company.

One day, when we were coming back from the office, it was raining heavily. We were not prepared for it and didn't have our raincoats. We were fully drenched, but we enjoyed the rain very much. In that cold weather, we even had ice cream. I love to go out whenever it rains. But my mom never allowed me due to the fear that I might catch a cold and fever.

We had two weeks' training at our staff training centre in Hyderabad. It was for the first time in my life that I stayed alone at the accommodation of the training centre—without any of my family members. That centre was located in a very beautiful place full of greenery. At night, we used to have some cultural events with other participants. My batchmate Lalitha helped me a lot. Early mornings were so beautiful there. I love nature very much. Whenever I get any chance to be close to nature, I leap at it.

We decided to complete CAIIB (Part 2) during our training period. We came to know that someone was taking classes for some of the tough subjects in Part 2. Thirumala Rao, Neeraja and some other batchmates and I joined those classes. As we were all in the same age group, it used to be like a college atmosphere. Sarala, our colleague, also joined those sessions. She became a good friend. Subsequently, we completed our CAIIB (Part 2) successfully.

13

The Hardships in Finding a Rented House

After getting a permanent posting, my parents and I decided to take a flat on rent near my office. My parents made all the arrangements at home to leave our native place and stay with me. My brother's house was in a far-off place. They could not shift from there as their children's school was near that house. I used to start early to be able to reach my office on time, as the journey took at least one and a half hours; and in the evening also, I used to start late from the office. As late evenings and nights were very busy in terms of traffic, I used to reach home very late.

After deciding to take a flat, mom and I went in search of a flat for rent every Sunday. We went on my scooter to all the places within a radius of 4 km from my office. We realized soon that getting an accessible flat for a person like me was not an easy task within our budget. It would be within our budget if it's located on the first[1] or the second floor

---

[1] As opposed to accessible flats on the ground floor or in a building with an elevator.

without an elevator. If it's accessible in all aspects, then rent would be on the higher side. Finally, we could find a flat on Saradhy Studio Road, and we took it. That was in Year 2000. It was within our budget and with an elevator. That road was always busy with heavy traffic. While coming home, it used to be a Herculean task to cross the road, as no one would care to stop for me, even after giving the right signal. After entering my flat, if I looked down through the window and watched the road, I would wonder how I had crossed that road.

Just beside our flat, there was a park. My nieces and nephews used to play there when they came for vacation. We waited eagerly for the summers when all our siblings would arrive at our place with their families to spend the time merrily.

After shifting to Hyderabad, my parents thought of consulting a physiotherapist. Until then, as I was in a town (my village later developed into a town) with limited services, we didn't get the opportunity to try physiotherapy on a regular basis. We found a very big physiotherapy centre near our flat. As I had a scooter, I agreed to go there regularly. After checking my condition, the physiotherapist told us that there was no use of doing physiotherapy at that age (29 years). It's very surprising for me now, as I know from my present experience that any type of physical activity started at any age will help in improving the condition of any person. Of course, there may be variations in the results depending on the age of the individual. But at that time when he told us that, I felt happy for escaping from the ritual of daily visits for therapy. Thus, I missed another opportunity for better health.

After buying the scooter, during weekends, mom and I used to go to Necklace Road (waterfront road along the lake Hussain Sagar) or to some other places where we could spend our time peacefully. If and when dad wanted to join us, we got an auto.

During Vinayaka Chavithi and Durgashtami festivals, people used to raise pandals at public places and install the idols of the deities. Mom and I used to go to different places to see those celebrations. The tallest idol would always be at Khairatabad. On the ninth day of the festival Vinayaka Chavithi, most of the idols of Lord Ganesha would be immersed in Hussain Sagar lake, which is centrally located. Likewise, the idols of Durga Matha would be immersed (*Nimajjanam*) in water, following a big procession. Generally, it would be a local holiday. On one such occasion, I had to go to the office. As processions generally start in the afternoon, the roads were free in the morning; I never saw empty roads in Hyderabad like that. However, while returning in the evening, it was very difficult for me to move forward due to the heavy traffic of people and big vehicles with idols.

After we shifted to the rented house, my eldest sister's son Sudhir got an admission in Gandhi Medical College in Hyderabad and came to live with us. We felt very happy to have him with us; it was a very good company for me.

My cousin Dr Kavitha's husband Dr Narendra was doing his super specialization in cardiology when we were in Hyderabad. He is very simple and humble and also an artist. He draws very naturally. As my mom had blood pressure (BP) problem, we started taking his advice. Till today, whenever mom or dad has any health issue, we call him even in the wee hours. With great patience, he gives his advice.

14

The Dream Posting

After completing my training, all my well-wishers thought I would request for posting in my native place. But my purpose of opting for promotion was to learn new skills and get more exposure. One of my ex-colleagues told me about our IFB in Hyderabad. He explained all the skills that we could learn if we worked there. From then on, I strongly wanted to work in that branch. My well-wishers were not happy with my decision. As per their view, for a person like me who needs support, it is better to stay in villages as people have concerns for others there. They were of the opinion that in cities, no one cared for others.

But that was not my experience during my training period in Hyderabad. Just like in my native place, people in Hyderabad were also very friendly and caring.

After the training, our personnel department enquired about my choice of place for the posting, as they wanted to give importance to my convenience. Since working in the IFB was my dream, I requested for a posting at that branch. To arrive at that branch, we needed to drive via a very steep path. That official enquired how I would travel to the branch. I told him that I had a scooter, and I would go by that. As the concerned official knew about that steep path, he suggested me to think about any other branch which was nearer to my house. But I explained to him about my strong desire to gain exposure in the area of foreign exchange and credit in that branch, and also told him that I had managed to go to that branch during my training period successfully.

Finally, they posted me to that IFB. I was the happiest person. I worked there during the training period for a few days. Regular posting is different from training period assignments. In regular posting, one has more responsibilities.

After taking charge, I found a huge difference between this branch's atmosphere and that of my previous branch. In ADB, customers were villagers and they treated me like their family member. I had to speak with them only in Telugu. But at IFB, customers and staff communicated mostly in English. The moment the Reserve Bank of India (RBI) issued circulars, the customers would come with a request letter based on those fresh guidelines. We had to be up-to-date, always. Some of the staff were so senior that their service years were more than my age. IFB was a computerized branch. I came from a manual branch. The section allocated to me was new for me, and I only had theoretical knowledge but no practical experience except working for a few months during the training programme.

When I joined the branch, it was a very tough time for me for some months. All the challenges came at once to me.

Our department head, Mr Santanu Mukherjee, was famous for his knowledge in credit and foreign exchange and his proficiency in English. I'd heard so many nice stories about him. Some colleagues told me that if he put up a proposal, rarely would it come back from the head office for any clarifications. He used to come very early to the office and leave in the late hours, as his position demanded a lot of attention. He didn't know Telugu. I was not used to speaking eloquently in English, that too after working in ADB, where there was no need to speak in English. So I had lost my grasp on the language.

As I was new in this position as well as in the branch, I had many doubts. One of my senior colleagues, Mr Hari Prasad, advised me to take action on every paper immediately, without any delay, as it was a very big branch and all the transactions were of high value. As I tried to act on all the documents without any delay, I used to go to my boss's cabin to get clarity on my doubts and seek his guidance. As I'd heard high praise about his proficiency in English, I would just forget even the simplest words in English due to fear while speaking with him.

He was very nice though. He understood my struggle. Even though I spoke a few words in English, like telegraphic language, with his experience and from my facial expressions, he used to understand the matter and guide me. Understanding others' English was not an issue for me.

I bought some books to improve my spoken English. But finally, I realized unless we practise speaking without worrying about making mistakes, we cannot acquire proficiency in any language.

Slowly with practice and with his polite behaviour, I could relax and come out of my fear. Once we are out of it, the brain starts to work in a better way.

I took it up as a challenge to learn about my section. I read a lot about my work. Simultaneously, I started learning how to carry out transactions on a computer. My section had two different systems. After doing the transactions in one system, it needed to be linked with the main system. In a few months, I picked it all up.

I used to come to the office very early. Many a time, I would reach even before our sweeper had completed her work. As I had to simultaneously learn the work and complete it as per the expectations of customers, I used to work for more hours.

Although the staff were very senior, they were very friendly and had a great sense of humour. Karunakar, Peter, Jaipal, Gopal and Babu were particularly jovial people. For every Raksha Bandhan (a festival when sisters tie a *rakhi*, or decorative threads, on the wrists of their brothers for the safety of their brothers as per the custom in some states in India), I used to tie a *rakhi* to Karunakar. When we meet some people, we get a brotherly warmth. Karunakar is the only person whom I tied a *rakhi*, other than my own brother/cousins.

Ms Nirmala and Ms Bhavani were in my section. Ms Bhavani was a little bit of a serious kind of a person. But later, we became good friends. We are in touch even now.

The foreign exchange department head was Mr Krishnan. I wanted to work there but didn't get the opportunity, as no vacancy was available at the time of my joining. During my training, I'd worked in that department though. Mr Ravindra, Gopal and Mr Ram Prasad used to teach me the work I needed to know in that department. Mr Krishnan gave me some very valuable advice in the beginning; he advised me to sign on any paper only after understanding it thoroughly. In case of any doubt, he advised me to check with the concerned official, however senior they might be, without any hesitation. He told me that senior officials would be happy to clarify the doubts. That would save us and the bank too.

While having conversations with Mr Krishnan, I came to know that he could speak in Telugu as well, since he'd worked in district branches. I felt very happy as I could escape speaking in English with him. After that, I spoke with him only in Telugu. My colleagues were surprised. Although they were working with him for some time, they didn't know that he spoke Telugu. As they were all comfortable in speaking English, they might not have been bothered about it.

Mr Madhusudhana Rao, whom I had met in the Paloncha branch, was posted as the head of our branch. I felt very happy to hear this news. Having a known person as boss is always nice.

Although I concentrated only on my section, I was eagerly waiting for an opportunity to work in the foreign exchange department. Once there was a vacancy in that section, and I was hoping that I would get the chance. But as the new lady officer who was posted to our branch was senior to me, she filled that vacancy. It was a great disappointment for me.

It was not that easy to get a chance to work in departments such as credit and foreign exchange in banks. My section was in the credit department. As mentioned earlier, our department head, Mr Santanu Mukherjee, was an expert in that domain. I felt that I was missing the opportunity to learn credit by always thinking about the missed opportunity in the foreign exchange department. Finally, I concentrated on learning about credit proposals. By that time, I became comfortable in handling my section. I shared with my boss about my desire to learn credit. He told other officials to involve me in that work.

Mr Sridhar joined our branch around that time. He was also an expert in credit, and I started learning from him and other field officers. Generally, field officers used to go out for inspections during the day and worked till late hours in the evenings in the office. By that time, I would complete my desk work and sit with them to observe what they were doing. During that time, trainee official Padma joined our branch. Her family was in Chennai.

After seeing my interest and enthusiasm, my boss gave me the opportunity to work on some credit proposals and also gave me a task: to do some research about certain industries for which we had some proposals. Apart from reading in newspapers and the Internet, I used to go to some places to know more about that industry along with Padma on my scooter. We used to feel like detectives. On a day-to-day basis, I used to give updates to my boss and got his guidance on what to do next.

Fortunately, I got the opportunity to work on a very big proposal under the guidance of Mr Sridhar and my boss. It was a great learning experience for me.

While working on another proposal, I was supposed to go to a factory for inspection. My boss gave me two options: either to go for inspection, taking another field officer to guide me, or get the inspection report from another field officer and work on credit proposals. I decided to go for inspection along with another field officer, Mr Nawaz. One place of inspection was a software office. I was able to go to that office successfully. But another place was a factory. It was not at all accessible for me. I waited on their ground floor and Mr Nawaz went inside and completed the inspection.

Then I realized it would be difficult for me to go for inspections due to the many inaccessible conditions that exist in our country for persons with disabilities. Time came for me to decide whether to work on credit proposals that were based on inspection reports given by other officers or to leave that work completely as it was not suitable for me with my condition. I was in a dilemma. Actually, I applied for an MBA (Banking and Finance) through Indira Gandhi National Open University (IGNOU) and started learning more on analysing balance sheets of the companies, etc. I found credit work very interesting. But, at that time, I didn't have much idea that the work could be split into many parts, with different people attending to different parts of the work. I saw that all other field officers were taking care of one account fully from pre-sanction inspection, working on proposals, disbursement of loans, post-sanction inspection, reports/returns, recovery, etc., and hence I felt it was not suitable for me.

However, with my present experience, I feel that I could have tried working in credit by taking the support from other officials in getting an inspection report wherever I could not go. Nothing was wrong in that. Nowadays, work is being split into so many parts and each is taken up by different people. Generally, bosses may not be comfortable in giving such work to colleagues with disabilities. When the boss was ready to give me the opportunity to work independently on credit proposals, I could not avail it due to my hesitation. Whenever I remember it, I feel happy for the confidence my boss had in my work and his attitude to accommodate me in a place where I wanted to work, by offering multiple options for me.

At that time, I got an opportunity to take care of one section in the foreign exchange department along with my regular section. Although it was hectic for me, I opted for it as I thought foreign exchange work suited my condition as it was a desk job. I worked under two bosses simultaneously. Although it was a challenging task, I could manage it successfully, as both the bosses were very nice.

On my request, Mr Krishnan suggested some books to improve my knowledge in foreign exchange. As ours was an Authorised Dealer[1] (AD) branch, we used to have RBI audits. From those auditors too, I got the details of some good books. I used to read them to improve my knowledge in foreign exchange. I started following the RBI website. It's very important for us. I appeared for the certification in trade finance (CTF) exam and cleared it.

One day, when I went to the bank, one of our customers came very early and was waiting with a request letter based on the latest circular issued by RBI on the previous day, late in the evening. It was very beneficial for them. I hadn't seen that circular. Therefore, I told him that it was not possible as per RBI guidelines. He immediately showed me the latest instructions from RBI. I could read his feelings at that time. After that, I never gave the opportunity to my customers to give me the information about RBI circulars. Before going to bed, I started browsing the RBI website regularly as they would release circulars late in the evening sometimes.

One day, our system administrator had to go on leave due to some personal emergency. He requested me to take care of his work in his absence. Although I had never done that kind of work, with the instructions prepared by him and the support from the systems department in the head office, I managed to do it successfully. The

---

[1] AD branch is a bank branch which is authorized to deal in foreign exchange transactions by RBI.

only challenge was that it required sitting late to do the EOD (end of the day) and coming early to do the SOD (start of the day) processes. I remembered doing that work a few times in the absence of the system administrator.

My boss Mr Mukherjee became the head of our branch. During that time, our bank MD came for a visit to our branch. It was a very challenging task to deal with him. We had heard stories about the struggles of heads of branches and departments when he visited their respective branches/departments, and with the questions he asked. He had vast experience in the field of banking, naturally. All the details of our branch were on the fingertips of my boss. My boss gave responses to all the queries raised by our MD and also supported other colleagues in responding to him. Our MD was quite satisfied. He understood that we knew where we were and what we were aiming for. Observing the way my boss handled the MD's visit was a learning and inspiring experience.

After a few months, a new official Ms Darahasa was transferred to our department in place of Mr Krishnan. She had plans to make me incharge of a section in her department which demanded more time from me. Finally, I got the opportunity to work fully in the foreign exchange department. Darahasa ma'am used to tell us that before leaving office at the end of each day, we should keep all the things in such a way that we would not show up the next day. Her intention was that in case of exigencies if we didn't come any day, other colleagues should not face any problem in continuing the activities. If we can follow this advice, not just in office, but also in our life, it would be great considering the unpredictable and uncertain nature of life.

Ms Koteswaramma and Mr Ramprasad were incharges for other sections in the department—very friendly officials. Mr Ramprasad had great patience and Koteswaramma ma'am was a highly qualified person. I worked in both imports and exports sections. Ms Nandini and Mr Gopal were working in those sections. I had to learn another new system called Society for Worldwide Interbank Financial

Telecommunication (SWIFT) to send messages to other banks. From the beginning, to learn anything, I love to go through the theory part, and while doing it practically, clear the doubts with the seniors. Mr Babu was an expert in that area.

Most of the time, customers came in the late hours with a request to do a transaction explaining their urgent requirements. Generally, we used to go home late due to those last-minute requests.

Meeting RBI auditors was also a great learning experience. As advised by Mr Krishnan, I never hesitated to approach RBI if I had any doubts in interpreting their circulars. Being an AD branch, we could approach RBI officials directly. As ours was a big branch with regard to foreign exchange transactions, generally we got the first opportunity to apply RBI instructions based upon our customers' requests. After that, if any other bank officials approached the concerned department of RBI, those officials, after explaining the theory part, referred my name to them to seek more clarity as I had already applied those guidelines in a practical situation. While attending the sessions arranged by RBI and International Chamber of Commerce (ICC), I got the opportunity to meet other bank officials.

One day, some company's chairman came to our branch. Generally, such senior people wouldn't come to a junior official like me. They would meet the head of the branch and leave. But he came to me. He told me that he had heard a lot from his staff about me. They told him that I was very cooperative in completing their transactions even if they came in very late hours. But at the same time they told him that even if there was any small deviation, I wouldn't do it without proper approvals. Generally, he used to get feedback from his staff about the officials either as supportive or non-supportive. But in my case, it seems that the feedback was mixed. So he himself came to see what kind of a person I was. As I was only a junior official and as it was a very big branch with high-value transactions, many transactions wouldn't be in my authority. Wherever I felt there was a genuine reason behind any deviation, I recommended quoting supportive relevant internal or RBI guidelines to my higher officials who had the authority to approve.

Whenever any opportunity came for sending me for training, concerned officials from our head office used to call me and check with me whether I was comfortable going for that programme or not. They thought that it would be beneficial for the bank to send an official like me for the training programme who was passionate to share knowledge with other employees.

When I was working in IFB, I was also doing my MBA. My examination centre was around 25 km (~15.5 mi) away from my flat. I used to go there along with dad on my scooter. When we went there to write the exam for the first time, as usual my room was on the second floor. In spite of so many requests from our side to arrange the exam for me on the ground floor, they didn't accept. They told me to get the approval from IGNOU. My father went out and searched for some people to help us. Finally, he found some workers at a nearby construction site. They helped in carrying my chair to the second floor. I was able to travel 25 km very easily on my bike, but to climb two storeys, we struggled a lot. To our surprise, when dad went to the IGNOU office to seek permission to arrange for a ground-floor sitting for me for the remaining papers, the IGNOU officials wondered why for such a simple arrangement, the college officials couldn't take a call themselves.

After Mr Santanu Mukherjee left, Mr Saswath Chowdhary took charge of our branch. I used to become very emotional during any farewell of officials for whom I had great respect. Mr Madhusudhana Rao, Mr Mukherjee, Mr Krishnan, Mr Sridhar, Ms Darahasa—all of them helped me a lot in gaining good knowledge in the areas in which I worked.

I became eligible for my next promotion again. At that level, there was no written test—only interview. With the first experience of my promotion, I thought I might face some challenges there. But this interview appeared like an appreciation for my performance. In the interview, the chairman asked me that while I was able to perform excellently in spite of my physical challenges, why some others were lagging behind. With that question itself, I could predict the result of that interview. For the agony I had experienced in my first promotion interview, this experience was like a soothing balm. There, the chairman doubted my capabilities to discharge my duties as an officer. But here, I won the appreciation of the interview board members for my performance as an officer. It was an exhilarating moment for me.

When I was working at IFB, a boy named Ram was working in our foreign exchange section. He took care of filing and other work. Everyone in the branch liked him very much. One day, while I was leaving the office around 9:30 pm, he came along with me till my vehicle. Around 12:30 am in the night, I received a call from my colleague, Mr Sridhar, informing that Ram had died. I could not believe that shocking news. The person who was with me till three hours ago was no more. After going home, while eating dinner, he choked. His family members immediately took him to the hospital, but it was too late. How uncertain a human life is!

Apart from learning different skills at work, I enjoyed a lot of pleasant time with my colleagues. We would always have treats from colleagues for some occasion or the other, like their child getting admission in a good college, or getting a job, or buying a new vehicle, etc. Considering the accessibility issues, I used to tell them to excuse me for not joining them. But they were also like my family members; they never left me alone. They used to find accessible restaurants to take me along with them.

One day, my batchmate Kalyan invited me along with a few of our batchmates to a five-star hotel to give a treat on the occasion of his wedding. As his wedding took place in a different city, we could not attend. The hotel, in which the celebration was arranged, was near my office. It was the first experience for all of us at a five-star hotel. When they gave a finger bowl with lemon water, we didn't know what to do with it. We observed what others were doing with that bowl and followed them. After that, the waiter brought the menu card. After seeing the prices, we almost got a heart attack. After a lot of discussion, we chose the cheapest items available and decided to order just two or three items to lessen the bill by sharing each item among all of us. We laughed a lot that day.

Saturdays were half working days for us. But generally, we used to work till 5:00 or 6:00 pm. Whenever we were free on any Saturday evenings, Padma and I used to try different restaurants/bakeries, following suggestions from our colleagues. Normally, we used to think a lot about the budget before selecting a restaurant. But on those days alone, we used to try expensive places. One day, at one place, when they told us that the cold coffee was for ₹100 (20 years back, it was a big amount), it was a big shock for us. But still, we tried. I enjoyed the freedom of having my own vehicle—no need to worry about going anywhere; no need to worry about the timings.

In 2004, I was transferred from IFB to the Sanath Nagar branch. Even at that time, concerned officials from our head office told me to verify the branches in the city with regard to accessibility for me and give them my choices. My bank always thought about my convenience. When I went to Sanath Nagar, even before joining there, AGM Mr Saiful Islam received me with a lot of affection. He promised to make arrangements for a ramp at the entrance and a Western commode in the toilet.

It was really very painful to leave IFB, a branch that had given me great exposure in areas I wanted to excel. The working environment was also very friendly there. Although the work was more, I always felt energetic in that cordial atmosphere. But transfers are inevitable for any employee. I left IFB with a heavy heart.

Numaish

Every year, from 1 January to 15 February, a very big industrial exhibition, Numaish, takes place in Hyderabad. We planned to go to the exhibition with my parents and brother's family for the first time. I followed them on my scooter with my mother riding as the pillion. At the entrance of the exhibition grounds, they stopped my scooter because vehicles were not allowed inside. We requested them to allow us as I could not manage to go inside without the vehicle. They told us to approach their seniors. Finally, after giving assurance from our side that I would maintain minimal speed and not honk much, they gave me permission. As we all went together, it was great fun initially. But later, even if one person went away from us, we had to search for that person in that huge crowd. Present generation cannot even imagine such a situation as everyone now owns a mobile phone.

I enjoyed looking at the different types of products. Dad gave some money to all the children to buy whatever they wanted. After some time, I was moving slowly while speaking to my family members. They were walking. I was going along with them on my scooter. Suddenly when I looked back, I could not find anyone. How could it happen within just a few seconds, I did not understand. I took two or three rounds of that ground but could not find any. I heard announcements from speakers at the end of every street. Then I went to the announcement centre and requested to make an announcement informing them that I was waiting for my family members. They asked me whose names were to be announced to come there. I gave my parents', brother's and sister-in law's names. No use! After some time, I requested them to announce the names of my nieces and nephew. Hearing their names, the children immediately became attentive to the announcement. Finally, we all reunited.

After buying the scooter, I got relief from transport-related challenges. But the problem of accessible toilets remained the same. Although I had a nice time at the exhibition, I had to control nature's calls as long as I was there. Due to this inconvenience, I could not enjoy it to the full extent.

As it was a very big place, whoever was tired would just sit on my scooter for some time.

On the whole, it was a nice experience.

Saved by a Whisker!

One day, I was going to my friend Sarala's house. From there, we had planned to go for a function at a common friend's house. It was a far-off place from my house. Just a few metres before Sarala's house, there was a signal. I had to take a right turn at that signal. When the signal turned green, I immediately tried to take a right turn. On the opposite side, there was a big lorry. A boy on a bike tried to go straight even though the red signal was blinking. Due to the lorry, he couldn't see me. He thought of jumping the signal before others could start. While he was trying to cross the signal with high speed, he hit my scooter. With that hit, my scooter was dragged to the side of the road and I fell down. Only because I was wearing a helmet then, I am alive today.

I got some scratches on my hands. Everyone there got angry with that boy. But as his bike's speed was high, he got more injuries. After seeing his condition, people helped him.

After I got to my friend's house, I didn't tell this to her as I didn't want to spoil the mood or the programme. She could not see the scratches on my hands since I was wearing a full-sleeved dress.

After the function, when we came back, I showed my injuries to her and we applied spirit and ointment.

After the accident, I travelled on my scooter almost 30 km on that day. Whenever I recollect that incident, I cannot say whether I was courageous or mad.

15

The Struggle to Gain Ownership

After experiencing the challenges in finding a suitable flat for rent, my mother was worried about a scenario where our landlords might ask us to vacate the house; how would we find another house immediately? That was her fear. She started asking me to think about buying a house so that we could live comfortably without such fears.

Due to pressure from her, we started thinking about buying a house. The first question was whether to opt for an apartment or an independent house. Initially, mom wanted an independent house, as being from a village we were used to that set-up. We looked almost everywhere in Hyderabad for a suitable house. For independent houses, the prices were too high. So my mom slowly accepted and habituated herself to the apartment culture. She also felt that a flat in an apartment complex would be safer than an independent house for the three of us. Thereafter, we started looking for flats. We faced the issue of accessibility and *Vastu Shastra* (a traditional Hindu system of architecture) everywhere. My father was very particular about *Vastu*. Getting an accessible flat in the city with perfect *Vastu* and within our budget looked like an impossible task for me. We even gave an advance in two or three deals, but later, as dad was not comfortable with the *Vastu* of those flats, we withdrew from the proposals, losing the advance of course. Another challenge was that if we gave advance in the beginning stage of construction, we couldn't be sure about its completion. And to get a constructed flat, no flat with *Vastu* and good ventilation was available as such flats were already booked. We faced many such challenges.

One day, one of my friends told me about a flat in the Kukatpally area. Mom, dad and I went there. The builder showed us three-bedroom flats. As the cost was exceeding our budget, we asked him to show us two-bedroom flats instead. No two-bedroom flat was available under the builder's share, so he showed us some flats which were under the owners' share. We found one of the flats suitable for us. *Vastu* was perfect, the cost was within our budget, it was within the city (6 km away from my branch) and was a well-constructed flat on the first floor. I wondered how we could find such a flat, convenient for us in all aspects. That place belonged to a family in which 14 cousins were partners. The owner of our flat was the eldest of them.

Later, we requested our cousin Durga Prasad, a civil engineer, to come and verify it. He also advised us to go ahead.

I started the process of applying for a loan in my bank. We paid ₹3 lakh as advance and entered into an agreement. One purohit informed us that an auspicious *muhurat* (an auspicious time for an enterprise to begin or for a ceremony to take place) was available on 10 February 2003. We requested the owner to complete the registration process before that date. But as the owner had prior commitment at another place, he told us to go ahead with the house-warming puja. He promised to register the flat after his return. He was a gentleman. Basing on his promise, we made all the arrangements. We invited our uncles and aunties with their families. I wanted to invite my colleagues separately, as I wouldn't be able to pay attention to them if they came along with our relatives. Two days before the event, the builder called my father and told him that he would not cooperate in registering the flat as there were some financial issues to be settled with the owner. As ours was the final flat that was to be sold, the builder didn't want to lose that opportunity. He told my dad that although he didn't have any grudge against us, he would not allow us to do the house-warming function. We informed the matter to our owner. He told us not to worry and proceed with our puja.

On the day of function, our sisters and aunties went to the flat to decorate it. We went shopping to buy some items for the evening function. At that time, the builder's posse came and asked our aunties and sisters to go out. They thought that these men had come to do some cement work. When they came out, the men immediately locked the door. We approached a minister from our area with a request to help us. He is my father's ex-student. We felt very embarrassed in front of our relatives. The purohit had come, and we had made all the arrangements as well. All of us were very tired due to the tension and suspense around whether the ceremony would happen or not—a million-dollar question. Like in the movies, three minutes before the *muhurat*, the police came and ordered the builder's men to open the door. We entered the flat exactly on time. After that, we performed the puja as planned. Although we had bought new clothes to wear for the function, except me, others didn't even have time to change.

Next morning, they threatened us to vacate the place again. Although we had to stay in that flat for two more days as per our tradition, we were so vexed with their behaviour that we decided to vacate the flat and enter it only after the registration was done. It took them almost six months to settle their disputes and complete the registration of all pending flats. My mom fell sick thinking way too much about that incident. More than the flat issue, I was worried about her health. We decided to shift to a rented flat in the same apartment complex. We felt that it would be helpful for us to follow up with them and mom might feel a little bit better if we stayed in the vicinity. During that time, our uncle Mr N. A. S. Raju and our cousin Kavitha Prasad gave us immense moral support. Finally, after completing the registration process, we could move into our own flat.

Although we were not part of their dispute, we faced a lot of mental agony, mom's sickness and embarrassment before our relatives. It is indeed a challenging task to become a homeowner.

Decorating the Apartment

Owning a flat is such a wonderful feeling. In my case, I was so exuberant that I had become the owner of a flat after so many struggles. Mom, dad and I went to various places to buy different items for our flat. We found shops in Secunderabad where we could get cheap and best items. We bought curtains, chandeliers, lights, etc. One day, while coming home from office, on the sidewalk I saw a beautiful Lord Krishna idol made from plaster of Paris. They had moulded and kept it for drying. Later, they would apply colours. I told them that I wanted to buy it in its existing state, that is, in white colour. I brought it and kept it in our showcase. I liked it very much. All of our guests thought that it was made of white marble.

I love to sleep under the open sky. But due to the prevailing conditions, it was to remain only a dream. Hence, I opted for radium painting on the roof of my bedroom—with stars, clouds and moon. After switching off the lights, I felt like I was sleeping under the open sky.

Later, on one auspicious day, I invited my IFB colleagues to our flat. They all liked it and appreciated my accomplishment very much. All that appreciation made me feel so proud.

Owning a Car

Although the scooter was very comfortable for me, I could not take both mom and dad at the same time on my vehicle to any place. I could only go with either of them. Finally, I decided to buy a car in 2003. I had the facility to apply for a loan at my bank. First, I had to do a lot of enquiry about the process as it's not a very common thing. In those days, only Maruti car company was modifying cars for the persons with disabilities. I approached a Maruti dealer. I started the process as advised by them on 18 December and got the car on 20 April. It took four months for them to deliver the car.

First, I had to get a medical certificate from a government doctor mentioning that I was fit for driving. When I met the head of the orthopaedic department, he enquired about my experience in driving. When I informed him that I drove a scooter, he was very impressed. But another doctor who was present in the room told the senior doctor that it might be risky to give a fitness certificate to me. As per his view, if I met with any accident in future because of my disability, the doctor who had given the certificate of fitness would be taken to task. But the senior doctor told him that he was confident that I could drive the car safely. Thank God, the other doctor was not the head of that department.

With the medical certificate, a learner license copy (I applied and got it from the RTA office) and DD for ₹25,000 as advance, I applied to Maruti to manufacture the car as per our requirements. At that time, they were doing necessary modifications for only the Zen model. Later, I got the manufacturing certificate from them, agreeing to modify the car. With that we applied to the Central government for exemption in excise duty. Within two weeks, I got the approval letter from them. After paying the full amount, I got my car. As the company wanted to keep the cost at a reasonable level, they did not install the AC while manufacturing. Even though we were ready to pay the extra amount, they didn't add that feature. We had to get it done from a private mechanic suggested by that dealer. The car did not have power steering either. The reason given by them was that power steering might be dangerous for a person with disability. But with my present experience, I don't agree with that view. For 13 years, I managed with the manual steering, struggling a lot while taking turns. Now, the power steering in my present car has reduced my strain to a great extent.

My nephew Sudhir had a driving license. During that time, my niece Sunanda had also come to Hyderabad to do her house-surgery in

OU. She started learning how to drive along with dad. Dad, however, never drove the car.

My car was like a toy car for Sudhir, as it was an auto gear car. With him, I made my first attempt to drive the car. Between car and scooter driving, there is a huge difference. Although road sense is common for both, estimating the distance between other vehicles/people in front of our car is a major difference. On a scooter, we can see everything very well. Another challenge was controlling the steering. Initially, I used to always move the steering wheel to drive the car in the correct direction. When I observed other drivers on the road, they used to move the steering only now and then. I could not understand how they were managing. We then hired a professional driver to teach me driving. He sat beside me and gave instructions, completely leaving the steering to me. He made me drive on the busiest roads of Hyderabad. In the initial days, I used to get scared if someone honked behind me and would give way to them immediately. My coach told me not to get disturbed by those honkings but drive at my own pace. He also told me that if others were in too great a hurry, they would overtake me and go. That was a great lesson for me.

I went for a driving test and successfully got through it.

16

Holy Places: Obstacles to Access

Although I strongly believe that God is omnipresent, I like to visit holy places (temples, churches, dargahs, gurudwaras, etc.). I tried to visit one or two mosques, but not all the mosques allow women. Women can only go to certain specific mosques, it seems. I love to be in spiritual environments. Any place in the lap of nature with a peaceful and serene atmosphere is among my favourites.

Visiting Chilkur Balaji Temple in the early hours was a wonderful experience. At that time, the temple was very peaceful. We could sit so close to the idols and observe the puja. At the Lord Shiva temple there, we were allowed to do *abhishekam* (a religious rite or method of prayer in which the devotee pours a liquid offering on an image or idol of the god or the goddess). Devotees could offer all their services to God without any charges. In that temple, we didn't see a single *hundi* (a donation box used in Indian temples to collect cash offerings from devotees).

At Srisailam temple too, people were allowed to touch the Sivalingam and perform the puja. To get to that temple, we had to pass through a ghat road. It's in a dense forest area. Travelling to that temple itself was an amazing experience.

Whenever I visit any place, I try my best to go to different places of worship in the vicinity. Although accessibility would always be an issue at most places, I got some very nice responses from people. However, I have had a few bitter experiences at some popular places.

Mahanandi was one such place. I went there with my parents and brother's family. When we went to the temple, we came to know that we had to walk for a long distance to reach the entrance of the temple, as it has very big premises. At that time, I used to walk with a walker. I thought I could not manage that much distance with a walker. So I told my family members that I would sit at the entrance near some shop. But they didn't accept it. Dad saw a bicycle inside the campus. Dad made me sit on the bicycle after taking the permission from its owner. Dad started walking holding the cycle. Suddenly, one senior person came to us and told us that we should not use a bicycle in the temple complex. Then dad explained to him that it was parked inside only, and he also explained about my situation. Even then, that man didn't accept. He told us that if it was not possible for me to walk, it was better for me to sit at home instead of coming there and troubling them. I told my family to leave me and go inside but they didn't listen. They went outside and brought one stool from a shop. They made me sit on the stool and started carrying me. It was really difficult to balance it without handles but they somehow managed it, albeit with a lot of strain. After reaching the entrance of the temple, I started walking with the walker. The same person approached us again and told us that the walker was not allowed inside the temple. The distance was very little, so I just crawled on the ground to go and pay my respect to the deities inside.

I could not understand how the temple authorities appointed such a heartless person there.

Some years ago, we went to Tirumala, which is famous for the Lord Venkateswara temple. Travelling via the ghat road was a thrilling experience. We got such humbling spiritual feelings on those seven hills. As I love nature immensely, I liked my stay there very much. We hired a vehicle and saw all the important places in Tirumala. We went to the main temple. For old and persons with disabilities, there was a shorter way. I felt very happy for the concern shown for people like myself. After going for some distance inside, they told me that walkers were not allowed. Then I asked them how I could walk suddenly without my walker. We enquired if any wheelchair was available with them. They told us wheelchairs were also not allowed inside. Then I asked how to manage the situation. They said that I could go with the support of either my family members or the temple volunteers, I had to be carried physically inside. Only my parents were with me at that time. They could not carry me for that much distance, and the female volunteers could not carry me either. I didn't want to be carried by the male volunteers. Finally, with a lot of effort, dad carried me in.

In case any temple authorities don't want to allow external wheelchairs, they can arrange for wheelchairs (with the material that is acceptable inside the temple as per their customs) to support people like me. But putting us in such an embarrassing situation is not at all fair on their part. I think that God won't accept putting us to such hardships.

Due to similar situations, I could not enter the Golden Temple at Amritsar either. I went there with my parents, WBFI joint secretary Shanthy, treasurer Vishal Kothari and his family, and our volunteer Subramaniam. As it was not accessible for me and Shanthy, others also didn't go inside. On behalf of us all, Vishal's wife Priyanka went inside to pray for all of us.

Guruvayoorappan Temple is a famous temple in Kerala. I went there with my parents and all my siblings' families. To a great extent, it was accessible. I felt very happy about that. By that time, I started using a wheelchair for long distances and the walker only for short distances. Inside the temple, the officials told me that a wheelchair was not allowed. Fortunately, they allowed my walker. Due to post-polio syndrome (PPS), my muscle energy levels were deteriorating. On that day, it became very difficult for me to walk inside the temple. By the time I came out, I felt like I would faint. All the concerned officials were observing my situation. I knew that they felt sorry for me but were not ready to break their rules.

Whenever I had such experiences, I would dream about constructing accessible places of worship for all possible religions at one place, where people like me could go and pray without any hassles.

As many holy places are very old constructions, I can understand the non-availability of accessible facilities for the persons with disabilities. Due to the efforts of many disability rights activists, many places are now becoming accessible.

The attitude of people at some places hurt me. They think that it would be better for persons with disabilities to sit at home and pray. But like any other person, they also want to visit the temples and pray to get some mental strength and peace.

Once I went to the Goddess Mariamman Temple in Samayapuram, near Chennai. I was surprised to see that the temple was fully accessible for wheelchair users. With my wheelchair, I could go to each and every corner in the temple—no objections whatsoever. It was such a great feeling!

17

Moving Out of My Comfort Zone

By the time I joined the Sanath Nagar branch, our branch head Mr Saiful Islam had made the arrangements for a ramp and a commode in the washroom. In my section too, he instructed the concerned people to keep everything within the reach of my seat. He thought that I might hesitate to tell him about any inconvenience. That's why he told other female colleagues to enquire with me about the facilities available there, or if I had any other requirements. He was such a gentleman.

My batchmate Balaram was also working there. He is always so cool; I never saw him tense. He is a very friendly and supportive person. In our section, except one male colleague, all were women. Ms Vijayalakshmi, Indira, Padma, Gowri and Kameswari from the credit section were all very friendly people.

At IFB, I was a learner. Here, as I came from a big branch, I got the respect from others for my experience there. They used to take my advice. Customers were with the branch from its inception; they had a strong affinity with the branch. I tried my level best to implement the best practices I learnt at IFB without hurting the feelings of the customers.

After coming to this branch, my walking reduced to a great extent, as everything was within my reach. As I was not doing any other exercise, walking with a walker was the only exercise that helped me till that time. As my walking was reduced, I started feeling some discomfort in my back.

We had many relatives and friends in Hyderabad. Most of my cousins had also shifted to the city. We used to meet each other frequently. My niece Sunanda and nephew Sudhir were with us. Sunanda's marriage was fixed—first marriage in the next generation in our family. During the weekends and after office hours, we spent most of the time shopping. Sunanda, like my mother, is very particular and was not willing to buy anything that was not up to her taste.

We went on buying something or other till the very last moment of the wedding. Even then we forgot to buy some important items. Shopping for marriage is a never-ending process.

We all had a great time during her marriage. Both the bride and bridegroom were doctors. Her husband Vamsi lived in the USA. After a few months, she went there too. After giving farewell to her at the airport and while coming back, I became very emotional. I love all my siblings' children as if they are my own children. She was travelling alone to the USA for the first time to join her husband. We were all in a tensed state till she met Vamsi, as there were many air travel restrictions during that time due to terrorist attacks in some countries. We felt great relief when she reached safely.

Another niece Padmasri joined intermediate in a residential college in Hyderabad. Earlier, Sunanda, Sudhir and Vindhyasri also studied intermediate in residential colleges. As they studied in different places, I didn't have the experience of witnessing their struggles directly. In both the Telugu states, most of the parents prefer to make their children either doctors or engineers. There are so many famous residential colleges in our area. Those two years, children would only study without playing any games or participating in any extracurricular activities. In the first year, Padmasri was very homesick. We used to go to see her frequently in the evenings after her college hours.

Although I gave much importance to studying my course material, simultaneously I continued reading my favourite books along with doing other activities joyfully. I remember dad taking me to a movie just a day before the night of one of my exams. He thought that as I was studying continuously, I should indulge in some relaxation. I strongly believe that children should take part in other activities such as sports and cultural activities along with their studies. They should not be treated like machines. We can't expect them to study for 20 hours in a day. Every parent must enquire how much importance any school/college is giving to sports and other activities, apart from studies. If parents start demanding these activities, which are essential for all-round personality development of the child, automatically schools and colleges would give importance to them.

Slowly, I started feeling the back pain and fatigue. Bearing the weight of the helmet also became very difficult. Even after buying a car, I used the scooter to go to some places as it allowed me to go nearer to the shops or made it easy to do shopping in narrow lanes. But now, I started using the car to avoid wearing a helmet.

I had no idea why I felt the fatigue even after taking good food.

Relationship managers from MNC banks used to come to our branch. I used to hear from them that working in MNC banks is more challenging than working in public sector banks. I could not understand the difference. I used to disagree with them. Although the conversations were in a friendly manner, I started thinking about it. If anyone challenges me in an area where I believe I am strong, I like to take up that challenge.

I heard about the Certified Documentary Credit Specialist (CDCS) exam from the Institute of Financial Services (IFS), UK, when I was at IFB through Mr Krishnan. I wanted to apply but I didn't because

I thought my knowledge might not be sufficient. No one in my bank had applied to it till that time. Through one of my friends, I came to know about one official in another MNC bank, Mr Nageswara Rao, who cleared this exam. I spoke to him over the phone. He was working in Chennai at the time, and his family was in Hyderabad. He told me to go to his house and collect the material available there for this exam. I collected the material from his house. Fee for that exam was around ₹40,000. I had never paid such a big amount as a fee previously to acquire any of my qualifications. Exam was in the second week of April; it was the second week of February when I decided to write the exam, that is, within just two months' time. I was in a dilemma whether I could clear the exam without any guidance, with just two months' preparation. After seeing the material, I became confident. Finally, I decided to apply for it. I remember that I requested the concerned official in the institute for extension of the due date to pay my fee.

The official, who gave me the material, told me that job opportunities would be more for me in the market if I cleared that exam. When I recollected the words of those relationship managers, my decision to take up a challenge had become strong. But at the same time, I loved my bank, in which I worked for 15 years. All the officials and colleagues extended their full support to me in all aspects. Still, I was in a dilemma. My parents and I were settled in Hyderabad happily among our relatives and friends. Was it required to change that set-up? But my quest for knowledge, urge for more exposure and crave for adventure by taking up challenges were telling me to try for the job in MNC banks. I kept all those thoughts aside and concentrated fully on my exam.

It was annual closing time in the bank. During that time, work would be more, and we couldn't apply for leave. After coming from office, I would read the material from 10:00 pm to 2:00 am daily. We went to Chennai to write the exam. At that time, Nageswara Rao introduced me to his boss. It was like an informal interview. He was impressed with my experience, knowledge and positive attitude.

After coming back, I became busy with my duties. Later, I was interviewed over the phone by officials of the organization in which Nageswara Rao was working. They gave me the offer letter. At the same time, another MNC bank also approached me. My results were announced. I had cleared the CDCS exam. I was the first official who acquired that qualification in my bank.

At that time, I was in a great dilemma whether to resign or not. I had to do a lot of brainstorming. My parents were always ready to support me in attempting choicest of things. Finally, I decided to resign, although half-heartedly. I felt so guilty while giving my resignation letter, remembering the support extended to me by my bank. When I gave the resignation letter, my boss Mr Suri was surprised. He told me to think for a few days and confirm to him. Till that time, he said that he would keep my letter with him safely. He also told me to inform him without any hesitation if I decided to change my decision. But I gave the letter only after taking my final decision. Generally, after taking a decision I don't go back. But I didn't want to confirm with him immediately, because it might have appeared as if I were not respecting his words.

Next day, I confirmed my resignation to my boss. By that time he understood that mine was not a hasty but a fully thought-out decision. Whoever came to know about my decision got surprised. Although resignations are not new, a person like me (a woman with disability) taking such a bold step was surprising for many.

Our relatives were also not very happy. They thought that it was a foolish decision, as my parents were old and I was a woman with severe disability. In that condition, leaving a government job in a familiar region and going to a new place with an unknown language and without any friends or relatives—and that too in the private sector, which many people consider risky—looked like a hasty decision to many. So many people tried to dissuade me. Only a few well-wishers who knew my interest in learning new things and knowledge in the area where I was working welcomed my decision. All the resignation formalities were completed smoothly. On the last working day in my bank, farewell was arranged. All the staff spoke very positive things about me and wished me all the best. To my surprise, my colleague Padma also spoke. I never saw her speaking on any occasion. On that day, she spoke very emotionally. She told me that though the meaning of my name Latha is a creeping plant, I was like a big tree under which they learnt many things, and then they were feeling like kids who were going to lose their mother. Her words touched my heart a lot.

I left the bank with a very heavy heart. I didn't know whether my decision was correct or not.

18

New City, New Experiences

The family of my father's friend Mr Ananthakumar's sister is in Chennai. He was our tenant in Sathupally. My father went to Chennai and with the help of uncle's nephew Vijay, he could find a flat on rent just beside Prasad Studio in Saligramam area. In Hyderabad, we stayed near Saradhi Studios for some years, and in Chennai, beside Prasad Studio, though we didn't have any connection with the film industry.

We travelled by car from Hyderabad. My nephew Sudhir drove the car; he loves driving very much. We stopped at Vijayawada and went to my youngest uncle P. V. S. Raju's house. He has a very friendly nature. So we, all my cousins, treat him as one among us. I met my paternal grandmother who was then living with him. She was around 95 years old at that time. Rarely can we see people like her. It appeared that she never tensed up for any issues in her life. In the initial stages, her mother-in-law took care of the challenges they had in the family; and later, her children. I feel that her cool nature might be the reason for her longevity. That was the last time I saw her alive. We lost her one year before she could complete her 100th year.

My uncle's sister and her family received us in Chennai very warmly. We stayed at their house that night and on the next day we went to our flat.

Our flat owner had given the flat on rent for the first time. He took all the precautions. He took a copy of my appointment letter, driving license, etc. He used to come to our flat every fortnight to see whether we were maintaining the flat neatly or not. He also used to come inside the house to check the bathroom, bedroom, etc. Although I got irritated, we allowed him considering his age.

As my neighbours came to know that we are Telugu, they introduced us to Telugu families in that complex: a young couple Prasad and Uma, and another resident, Priya. Kausalya in our block also knew Telugu as she was brought up in erstwhile united Andhra Pradesh. For mom, it was a great relief as she was struggling to speak with the neighbours due to language barrier.

We let out our flat in Hyderabad. Dr Ravishankar, a surgeon in gastroenterology, stayed in our flat with his family. He was a gentleman. At a very young age he acquired many qualifications and studied in very reputed institutions like AIIMS. Later, I introduced him to my nieces and nephews so they could get inspired. We are still in touch with him. He gives suggestions whenever we approach him with any health issue concerning his area of specialization.

On 30 August 2006, I joined my new office. It was an entirely new atmosphere. Mr Johnson was the head of our trade department, and Mr Khan was my section head. Both of them had interviewed me before I joined. In the first few days, they gave me time to get acquainted with the new place and feel comfortable in the new environment. All the places I saw were accessible for me. I felt very happy. My colleagues Sangeetha and Sona showed me the rest room on the first day. Till that time, I used only common toilets. But here, there was a separate restroom for persons with disabilities, and it was very much accessible. As I was the only staff member with a disability at that time in my department, I was the only person using that toilet. I was so thrilled with this experience.

In the initial days of my joining there, I would talk more about the toilet facility with all my friends and relatives in Hyderabad and Sathupally. They used to laugh at me saying anyone else would talk about salary or other facilities in the new job, but I only knew the struggles I faced with regard to toilets from my childhood. No one knows how many times I controlled nature's call for hours together due to non-availability of accessible toilets, and how so many times I could not enjoy any function or other occasions fully due to this. Hence, for me, this matter naturally became the most important one.

Here, everyone calls others by their first names. Until then, I was habituated with being called 'Madam'. I found it difficult to call my seniors by name. But I had to follow, as it was common practice. And at the same time, accepting very junior colleagues calling us by name was also not so easy to accept. One of my colleagues, Govind, had also worked in the same bank where I worked earlier. He is a very friendly person. I used to have chats with him about the differences in both the environments. I was more comfortable in communicating with him, as he was also from my previous bank. Slowly, I got habituated to the practice. Now I find it difficult to call others as 'Sir' and 'Madam'. But, depending on the situation or place where we are, we have to follow the norm. Be a Roman when you are in Rome, so goes the saying!

In the initial days, I had a culture shock, though everyone was friendly. If this was the problem I faced just for changing the state, I could only imagine how people feel when they go abroad! If I came out of my house, I had to speak only in English. Although I had become comfortable with speaking in English by that time, I used to miss speaking in Telugu and cracking jokes with friends happily in my mother tongue. I missed my siblings' families, ex-colleagues, friends and other relatives very much. When other colleagues were speaking in Tamil in a jovial manner, I could not enjoy those jokes as I didn't know Tamil. Before coming to Chennai itself, we bought a book titled *Learn Tamil in 30 Days*. But we can't learn how to speak a language unless we practise speaking in that language with people. As all my colleagues communicated in English, I couldn't practise my spoken Tamil initially. When we speak to people who know only one common language with us, then only we would try to speak with them in the language known to them, even with mistakes.

My new job gave me a great opportunity to learn more in my subject. I got the opportunity to deal with certain types of transactions which I read only in books. In my previous organization, I worked in various areas. I knew very well what would happen from the moment a customer entered a bank to open a simple account, take a loan, etc. I knew the reporting part as well. I worked in a manual atmosphere too. As I worked in different branches, I got the opportunity to do banking work of all aspects. But, as the present organization is a back office of a big MNC bank, due to heavy volumes of transactions, there are a lot of super specializations. People who are working in a particular area will have a fair knowledge about that area alone, and getting an idea of all the other sections will take more time. As I came here with the experience of working in various fields of banking, it became easy for me to do more specializations.

One important thing that I missed was dealing with customers directly, as I was working in the back office. I became habituated slowly to this new environment and found many opportunities to learn new things. Here, branches of our bank are our customers. Initially, I worked with the Middle East team. As per my work-related requirements, I had to speak to relationship managers from different countries. I could now make friends from different countries.

Our trade head Johnson remembers the names of all the staff. If anyone looks dull, he can identify it and enquire with that person about the problem. The staff likes him very much.

Our section head Mr Khan was very supportive by nature. Slowly, other colleagues became friends. As I was working for Middle Eastern countries, my week off was on Friday. It took some time for me to adjust to this new calendar. As my parents stayed mostly at home, it didn't bother me much though. Meeting friends became a challenge, as I had to go to the office when others had a holiday.

One day, one of our senior officials, Steve Thompson, came from the Middle East. He planned to do a session for our team. As the team size was big, it was arranged in another building on the first floor, where capacity of the meeting room was more. As there was no elevator to that room, my boss and other team members apologized to me for not being able to take me to that meeting (later, we came to know that there was a way to go there through the elevator). I was sitting at my desk and doing some work. After the session, that official was the first person who entered our department. He saw me sitting alone and working. Then he enquired with my boss about the reason for me not attending. After the reason was conveyed to him, he immediately told my boss that he would take the session for me again. My boss came to me to check whether I would go to his cabin for the session or he needed to come to my desk. In the beginning I could not understand what he was asking. After understanding, I could not believe it. I felt immensely happy for his concern. I thought that he might brief the highlights of his presentation to me. But to my surprise, he repeated the whole presentation of his first session. I was overwhelmed with his compassionate nature. Even today when I remember that incident, my eyes turn misty. I don't remember how many times and to how many people I have narrated this incident. I shall never forget him.

Singara Chennai: Imagination to Reality

In many of the books I read in my childhood, there were always many references to *Singara* Chennai (Beautiful Chennai—erstwhile Madras). As it was the capital of the composite state of Tamil Nadu and Andhra regions, many freedom fighters, poets and writers from

Andhra region stayed or studied in Chennai. I read names of so many places in Chennai in those books. Whenever I saw boards displaying those names, I got very excited. I felt as if I were seeing the places from my previous birth. Chennai is very famous for arts. In the popular book *Mahaprasthanam* written by great Telugu poet Srirangam Srinivasa Rao (fondly called by people as Sri Sri), names of many places in Chennai were mentioned. As I remember those verses very well, I remember all those names.

As the Telugu film industry was also based in Chennai for many years, I read about the struggles of my favourite character actors in the initial stages of their careers. They used to take rest during their leisure time on the benches at Panagal Park. I have read so many stories about that park. When we came to Chennai, we went to see the park. As we could not park our car near the park, we had to park it somewhere else and come to the park by an autorickshaw. As it was already evening, there were so many mosquitoes. We felt nostalgic remembering all those great actors, although we could not stay for a long time due to mosquito bites. We went to many famous temples in Chennai. The beach is my favourite place anyway. Although I could not go near the water, I always enjoyed the cool breeze at the beach.

Kodaikanal Trip

Our team in office planned to go to Kodaikanal during one weekend. I hesitated to join them as I didn't know how accessible that place would be. But Govind and my boss encouraged me to join them along with my parents. By that time, I had started using a wheelchair for travelling long distances. And for short distances, I used my walker as usual. I always remember the affectionate support from my team members towards me and to my parents. They didn't allow my parents to carry a small handbag even. Whenever it was required, my boss Khan, without any hesitation, pushed my wheelchair. It was a very beautiful place. Being a nature lover, I enjoyed our stay there a lot. Govind encouraged and supported us to go for a boat ride. My parents and I enjoyed that ride a lot. Thanks a ton to Govind! Our team member Kevin was with us for most of the time during that trip, taking care of us very well.

Visit to Puducherry and Thiruvannamalai

Sudhir and Vindhyasri came to Chennai during vacations. We all went to Puducherry, Auroville and Thiruvannamalai in our car, driven by Sudhir, during one weekend. I was very surprised to see the cleanliness of Puducherry roads. Flower sellers were also speaking in English there, which is not common in other places. I roamed about Auroville in a battery-operated car. At Thiruvannamalai, all the devotees go for a circumambulation around the hill during full-moon nights. As my parents and I could not walk that distance (14 km), we went in my car. It was a great experience. We also went to Ramana Maharshi Ashram and experienced a deep feeling of serenity there. We enjoyed watching the beautiful scenery throughout our journey.

19

A Rude Shock: 365 Days to Live!

Deterioration of Health

Although I was trying my level best to stick to my daily schedule, day by day my energy levels were falling down drastically. Sitting for hours together started becoming painful for me. I started feeling severe pain in my lower back, and it began to spread to the toes of my right leg. Even small activities were proving to be extremely strenuous for me. I lost all enthusiasm, which had been a prominent trait of my personality. The pain was such that I could not even hold a book for a few minutes. At times, I started feeling breathlessness and a twist in my tongue while speaking, as if I'd lost control of my tongue movement. I didn't know why I was feeling like that. Earlier I used to get irritated if I saw anyone sitting idle without doing any productive work. But due to the deterioration of my health, I wanted to be idle. At that time, such idle people appeared to be very lucky to me.

From the beginning, I am used to taking up additional responsibilities at work. But in that condition, I didn't know how to manage in a new organization. One weekend, I decided to go to an orthopaedic surgeon in a famous hospital near my house. After examining me, the doctor suggested that I go for an X-ray of my spine. After seeing my X-ray, I was scared. It was like an 'S' shape. I could not understand how anyone could be alive with such a curved spine. The doctor scolded me for not wearing callipers. He suggested that I go to a rehabilitation centre. I didn't like his suggestion. How could I just leave my job and go to a rehabilitation centre? I thought of consulting another orthopaedic surgeon. Dad and I went to another hospital known for their specialization in treating severe orthopaedic cases. We took an appointment with the head of that hospital. We showed the X-ray and explained to him my health condition. The doctor didn't say anything to me. Instead, he turned towards his assistant and started dictating to her, saying that he had examined me, who had come to him with severe back pain in sitting posture, and he observed that after some days I would start experiencing the same pain in the lying posture as well, and that I would face breathlessness in the near future, which will be followed by the collapse of my digestive system and eventual paralysis of my legs within six months. The suggestion given by him was: spinal surgery by instrumentation.

My mind became blank. I went to him expecting a better suggestion than that of the previous doctor. But he gave me almost a death sentence. It was a bitter shock for me. Tears rolled down my eyes incessantly. There was no effort from the doctor to prepare me for listening such a horrible prospective diagnosis, or at least to console me after sharing his opinion. With great effort, I controlled my tears and checked with him about the chances of success of the spine surgery. He told me that at my age, chances might be minimal. When I asked if there was a way to improve the success chances of the surgery, he told me that he could not do anything as I approached him too late. I was 37 at that time. We came out. Even in that depressive mood, I drove the car myself. As mom was under medication for BP, we thought of telling her the news slowly. It became very difficult for us to pretend as if everything was normal. But after seeing our faces, mom understood that something was wrong.

She insisted on us to tell her what was going on. We tried to tell her about the matter as lightly as possible. But she understood the situation and cried a lot. All three of us were in great distress. We informed all our siblings about the situation. They came to our place immediately and were very anxious. As we have many doctors in our family, we consulted them immediately and understood that due to spine compression, one of my lungs was not working at all and the other was working only partially. Spine is the most vital part of our body; it is because of the spine that the human body remains straight and all other vital organs are placed in their proper positions and work efficiently. But in my case, the spine was in a very bad condition. Due to its severe compression, my heart, digestive system, kidneys and so on were in danger of getting affected.

What would be the impact of this report on my future? Would I survive beyond one year? What does the future hold for me?

The Aftermath

Slowly I came out of the shock and started thinking about the situation. Generally, I don't spend much time worrying about challenges. Being a human being, I may experience natural feelings such as anger and worry, but I can't stay in a negative mood for a long time. I always try to find a way to overcome the challenge. However, in that situation, I did not know what to do. As per the doctor's words, going for surgery seemed to be very risky. Without that surgery, my lifespan might be reduced to one year. Even in that one year, I might become bedridden. I am not the type of person who tries to multiply money or save a lot. I had just started a new job. In the present condition, I didn't have any idea how my new management would respond. In case they were not supportive, what would I do? I even recollected the words of my well-wishers who strongly opposed my decision to leave a secure government job. For some time, even I thought that had this happened to me while I was still working in my previous organization, they might have taken care of me as they very well knew my hardworking nature, sincerity and commitment. But as I had joined my present organization just a few months ago, I couldn't guess what they would think about me. If I become bedridden, how would my parents manage? In my childhood, they were young and energetic, so they could take care of me. Now, due to old age, they wouldn't be able to manage. Many such thoughts kept rushing in my mind. I called my boss and expressed my condition in brief and requested for leave. I could not control my tears while speaking to him; my voice choked. From the brief update I gave him, he could understand the seriousness of the situation. He told me to take care of myself and permitted me to go on leave.

By that time, Sudhir had completed his MBBS and was preparing for his master's entrance exams. When he came to know of the situation, he immediately rushed to us. Whether to go for surgery or not was the million-dollar question for us. We broke our heads on that point. Finally, my parents told me that they were not ready to see me dying on the operation table. If not the operation, then what would we do? We thought of trying Ayurveda and homoeopathy medicines. As Kerala is famous for Ayurveda, we thought of going there. Someone told us to go to an Ayurveda centre run by Kerala Institute in Chennai. If required, they would refer me to their head office in Kerala. We went there and showed them my medical reports. The female doctor told us that for polio, treatment could be done effectively at a young age. In that situation, with some medicines, patients could only get temporary relief, and there was no permanent cure. We somehow came to know about Dr Mathews Jo, a homoeopathy doctor. I started consulting him.

20

The Lifeline

Meeting Mr Ananda Jothi

My niece Sunanda, who is a neurologist in the USA, suggested that I try physiotherapy. My sister Nirmala and brother-in-law who came earlier from Sathupally stayed with us for a few months to support us. They both take care of all our siblings like their children. As and when we are in need, they will come to help us. We went to a physiotherapist. He spoke to us in a very positive way. Sudhir and my sister accompanied me to the physiotherapy centre daily. We went there for a few days. They tried traction and ultrasonic therapy. When it was done, I felt a little bit of relief from pain. But after some time, the pain still persisted.

At that time, I got my ex-student Rajesh's contact number. He was the principal of a physiotherapy college in Hyderabad. After hearing about my health condition, he suggested that I go to Ananda Jothi, an experienced physiotherapist who is in Chennai itself. Rajesh had attended his classes, and he strongly recommended him. We contacted him and took an appointment.

While going to him, my mood was very low. I was on leave at that time and a few thoughts bothered me: How many days could I be on leave like this? In case my organization asked me to resign, what would I do? How would I manage this one year? I wanted to ask Mr Anand mainly one thing: Would there be any possibility for me to continue with my job till I died? It might look foolish now, but it was a fact then, and that was my main concern. I didn't want to be a burden on my family, both financially and physically. My only desire at that time was to be on my own during that one year, my remaining lifespan as per the doctor's words.

We went inside and met Mr Anand. He had a pleasant and friendly smile. After seeing my report, he kept it aside. He told me not to worry about that report at all. He assured me that he would guide me in improving my health condition, and that I would live a long life if I followed all his suggestions. He enquired whether I had participated in any sports earlier; I told him that I hadn't. I could not understand why he was asking that. How could I participate in sports? Maybe indoor board games were possible for me to play, but he was talking about athletics, swimming, etc. He told me that after a few days of treatment, and after I start feeling better, we would decide which sport I would like to participate in. I was clueless. I had gone to him to ask how I should manage my day-to-day activities until I died a year later. But instead he was talking about me participating in sports. He talked about paralympic sports. I forgot about my pain, my lifespan, etc. As I love sports very much, I saw a feather of hope, a possibility of me participating in sports. At that time, I didn't know that his treatment had started already. He could successfully change my mood by giving me the hope of participating in sports.

He suggested a few simple exercises with a combination of breathing techniques and advised me to see him again after two days. He also suggested that I should wear a spinal brace as I was struggling to sit even for a few minutes. He called the orthotist to take my measurements. Actually, at that time too, I was not interested in wearing it. In my childhood, I hated it very much. I told him how painful it was. He told me that it was not for the entire body but only for the spine.

He also told me if it was painful, we could ask the orthotist to make the required changes to it to make it more comfortable for me.

He also enquired about my profession. When he came to know about my job, he asked me how I could come to him during working hours? Again I was surprised. Even after seeing my health condition, he was asking me about my office hours. I told him I was on leave. Then he enquired about the reason why I had taken leave, and I didn't know how to respond. Frankly speaking, I was just sitting at home and thinking about the upcoming future. I told him that after seeing the medical report, my family and I were in shock and we decided that I should apply for leave. He smiled and told me to cancel my leave and join work as soon as I got the spinal brace. In certain conditions, bed rest is required. For my condition, he told me that bed rest was not required.

But sitting for so many hours was not good. He suggested that I sit for around six hours only. He told me that sitting idly at home would worsen my condition as I would spend all the time worrying about my health.

By the time I came out from his clinic, my mood had changed entirely. I started dreaming about participating in sports. For some time, I had completely forgotten my pain.

The exercises suggested by him were also very simple; I could do them on my own. I no longer needed to trouble anyone. In my childhood, all the exercises that were suggested to me needed support from others.

I immediately called my boss and told him about the physiotherapist's advice and expressed my intention to come to office within a few days. He was fine with that.

I got my spinal brace. It was an expensive one, but very lightweight. Wherever I had pain, the orthotist kept some cushions in it to make me feel comfortable.

I started going to the office from a Sunday (week beginning as I work for Middle East countries). Johnson was not available in office; my section head, Khan, was there though. When he updated Johnson about my decision, he told Khan to allow me to go home whenever I wanted. That's why on that day Khan asked me many times whether I would be able to sit or leave. I was so touched by their concern for my health condition. I sat for a few hours and then came home; Sudhir drove the car. As my hands and neck were hurting a lot, I temporarily stopped driving. Sudhir was the one taking care of that part.

Support from My Organization

The next day I met Johnson. I showed him the reports, explained my situation as well as the physiotherapist's advice. Actually, I hesitated in telling him the suggestion given by the physiotherapist to sit just for six hours in the office. With great hesitation, I told him about it. I myself was not happy with it. While working, how can I be in the office for just six hours? That was the question I had in my mind. Never had I worked like that. Then Johnson told me to stop thinking about all these things. He advised me to concentrate fully on my health, and not to worry about office work, and he permitted me to stay in the office for whatever hours I was able to manage, and to leave whenever I wanted without any hesitation. He told me that life is more important than anything else. He made it very clear to me that our organization would be with me in overcoming my health challenges.

I was so incredibly moved by his compassionate words and support. They gave me great relief. I didn't have much idea about the culture of MNCs as I had joined there just a few months ago. As believed by my well-wishers, government jobs have security, whereas private sector organizations do not give job security and may throw out their employees at will.

However, that was not the case. I had a different experience altogether. I got immense support from my organization.

Hydrotherapy: My Lifeline

On the next visit, Mr Anand suggested that I start hydrotherapy. I could not understand what he was talking about. He explained to me that hydrotherapy was doing exercises underwater. Whenever I went to him, he gave me pleasant surprises. I have immense fascination for water, but until then no one in my family had allowed me to go near the water, let alone enter it. But here, he was suggesting that I enter the water. My heart jumped with joy. Dad had his concerns about my safety in water. I applied brakes on my happiness and eagerly waited for his response. Mr Jothi told me that he would come with me to the pool and show me the exercises. He asked me not to worry. As he knew we were from erstwhile Andhra Pradesh, he asked us to find the possibility of going to the pool at Andhra Club in Chennai.

Mr Anand also suggested changes for my shoes. Due to the bend in my spine, my body was in an uneven position. One side of my body was taller than the other. Accordingly, he arranged for increasing the height of the shoe on the shorter side. As my left leg was weak, a brace was arranged for the knee and shin part. With the height change in shoes and with the knee brace, I could get support to walk with less strain on my hands. But my elbows had pain due to overstrain. It was tennis elbow. During a conversation with Anand (we became friends by that time and started calling each other by our first names), I came to know that my situation was called post-polio syndrome. I immediately googled about it. After reading about that syndrome, my mind became blank again. As per the information available on the Internet, it is caused due to improper or excessive use of limbs by polio-affected people. Until then I had thought that polio would affect me only one time (when it actually occurred) and then leave me to my fate. But due to its lingering effect, after some years, some polio-affected people like myself would start getting muscle deterioration; the muscles would become weak slowly. It was only then that I realized the importance of muscles in our body. Our tongue is the strongest muscle in our body. As that became weak, I had felt the problem of tongue-twisting earlier. Even breathing is supported by the muscles near the lungs. After reading all that research, I understood how horrible my situation could become in future. I felt very bad. I couldn't sleep for weeks. I started having dreams in which I was struggling to even swallow.

Only when we have a problem with any part of our body do we realize the importance of that part. I suddenly realized the importance of the spine and muscles. When I shared all the knowledge I'd acquired through the Internet with Anand, he told me to stop reading all that. He assured me that I would feel better with the treatment he was giving. I had my own doubts but kept quiet.

My family and well-wishers were shocked when they came to know that Anand had suggested hydrotherapy for me. They all thought that he had gone mad. They wondered how a person like me with severe disability could manage in the water. As I like water very much, I convinced all of them for a trial. We didn't have any other choice anyway. I didn't want to lose this opportunity to be in water at any cost. I even started loving my health condition for giving me this opportunity.

Our ex-tenant Krishna Kumari aunty's daughter Gowthami was staying in Chennai with her family at the time. Through her husband Sarath (he is also from our area and dad knew his grandfather very well), we got a letter from one of the Andhra Club members to use the swimming pool as his guest. One day, we went to the pool. My parents, sisters, their husbands and Sudhir came to the pool with me, harbouring great anxiety. Even today, Anand teases me by reminding me of the full attendance of my family on the day of my first encounter with water. Anand also came with his family to the pool. I met his wife Preetha for the first time on that day; she was also affected by polio, but I couldn't recognize much difference in her movements. In her childhood, before completing the age of one year, her parents had started physiotherapy. Due to that, her condition had improved a lot.

She was also a physiotherapist. They had a girl child at that time—a very sweet family indeed.

I entered the kids' pool after taking required approvals; it was just two-feet deep. The moment I entered the pool, I couldn't balance myself in the water. But I enjoyed the feeling of being in the water so much. Anand showed me some underwater exercises; he came to the pool to teach me for three days. Later, he went out of town to take classes. On the fourth day, the in-charge of the pool objected my entering the kids' pool. The pool was very small and I was occupying it fully, it seems. He suggested that I should go to the big pool. Anand was also not there to give proper advice. After seeing our fears, the in-charge, Ravi, told me that a lifeguard and coach were available, and that entering the adults' pool with a floater wouldn't be risky. Finally, I entered the adults' pool with a floater. As I entered the big pool, my body was fully submerged in water. I felt very light underwater. Like a miracle, I felt relief from pain immediately after entering the water. It was like magic for me, an amazing experience. Finally, I could enter water, a cherished desire fulfilled. But my parents' feelings were exactly opposite to mine. They were fully tensed. If air went out from the floater, I might drown—that was their fear. My father told me to stay near the edges so that he could save me, should any mishap occur. He didn't enter the pool as he doesn't know how to swim. Otherwise he would have been in the pool taking care of my safety.

On that day, I couldn't sleep as I was overjoyed. Slowly I was able to make some movements in the water. I was extremely happy when I was, for the first time, able to complete one lap in that 15-m pool with the help of a floater. My parents' schedule became very hectic though. Making fruit juices and special dishes that were very nutritious for me, coming along with me to the pool and sending me to the office, and everything else that they did—I felt very sorry for them. Finally, I could somehow stop mom from coming along with us to the pool as it was becoming very strenuous for her to prepare food after going back. My parents were not, and never have been, comfortable in hiring a cook. They are habituated to working hard. Even if I wanted to give them rest, they wouldn't be ready to take it.

Initially, I used to go for a swim in the morning. From the pool, I would go home, and after having breakfast I would head to the office. I took permission to go to the office in the afternoon to complete my swimming and other exercises and stayed at work until late evening.

Concerns about My Skin

After I had started swimming, my complexion started becoming dark due to tanning. Whenever I looked at my hands, I would wonder if those hands were mine. Although I felt bad about it, I wanted to continue swimming not only because it was becoming my lifeline by the day but also due to my love for water. Although I compromised on the complexion part, I struggled with very dry skin; I developed some allergy on my ankle too. So I went to a dermatologist. I thought she would give some medicines including antibiotics, etc., but to my surprise, she told me to use Efaderm (a moisturizing cream) after bath and olive oil half an hour before swimming. I have been following her advice since then religiously and have never faced that problem again.

Wearing Spinal Brace

As suggested by Anand, I started using the spinal brace. When I wore the brace, my height would increase by a few inches as it gave support to my spine. But I couldn't wear it for long. If I wore it for some time, due to the hump in my back, muscles would get compressed and I would feel pain. If I removed it, I would have back pain. So I had to wear it for some time so as to give relief to the back muscles and remove it for some time to give relief to my muscles at the hump. Whenever I made these changes, I had to change the height of the chair and my walker because my height would change with the wearing and removing of the spinal brace. I had a very, very tough time. As I had to remove and wear it frequently, I used to wear the brace over my clothes. It was not possible for me to tie the straps and change the height of the walker on my own. My female colleagues used to help me; Sangeetha and Sona helped me most of the time. As I had to put it on and take it off many times, I used to feel awkward troubling them. But I never saw any inconvenience on their faces. They were so supportive; I am very thankful to them for their affectionate support.

Wearing a spinal brace, elbow braces, knee brace and removing them whenever I felt inconvenienced and wearing them again in the office are generally embarrassing. But due to the friendly nature of my colleagues, I never felt like that. I felt my office as a second home. Incredible support was extended to me by my bosses and colleagues during those trying times. I am extremely grateful to them for their graceful support.

I was going to Anand's clinic three days a week by then. Practising the exercises suggested by him at home religiously, swimming, physiotherapy and office—days became very busy for me. Even during that busy schedule, now and then my mood would take a dive when I thought about the consequences of having PPS.

Anand is from Vellore, a town near Chennai. He had worked previously in Christian Medical College (CMC), a very famous hospital in Vellore. He suggested that I visit Vellore CMC Rehabilitation Centre and meet his friend Suresh. During one weekend, we planned a visit and went there. Anand's family also came along.

At the spinal cord injury department in CMC, we met some patients. They had all lived very active and dynamic lives before they met with the accidents. After accidents, they faced drastic changes in their lives. Their heart-rending stories moved me deeply. When we went to one particular bed, people around it were all very happy. The girl on the bed was studying her master's when she met with an accident; on her way to college, a bus had hit her scooter. She had spinal injury in the neck area. Her body below the neck was completely paralysed. On that day, she could hold a pencil with her fingers. So everyone was celebrating her achievement. I was so moved after meeting all of them.

I met Suresh who has muscular dystrophy. In his entire body, only a few fingers work a little bit. I saw a person in such a condition for the first time in my life. He is a great inspiring personality. When we met him, he and his father were staying together. As his father's health was not well due to old age, some caretakers were taking care of them. Suresh is working as a financial consultant and also as an occupational therapist at CMC. He uses painting for rehabilitating his clients. He manages to do everything from his bed. Suresh told me that he would only plan everything for a short term, for instance, a week. He unfortunately lost his father soon thereafter. Knowing what Suresh is doing in his life, like building a house for himself and leading an independent life, etc., always gives me a great feeling of amazement. I never thought that a person in such a severe condition could live that much independently. It gave me confidence to lead my life independently even if my condition becomes worse in future due to PPS.

I also got a great opportunity to meet Sri Ramakrishnan, founder of Amar Seva Sangam in Tamil Nadu. While studying engineering, he attended a naval officer job-related test. During a physical test he injured his neck following a fall and incurred cervical spinal injury which left him paralysed below his shoulders. After a few years of this incident, he started an organization through which he has been supporting hundreds of children with disabilities in getting education, employment, etc. Mr Shankar Raman joined hands with him in his endeavours later. I got the wonderful opportunity to meet both of them.

Although I am also a person with disability, I am habituated to a certain level of disability. Due to PPS, when that level started increasing, I could not understand how to adjust to it. Going to CMC Rehab Centre and meeting all those people living dynamically with their disabilities helped me in accepting my condition.

Many times, I compared Anand's treatment with that of my childhood doctor's and physiotherapist's treatment. Anand tried to treat me with a holistic approach. He is very positive. He explained to me my condition very clearly but in a positive way. All the activities suggested by him have had a positive impact on my health. Introducing me to hydrotherapy motivated me greatly to be active and my love for water made me religiously practise swimming. When he introduced his wife to me, I realized that physiotherapy could have done wonders had we started it in childhood itself. I had wrongly felt that these therapies wouldn't be of any use since the doctor, in my childhood, had told me very bluntly that I had to wear callipers throughout my life. Even though Anand had also suggested braces, because some modifications were done to reduce my pain, my feelings were taken care of.

I strongly feel that accepting one's own condition as it is is the biggest and foremost step in rehabilitation. If a person likes the suggested fitness activities, that acts as a self-motivating factor. In my case, my love for water motivated me to continue swimming. Anand's way of treatment made me realize how the process of rehabilitation should be.

An Autobiography of a Yogi

Dad had brought a book titled *Autobiography of a Yogi* when my mood was very low due to health issues. I started reading that book. Although I was not able to hold the book for a long time due to pain in my hands, I tried to spend some time reading that book daily.

Generally, we feel that seeking the blessings of God requires years of wholehearted devotion and sincere prayers. But after reading that book, I realized that God will always be with us to listen to our smallest wishes and help us if we are sincere in our hearts. Through that book, I understood well that it is possible for any person to become a yogi through his/her devotion. It is a greatly inspiring book which helped me a lot in coming out of my depression.

21

Finding Work–Life Balance, Literally!

Membership in Andhra Club

As swimming had become an essential need for me, we thought that it would be better to take membership in Andhra Social and Cultural Association (ASCA, popularly known as Andhra Club). And I got a membership there. Due to its good name among Telugu people, having membership in that club is considered a privilege. On Saturdays, they play Telugu movies in their auditorium and for all the Telugu festivals they arrange good programmes by inviting prominent Telugu celebrities. By attending the programmes, mom felt happy as she could speak in Telugu with the members there. We could get Telugu food in authentic taste at a very reasonable price. Apart from swimming, speaking to other members who came to swim also worked as a stress buster. I made many friends there.

Learning to Swim

Anand advised using swimming dumbbells. We called up many shops to find them. No one knew about it; everyone would ask me what it was. I had to explain it to them all the time. After many trials, we realized that it was not easy to buy them. Luckily, at that time, my niece Sunanda was coming to visit us from the USA, and she brought swimming dumbbells, swimming training waistband (belt) and some other equipment for legs, among other things. The waistband made my movements more comfortable than the floater, which used to restrict my hand movements.

After entering the pool, one can't stay still at one spot. I slowly started moving from one place to another with the support of the belt, after completing the exercises suggested by Anand, of course. After some days, I started feeling more comfortable in making movements freely. I wasn't always content with what I achieved though; I would look forward to the next step. I wanted to learn swimming, but I had so much hesitation in expressing the same. I thought that they might laugh at me, thinking I was overambitious. After speaking to Anand, everyone in my family was also thinking that doing exercises underwater would help me a great deal in improving my health condition. No one was thinking beyond that. Finally, one day, I asked the coach at the pool if he could teach me how to swim. He told me that he had never seen a person with disabilities like me swim before, and that he had no idea how to teach swimming to me. But I didn't lose heart. I continued my efforts with the help of the belt. I observed one thing: Whenever I could not go to the pool due to some reason, my mood would be off that day as I would not get the relaxation that water gives me and would always be thinking of my health condition. I understood that spending time in the pool would always bring me out of my dullness. I tried to observe my mood while entering the pool and while coming out of the pool. I found a very big difference. While coming out, I was more hopeful and positive. For me, it was like a miracle. Later, I came to know that this change was due to the result of the release of a 'feel-good' hormone called serotonin. After understanding this magic, I tried to go to the pool without fail on all the days, except when the pool was closed.

After some months, I wanted to remove the belt and try it out in the pool. But it took some time for me to convince my parents about it.

It was very difficult for them to accept it. I told them that I would try in the kids' pool first and then only move to the adults' pool. They agreed reluctantly. Finally, one day, I tried in the kids' pool without the belt, and found out to my utter joy and disbelief that I could manage without the belt. With that confidence, I convinced my parents to allow me to swim in the adults' pool. They told the lifeguard and the coach to help me if required.

I entered the adults' pool without any external support for the first time, and it was a wonderful feeling. I could manage swimming without any support in a proper pool. There was more freedom to move my body. Till that time, I was unable to freely move my body due to the belt. Now, I was able to swim in the way possible for me. I used to update Anand about the developments at the pool. One day I tried to walk in the pool as suggested by Anand. I was able to walk holding my left knee with my left hand. It was an amazing experience. For the first time in my life, without the support of any external devices like callipers, crutches, walker, etc., I walked (of course, I had the support of water). All my family members felt extremely happy. They took videos of me walking and shared it with our family and friends. We celebrated that happy moment.

Every day in the morning, I'd go for a swim (going to the club, coming back home and taking bath was around three and a half hours' job) and after coming home, taking fruit juice and breakfast, and then taking rest for two hours was my regular activity in the forenoon. After having lunch, I used to go to the office and come back home around 10:00 pm. I'd go to bed after having my dinner. This was my routine in those days. After seeing some improvements, I felt that some change was taking place in my spine; it was slowly becoming straight. When I checked with Sudhir, he smiled at me and said that even to get one mm change in spinal position, it would take a lot of time. So he told me not to expect any change overnight. But it was my firm belief that some improvements had taken place in my spine through breathing exercises and swimming. After one year, Anand told me to get a spinal X-ray done to see if there were any improvements.

I went to a scan centre. Seeing my X-ray, the doctor was perplexed. She might have thought how it was possible to be alive with that severe curve in the spine. I told her that the position of my spine was the same in last year's X-ray too. She asked us to bring it. Till then, she hadn't given her report. Dad went home and brought it. Seeing it, she might have got confidence that people could be alive even with such a curve in the spine. Although I was feeling better, actually there was no improvement in my spine. I understood the reality of Sudhir's words. After that, I never went for a spine X-ray. I decided to go with my comfort in managing things, not with an X-ray. Anyway, I had been doing the best I could do. There was no point in taking X-rays and feeling sad about it.

During that time, my niece Vindhyasri joined our office. I was very happy. I had really been missing all my nieces and nephews after coming to Chennai. While coming home, one of my colleagues used to come along with me and Vindhyasri, as his home was near my house. One day while coming home, we stopped at a bakery to buy a cake for dad's birthday. I was sitting in the car. Both of them went inside to bring the cake. After making us wait for a long time, they told us coolly that it was not possible to bake the cake. I was very tired by that time and was irritated. In that mood, after starting the car and without confirming that there was no vehicle behind us by checking in the rear-view mirror, I got on to the road. Two traffic police were coming just behind our vehicle. Because I came suddenly on to the road, they had to move to their right suddenly. It was my mistake. They were extremely angry. They signalled for us to stop the vehicle; I stopped. My colleague got down from the car and went to them. When he came back, seeing his face, I could understand he was admonished with harsh words by those officials. He didn't tell me anything and asked me to move on. But I insisted him to reveal what had happened. He told me that I might feel bad after listening to their comments. But after some insistence, he said that after knowing that the person in the driving seat was a woman with a disability, they told him that if I didn't know how to drive on the road I should not have driven a car. The reason for sharing this incident is because I've observed that many people have a very inferior opinion about the performance of women in driving. If the driver is also with disability and commits any small mistake, the first comment people make is that it was not proper for her/him to drive a car with that disability. But we normally see many people committing mistakes while driving. It's not specific to women or the persons with disabilities. But comments are easily and freely passed on the driving skills of women or the persons with disabilities.

After seven to eight months, I was slowly able to sit without using the spinal brace. But fatigue continued. Later, Anand suggested changing my schedule as going to bed late and waking up early to go swimming was not giving the required rest to my body. Anand suggested that my day should start with sunrise and end with sunset. I requested my boss to change my timings; he accepted my request immediately. I started going to the office in the morning and, from there, directly to the pool in the evening while coming back from the office. By that time, Dad would come to the pool from home. After my swimming, both of us would head back home. Due to heavy traffic, it used to take one and a half hours to reach home, although the distance was just about 7 km. I was losing a lot of my energy in driving itself. But still I didn't want to engage a driver. I love to drive. After a few months, with great effort I convinced my father not to come to the pool as it was strenuous for him. By that time, we knew the staff at the pool very well, and they were very supportive too. I got the confidence that I could manage with their support in the absence of dad.

We thought of shifting to a place near my office. The agents we contacted could not understand my physical condition, and we started getting options from them that were unviable for me. One day, one agent told us to come to a place to see a flat that was on the first floor without a lift. At another place, I had to park my car at a far-off place and walk to the flat. Then my parents started to look for an accessible flat themselves. It didn't work well either. I realized that the situation was the same in every city. We even published a newspaper ad. If we found one or two accessible flats, the rent would be on the higher side. Thus, finding an accessible flat within our budget and that too near my office became a Herculean task. Due to this search, even during weekends I could not take rest. After many trials, we gave up.

Deteriorating Health: Clash with Ambitions

At the workplace, there was always a great scope to learn. From the very beginning, any task that I take up, I would do it with intense focus and concentration. After entering the workforce, I started loving my job more than anything else; I wanted to perform with perfection. I updated myself on the latest developments, acquired professional qualifications and learned different types of skills in the organization. In this process, I became a workaholic. But with the deteriorating health condition, the situation had changed. Although I wanted to sit and do many things, my back pain was not allowing me to sit for long hours. I had to apply brakes on my enthusiasm. Till that time, I had enjoyed the status of a star performer. But with the current health issue, I did not know how to adjust to this new situation. Although my bosses and colleagues were very supportive, my mind was not able to digest this fact, because my work demanded sitting for a longer time than I was doing.

On the one hand I was putting in sincere efforts to improve my health, and on the other, I was adjusting to the new situation with regard to office work—I think this was the most difficult time I faced in my life.

At that time, I came to know about the Certified Anti-Money Laundering Specialist (CAMS) exam from the Association of Certified Anti-Money Laundering Specialists (ACAMS), USA. Although I didn't have the energy to even hold a book, I applied for it. As my work is related to operations, it demands more working hours than that of other departments, and the volume of transactions is also more. I thought that this certification may give me an opportunity to work in any other department where the work I would do and my expertise would be considered 'normal', like any other official, even with the requirement I had with regard to flexibility in working hours. The fee for this exam was around ₹60,000 (now, it is more than double this amount). After making the payment, I got the material. As I was unable to hold the entire book, I arranged for photocopies of it. At a time, I used to hold only one or two pages. If I looked into those pages continuously, my neck would hurt. This exam was online and results would be known immediately. I cleared it successfully. It stimulated my mind. Among all the other qualifications, this is something special for me. Only I knew how much I had struggled to prepare for that exam overcoming my severe health problems.

My student Aruna became my mentor from that time. I used to share all my feelings with her. Driven by my passion for teaching, I started extending support to our training department by taking sessions related to our department. This was in addition to my regular duties. The very first time I conducted a session for CDCS aspirants in my office, I remembered all the challenges I'd faced in preparing for it without having anyone to give training to me. My sessions won the appreciation of the participants. Our training department recognized my efforts in facilitating many sessions and gave me an award for my services.

My niece Vindhyasri worked for almost one year in my office. We found a good marriage alliance for her. Dad and Vindhyasri went to Hyderabad to meet the boy's family at my brother's house. Meeting, engagement and wedding—everything happened in just 20 days! It was a pleasant surprise for all of us. After their wedding, she resigned from her job and went to the USA to be with her husband, who was working there. At that time, I hadn't travelled out of Chennai for almost three years to anywhere due to my spinal issues. We travelled to Hyderabad after a long gap to attend her wedding. Meeting my friends and relatives was a pleasant experience.

A Beautiful Birthday Gift from My Niece Sahithi

My niece Sahithi presented me a unique gift on my birthday in 2009. She wrote a nice story about me and presented it to me. At that time, she was only in high school. We were all surprised by her idea to write about me with great love and affection. After seeing that, all my siblings started insisting on me to write a book with my experiences in life. But due to my hectic schedule, I couldn't take it up at that time. My dad and sister Mythreyi started writing my biography. But they could not take it forward due to some other commitments they had.

Family Olympiad

After a few months, my niece Sunanda came from the USA. As I was not travelling much, she came directly to our house. All our siblings' families came to our house too. After a long time, we all (except a few) could meet at one place. We wanted to celebrate the occasion in a unique and memorable way, for which we planned a fun-filled series of competitions and named it 'Family Olympiad'. The entire event was organized by my niece Pranavi. We conducted many indoor games such as chess, dumb charades and impromptu speeches for all the family members. We also conducted a general quiz for which my dad was the quiz master and myself a scorer. I was a neutral observer throughout, and we divided everyone into two groups—Grand-Ma Team and Grand-Pa Team—with my parents mentoring their respective teams and everyone participated with true sportsmanship spirit. Based on the scores in various games, the Grand-Pa team won the title. The final day was celebrated as ethnic day. My sisters and sister-in-law helped me wear a sari. My parents presented gifts to all the participants. We had a delicious lunch with many of our favourite traditional dishes. It's an unforgettable sweet memory for all of us.

Opportunity to Work on a Project in Office

In my office, I got an opportunity to work on an important project (let's call it Project-1). My CAMS certification was useful for that project. My boss Tim was from the UK, a very nice person. Other team members were Niranjan and Sundar. We had a very good bond. Each one had expertise in a specific area. It was a new work for me; I love to learn new skills, as you, the readers, know well by now. And most importantly, this work could be managed by me efficiently with the hours I was able to spend in office. It required more skill and expertise than the number of hours I sit in office. My team and I got amazing recognition from the higher officials for our work.

Importance of Hydrotherapy

I could see great improvement in my health condition with regular swimming and other exercises suggested by Anand. I realized the importance of hydrotherapy in my life. Many people with very limited energy levels, for instance, persons with disabilities, elderly people and people with arthritis, are struggling to be active. Hydrotherapy is a wonderful treatment for all of them, as they can make movements with less effort underwater. But unfortunately, it's not very popular in India. Initially, I thought it was only me who had experienced these benefits. Later, when I searched the Internet, I realized that these benefits have been mentioned in medical books since many years.

After knowing these things, my parents felt very bad. Had they known about all this in my childhood, they would have arranged a cement construction to store water in our backyard in which I could have done all the required exercises. Moreover, I could have played in water too. It could have made their life easy in convincing me to be physically active.

The Visits of My Siblings' Families during Vacations

After coming to Chennai, we missed our siblings' families very much. They used to come during their vacations to our place. We always waited eagerly for their visits. As all the children had grown up, their vacation timings were different. Hence, they were not able to come for my birthday like earlier. But my sister Mythreyi makes it a point to come for my birthday with her family every year. Although my brother-in-law K. V. S. G. K. Raju is a college principal by profession, he is an expert in repairing electrical and electronic goods. We trouble him with repair works whenever he comes to our place. All other sisters' and brother's families come as and when they have holidays.

22

The Discovery of an Unknown Talent

One day in my office, I saw a notification regarding a corporate Olympiad. They were inviting nominations. Generally, I never looked into sports-related notifications. But I happened to look into it that day. While reading it, I observed swimming was also one of the disciplines. Then I thought of giving in my name. I immediately registered for the swimming competition. Even today when I recollect that incident, I wonder with what courage did I give my name? When I told my parents, they told me to prepare well. My boss Tim also encouraged me to perform well in the competition.

The venue of the competition was the Sports Development Authority of Tamil Nadu (SDAT) Swimming Pool, Velachery Road. It's an international standard pool—50 m in length and 10 feet in depth. I thought of going there to practise before the event but could not. The night before the day of the competition, I couldn't sleep due to anxiety. My regular pool was just 15 m in length and about 4–6 feet in depth. Without any practice, how could I enter a pool that was 50 m long and 10 feet deep? In my pool, I would just stand whenever I wanted to stop because it was only 4-feet deep. How would I manage in a 10-feet deep pool if I wanted to halt? I had so many doubts.

Next day, my parents, Sudhir and I went there. No one thought that I was one of the participants. Everyone thought that I was a spectator. After seeing me, the organizers also had many doubts about allowing me. Till that time, they didn't know I was a person with disabilities; none of the other participants were persons with disability. They could not say no to me after seeing my confidence and enthusiasm. I went inside the changing room. When I came out in my swimsuit, everyone was surprised. To be on the safe side, the organizers arranged for two expert swimmers to swim in front of me and two more behind me. After seeing so many precautions taken for my safety, I felt amused. They might have been thinking that I might drown immediately after entering the pool.

With the support of my dad and one of the swimmers, I entered the pool. I held the bar and stood on a step-like slab inside the pool. I participated in the 100-m freestyle competition. All the spectators and other participants who were not in the competition were clapping throughout my swim to cheer me up. I was able to complete 100 m successfully. After coming out of the pool, the way spectators praised me made me feel like I had won an Olympic gold medal.

The champion of that competition came up to me and said that I was the real winner. The organizers gave me the 'Most Encouraging Sportsperson' award. My joy knew no bounds. I was on cloud nine! It is one of the most euphoric moments of my life. That night, I couldn't sleep again, but this time due to being overjoyed. In the middle of the night, I felt as if I were in the air just two feet above my bed. I felt my body to be so light, like a feather. I remember being in that euphoric mood for at least 10 days. I love the city of Chennai which has given me birth as a sportsperson. I treat it as my second native place.

23

The Dawning of 'Yes, We Too Can!!!'

Creating Awareness on Hydrotherapy

In that competition, I could not participate in other styles of swimming such as backstroke, butterfly and breaststroke, as I didn't know them. After this competition, I checked with our coach at Andhra Club. By that time, a new coach named Gopi had joined there. He taught me all other swimming styles.

Slowly, I started thinking about other persons with disabilities, particularly kids. At around 40 years of age, if I felt that much happiness, I wondered how much fun and joy and how many benefits of hydrotherapy or participation in sports were the children with disabilities missing in their lives? It's easy to motivate people through sports to be active, which in turn improves their physical and mental health. And participation in sports gives confidence, a lot of recognition, exposure and satisfaction. Anand had told me that had I started hydrotherapy and other exercises in my childhood, I would have been able to walk with the help of elbow crutches. After knowing this, I wanted to create awareness about these benefits among children and youngsters with disabilities.

What could I do to create more awareness about these benefits? How could I help other persons with disabilities? So many questions ran through my mind. If I didn't share all my knowledge and experiences with others, they would die along with me. I didn't want that to happen. Considering my health, I didn't know the span of my life. Before I leave this world, I must do something for people like me. But what could I do for them and how—I didn't know. This fire in me was not allowing me to keep quiet.

Whenever I came across any person with disabilities, I started telling them about the benefits of hydrotherapy. Even if I didn't know them, I would share my experiences with them. But most of the people came back to me explaining their challenges: no support from family, expensive, no pools nearby, transport challenges, inaccessible pools, facility owners not allowing persons with disabilities to swim in their pool due to fears of drowning—you name it! I realized that if I tried to educate only the persons with disabilities, it wouldn't be of any use. I started thinking about what to do next.

I started my research. While browsing the Internet, I saw a video of a sports centre for the persons with disabilities in Israel. I felt that if I could arrange for founding such a sports school for the persons with disabilities in India, it would help many people. So, it became my dream project. Whenever I expressed my desire to any of my friends, they laughed at me saying, 'You don't have a house in Chennai for yourself and you have been struggling to find an accessible house for yourself to buy/stay at, and you are thinking about founding an accessible sports school? What a big joke!'

One day, when I was discussing this matter with Anand, he suggested that I use government facilities to arrange training for the kids. I thought it to be a practically possible idea.

SDAT is the concerned government entity in Chennai. I found their contact number on the Internet. I called them and explained my idea. They told me to come and meet the member secretary who was an

IAS officer. At that time, Sudhir was with me. We went there as per the appointment given to us. My father had great respect for IAS officers and met a few in his working life, being the headmaster of a school. He advised me to follow certain norms while speaking to a senior government official. The officer whom I was going to meet was a senior IAS officer.

As cautioned by dad, I felt tension before meeting him. Would such a senior officer listen to me and believe my words? With the apprehension that the officer would not believe my words, I brought along the medical report given by the orthopedic surgeon, my spine X-ray and my chest X-ray. On our way to the SDAT office, I felt like giving up and returning back. I told Sudhir to take a U-turn to go back home. But Sudhir insisted on continuing. He suggested we meet him and see what happens. My tension was increasing. We reached his office, which was on the first floor and without an elevator. Sudhir, with the help of three other persons, lifted me along with a chair and carried me to the first floor.

We were waiting in the hall to be called in; I was anxious. When they called us, we went inside. At that time I was walking with my walker. After seeing me entering into the room with a walker, Mr Sahoo, Member Secretary, SDAT, stood from his seat and welcomed me with a pleasant smile. After seeing his gesture and his pleasant smile, I was relieved from all my anxiety. I went near his table and sat in a chair. I was gasping a little due to the strain caused by walking, and also due to the anxiety. He gave me time to make myself comfortable and offered a glass of water to me. Once he felt I was ready to speak, he enquired about the reason for this appointment. I didn't know where to start. But as he made me feel very comfortable, I told him that it was the first time I was speaking on this topic with such a senior official, and so I was not able to understand where to start. He encouraged me to tell me in whatever way I could. I explained my health condition in 2007, showing the reports and X-rays, and told him how hydrotherapy helped me in improving from that horrible condition and expressed my wish to support my fellow persons with disabilities by arranging training in swimming in their pools. I requested for his permission to arrange the sessions free of cost. He was very impressed with what I had just told him. A person in my condition, making the effort to come to his office to support others—he appreciated my intention and my efforts a lot. He promised to support me. He told me that it might be difficult to give swimming permissions free due to the operating costs involved but he promised to give the maximum possible concession. I came back in a very happy mood.

When I shared this experience with some people with great joy, they told me not to feel so happy as things wouldn't move that easily in government offices. They also told me that the officer might have forgotten me by the time I had stepped out of his office. But to everyone's surprise, after a week, we saw in our mailbox the approval letter from their office, giving a 50 per cent concession to arrange training sessions in one of their pools. That gave me more confidence in the system.

Now, I had the sanction letter from the government in my hands. The next step was to find participants to arrange for training. Where would I get the participants? Loyola College came to my mind immediately. I used to go to the office via Loyola daily. During my weekend (which used to be on Thursday and Friday), I went to Loyola College with Sudhir. I enquired the staff there about getting an appointment with the principal. They told me that it would be very difficult as he was extremely busy due to admissions. After seeing the disappointment on my face, they enquired about the reason for asking for an appointment. I explained it to them. Then they told me that for such a matter, I need not go to the principal, but the vice-principal (Outreach) could help me; they directed us to his office. When we went there, he was in a discussion with some people in his room. After seeing me waiting outside in a wheelchair, he came to me. He didn't want to make me wait for a long time. But I told him that I would wait as the matter could not be explained in a few minutes. Then he called me inside after the previous visitors left. The vice-principal, Father Antony Samy, was very impressed with my idea. I requested him to give me an opportunity to address their students. I was expecting him to give me a date in future. But to my surprise, he checked with me if I could give a 15-minute presentation in the conference that was happening on that day itself. I didn't expect this at all. Luckily, I had my laptop with me. Although I didn't have any readily available presentation, I had some videos and photos of me swimming, and some other YouTube videos. For sharing my personal experiences, I didn't need much preparation anyway. I waited there for one hour to give the presentation during the post-lunch session. During that time, I saw the infrastructure facilities there. Everywhere I could see ramps and elevator facilities. In one building, because there was no elevator, they had attached a chair to the stairs. If a person sat in that chair and switched it on, it would take the person upstairs. I felt so happy. If such facilities were operational during my childhood, I also would have gone to a college. I got a strong urge to join any course and study at Loyola.

Post lunch, they invited me to give a presentation to around 300 participants. It was my first talk on hydrotherapy. At that time, I didn't know that it would be the foundation for all my future activities. It was very well-received by the audience. They gave me a standing ovation. A few students with disabilities came forward to join our training session immediately. Some of the students with visual challenges came till my car because they were very excited to know that I was driving a car. They touched the steering and other parts of the car and enquired with me how I could drive.

These two meetings gave me more confidence. Another requirement was financial support to pay pool charges, fee to the coach, transportation cost for the participants and swimsuits, goggles, caps, etc. Where would I go for support for all that? I knew that there was a team in our office that took care of CSR activities. That team was headed by Ms Gita. One day I took an appointment with her and requested for her support in this. I showed her the government sanction letter and informed her about the interest of students in Loyola. She gave me an opportunity to meet our CEO Edwin Nevis in one of our CSR meetings. I felt tense to speak in the presence of our CEO; I had never met him before. And the time available for me to explain to him was only a few minutes. My strong desire to arrange for the training session surpassed the anxiety to speak with him. I explained in brief how hydrotherapy had helped me to come out of a life-threatening situation and why I wanted to arrange for this training session, the support I had garnered till that time and my desire to create more awareness about hydrotherapy. With great hesitation, I requested for his support to arrange for training sessions for 10 students with disabilities. He immediately agreed and extended his support for many more events in the days to come. He is a great visionary, and a very simple and humble person. He is a corporate yogi. He told us to make a difference in the lives of others with our activities. He always suggested that I always think big. He might have visualized the benefits of hydrotherapy and how we could offer our support in creating more awareness, and to enable the persons with disabilities to practise hydrotherapy in a big way.

The positive attitude and encouragement from Mr Sahoo, Father Antony Samy and Edwin gave me great confidence, sufficient enough to take this initiative forward till my last breath. Had any of them discouraged me during that stage, when I didn't have much confidence in myself to take up this big task, I might have stopped moving forward with so many fears and hesitation. Hence, I have great regard for all of them.

My parents always taught me not to ask others for any financial support. They were of the opinion that one should manage with what they have, and that seeking support from others is not respectable. Till that time, I believed I could only extend support to others from whatever resources I had. But with these three meetings, I realized that in spite of not having any resources, I could (and we all can!) support more needy people if I am able to bring together all the like-minded/relevant people.

From that time onwards, I have been working with the government, corporates, educational institutions, NGOs working for the persons with disabilities and some other organizations that have been supporting the persons with disabilities.

'Yes, We Too Can!!!' Movement

We decided to give a name to the movement I had started. Inspired by Obama's campaign slogan 'Yes We Can', I named my movement 'Yes, We Too Can!!!'. Some people asked me why the word 'Too'. As many people expressed doubts about the abilities of the persons with disabilities in doing certain things, I felt that 'Too' will emphasize our abilities.

Although I got all the required approvals, students didn't turn up for the training session as parents had many doubts/fears about the safety of their children. But I didn't lose hope. I wanted to create more awareness. I thought about the following avenues to create awareness about hydrotherapy—first to give talks at educational institutions, corporates and other platforms where I could reach out to many people and second through media.

With regard to talks, I went to various schools and colleges during my weekends (as my weekends were working days for others, it helped me in reaching out to many organizations) and getting their permission to give talks. One day I went to the office of the English newspaper *The Hindu* and met a journalist there. I explained the entire story to her and showed her the evidence in support of my words. In those days, I used to go everywhere with my doctor's report, X-rays and laptop to show my swimming videos. Ms Anusha Parthsarathy wrote a nice article on me with the title 'Look, I Can Swim!' It really created great awareness on hydrotherapy.

Many people approached me through the contact details given in that article. One lady, Ms Sudha, contacted me from Malaysia. She came to Chennai later and met Anand to learn hydrotherapy. I received a mail from one Mr Singaravel, appreciating me and expressing his interest in meeting me along with his wife

Dr Rema Devi, who is also a polio-affected person, and a (now retired) senior scientist from Zoological Survey of India. And she is also an artist. At that time, I didn't know we would work together in the future for this cause. As many people approached me to know more about the benefits of hydrotherapy, we arranged a get-together with all of them at Anand's clinic. Everyone was impressed. Ms Uthira, another swimmer, had also joined us. She is also affected by polio. Sai Krishnan, an Abilympic[1] gold medal winner in photography at international level came to my office one day after seeing that article. He also wanted to know more about hydrotherapy. I learned about Abilympics for the first time. Later, we all became good friends.

One boy named Venkateshan also approached me. He had lost both his hands due to an electric shock. In spite of so many challenges, he could complete his postgraduation in Tamil. He learnt swimming in his village and wanted to continue practising it in Chennai but was not able to go due to financial challenges.

For him, I met Andhra Club President Mr Narsa Reddy for the first time. I requested him to allow Venkatesh to swim in their pool for free or with concession in the fee. Also, I sought his support to allow some more persons with disabilities. I showed him a few steps at the entrance and at the restroom of the pool and requested him to arrange for ramps to enable the other persons with disabilities to use the facility without any discomfort. He responded positively to all my requests. Next morning, when I went to the pool, ramps were arranged at both the spots I had shown him. He is such a nice person.

I also approached some TV channels to talk about the importance of hydrotherapy. They told me to give them a small video that they could broadcast on their channel.

---
[1] Abilympics is an international non-profit movement that originated in Japan and has been developing around the world since 1971. The movement holds championships on professional skills among persons with disabilities (Source: Wikipedia).

At that time, our neighbour Mr Prabhu had an ad film institute. I requested his support. He allocated one day for me and brought some hired cameras. He covered my driving, swimming and took a video byte from Ms Gita. He made a film *Yes We Too Can* free of cost at my request. I used that film for my presentations at various places. It was of great help to me. While editing that film, I sat with him. At that time, I realized how much time and skills are required for shooting and editing. I loved that work very much for its creativity. I got more respect for the technical people involved in making films.

Formation of a Trust

My well-wishers suggested that I start a trust to take up the activities I wanted to do. As it was difficult for me to take care of all the expenses by myself, they told me that if I have a trust with income tax exemptions, it would be helpful to get support from like-minded people. I didn't have any idea on how to start. One chartered accountant Mr Ganesh came forward to help me in this regard. He had read articles about me in newspapers and wanted to help me with his expertise. When he asked about the name, I thought 'Yes, We Too Can!!!' But as it was too lengthy, we took only the first letters and because it was going to be a charitable trust as per the income tax rules, we named it YWTC Charitable Trust. My friend Ananth and his brother came to the Registrar's office to sign as witnesses. We completed the registration process. At that time, Deepak was working at Mr Ganesh's office as an intern. He helped me a lot with regard to applying for trust-related income tax benefits. Till today, Mr Ganesh has been supporting us with regard to accounting-related matters. And from that time, Deepak has been extending support for my initiatives.

Exposure to Adapted Physical Education

I attended the captioned seminar which was conducted at Ramakrishna Mission Vivekananda University (Vidyalaya), Coimbatore. It was a very big campus, with very good infrastructure and academic facilities. I also saw Differently Abled Human Resources Development Department there; in that department, very good facilities were available for persons with disabilities. I even met some adaptive sports persons and medal winners there. However, I could not find any hydrotherapy facilities there.

I gave a presentation using the short film along with Anand and got a very good response from the audience. Many people approached me after the presentation and enquired about things related to swimming. Dr Shayke Hutzler, President, International Federation of Adapted Physical Activity, Israel, came to me after the presentation and told me that they had been trying hydrotherapy on the persons with disabilities for the last 30 years. He also promised me to extend his guidance and provide material in this respect. At that time, I didn't know I would seek his guidance for submitting proposals to the government for accessible swimming pools in the future.

Attending the seminar was a fantastic experience. I could interact with many great people related to Paralympics, Special Olympics and also educationalists. Swamiji enquired about our movement and appreciated the initiative.

After the event, my parents and I went to Ooty, a hill station, which is located near the university. As it was difficult for mom (due to knee pains) and me to get down from the vehicle to see the scenery, we saw it all from inside our vehicle only. Hence, it took just one hour for us to see entire Ooty. When I told this to my friends, they were surprised. But I enjoyed the journey to Ooty on that ghat road. Going on very steep roads on the hills surrounded by greenery was an awesome experience for an avid nature lover like myself.

Swimming Pool Lift, IIT Madras

After seeing the very many challenges I faced in getting into a pool and coming out, and also after listening to the challenges other people faced, I researched a lot on the Internet and found many videos on accessible ways to enter a pool, like a ramp or a swimming pool lift.

At that time, no one was manufacturing those lifts in India though. I didn't know whom to contact in this regard. I thought about approaching the Indian Institute of Technology Madras (IITM), a premier university in this field. I decided to go and meet the head of their Mechanical Engineering department. Sudhir and I went on one weekend to IITM. It was a great feeling while entering the IITM campus. For many students, it's a dream to study there.

We enquired where that department was and went there to meet the HoD. By the time we reached there, the HoD had gone for lunch. The staff were surprised to see me. When they asked me why I was there, I told them that I would tell that to the HoD, as I felt only he could understand the purpose of my visit. They called him and informed him about me. He also didn't have any clue why I had come to meet him. After a few minutes, he came to his office and immediately called me in. They were all very courteous and polite. I told him my story in short. He didn't understand why I came all the way and told him my story, even though he was impressed with it. I told him about the struggles of people like myself in entering and coming out of pools, and showed some pool lift photos and videos to him. I enquired with him about the possibility of advising his students to design a pool lift at an affordable price. He was surprised. He asked me how I got the idea to meet him. I told him that as their institute is a premier institute in this field, I came there to request for his support. He called Associate Professor Sujatha who had been working in the field of assistive devices. She is a very humble person. She liked this idea and promised to discuss it with her students. From that point of time till today, she is a very good friend of mine. I worked with her and her students to bring out the prototype of a pool lift.

24

The Ventures That Struck Gold: Becoming a National Champion

Many of my friends suggested that I try my luck in Paralympics. I learned from the Internet that Dr Dabas was the head of Para Swimming Federation of India. His contact number was also available on Google. So I contacted him and expressed my wish. He informed me that he used to frequently visit Chennai for some work and promised to let me know when he would plan his next visit.

After a few months, I contacted him again. He told me that he was about to call and inform me about his forthcoming visit to Chennai. I thought it would be great if I arranged a get-together with all our well-wishers when he would visit Chennai; I needed a venue for the same. So I requested Gita, the head of corporate affairs at my work, for her permission to arrange the meeting in our office. She accepted my request and also agreed to make all the arrangements, including to provide refreshments.

I invited all our well-wishers and the people who had approached me after reading the article in *The Hindu*; Anand, Dr Karthik (who was my pool mate), Mr Narsa Reddy, Father Antony Samy, Dr Rema Devi, Ms Uthira and Sai were also there. Dr Dabas attended the meeting and explained his efforts to promote para swimming in India through a nice presentation. We then explained our contributions so far and elaborated on our plans to create and increase awareness on hydrotherapy/swimming in Tamil Nadu. The guests also shared their experiences in supporting our efforts. Dr Dabas suggested us to form Tamil Nadu State-level Paralympic Swimming Association and send the participants for the forthcoming nationals to be held in Kolhapur, Maharashtra.

We took Dr Dabas to the Andhra Club pool. Our swimmers exhibited how we practised swimming and sought his guidance to improve our skills. He gave his valuable suggestions to us and appreciated our efforts. We also introduced our coach Gopi to him.

I had a discussion with Anand, Preetha, Dr Rema Devi, Ms Uthira, Sai and other well-wishers. We started the Paralympic Swimming Association of Tamil Nadu informally, with Dr Rema Devi as president, Ms Uthira as vice-president, Preetha as treasurer, myself as the general secretary, Sai as joint secretary, Dr Ponraj as medical director and Anand as technical director. With great efforts, we convinced Rema Devi aunty to be our president. They treat us like their children, so we all thought their guidance would help us in taking this initiative forward successfully. Mr Narsa Reddy accepted to be our patron. We started to practise swimming vigorously. We tried hard to find more people to train but ended up with only four swimmers: Uthira aunty, Venkatesh, Jyothi and myself.

We all went to Kolhapur along with our coach Gopi. At that time, I was feeling a little under the weather as my stomach was upset. I consulted a doctor and took the prescribed medicines. My friends asked me to reconsider my participation but I didn't want to lose the opportunity. Our transit time from Chennai to Kolhapur by train was almost 2 days, with a 10-hour layover at Bengaluru. During the layover, we had to wait at the railway station itself. We were all very tired by the time we reached Kolhapur.

Local organizers told us that they could not make the arrangements as planned, as they did not receive the promised funds from the sponsors. We decided to find an accessible hotel for our stay, as we were not comfortable with their stop-gap arrangements.

By the time we reached there, I started to feel better. It was the 11th National Para Swimming Championship, and our team won eight medals. Venkatesh and I won the championship in our respective categories. It was an amazing moment in my life—winning three gold medals (50-m freestyle, breaststroke and backstroke) and becoming a national champion at the age of 40+ years. It was an unbelievable achievement even for me. My joy knew no bounds.

There, I could see persons with different types of disabilities to swim with ease. When I saw blind swimmers maintaining a straight line in the pool, I was very surprised. If I close my eyes for a few seconds, I cannot maintain the line of direction in the pool. I was unable to understand how they managed to do it.

We noticed that there were very few participants from South India in the championship. I thought that it might be due to the general notion that these sports are dangerous for persons with disabilities. In my experience, when I tried to encourage participation of children with disabilities, often their parents were reluctant as they thought that swimming was risky for their children. If I tried to convince them by giving my example, they would respond saying that it was possible for me because I was a superwoman and it may not be the case for their kids. As I drive, swim, work for an MNC etc., they thought that I had some extraordinary skills.

Dr Dabas put up the proposal to host the next nationals to various states; I strongly wanted to accept his offer with three aims. First, to create more awareness in South India. Second, to give confidence to the parents of children with disabilities, officials, and the general public. Parents because, I hoped that by seeing the participation of persons with different types of disabilities and different levels of abilities, they would understand the benefits of hydrotherapy and participation in sports. Also, if the concerned officials understood the benefits and the possibility, then the persons with disabilities would get more support. Finally the third, to conduct championships at par with other Olympic sports events. I observed an inferior feeling and sympathy towards adaptive sporting events among the public instead of treating it like any other sporting event.

Anand also agreed with my views, and we thought of discussing with our association members. On the way back, our coach told us that IITM had a pool with international standards, and if we requested accommodation there, it would be easy to host the event in Chennai. After coming back to Chennai, we called for a meeting with all our members. We all knew that it was going to be a very challenging task. In the meeting, we decided to first register our association officially, and soon thereafter started that process. Dr Rema Devi, with the support of her husband, arranged for an office address and to fulfil all the statutory requirements to register the association and for its functioning.

Also, after coming back to Chennai, we got a lot of media coverage on our achievements in the championship. I gave so many interviews. Everyone wanted to take a video or a photograph of me while swimming for an article. It gave me an opportunity to create more awareness about hydrotherapy/para swimming. Till then, I was the one to reach out to the media, schools and colleges. But now, they started to approach me. It made my job to create more awareness much easier. These articles reached a wider audience, and I received a few invitations from outside Chennai.

At that time, I got an opportunity to give a talk at IITM. I felt very happy. I was looking for an opportunity to connect with them so I could request them to allow us to host the national championship in

Left: Participation that made us champions Right: PSATN family (Standing from left—Preetha, Anand, Dr Ponraj, Ms Uthira, Sai Krishnan, Sitting—me and Dr Rema Devi)

their pool. My talk was received very well, and I got a standing ovation. Later, I came to know that their pool was under renovation. All my hopes were shattered.

After my talk, many professors wrote to the director of IITM, Professor Bhaskar Ramamurthi, to incorporate the suggestions I gave in my talk to make their pool accessible; he responded to their suggestions positively. The concerned staff from IITM were in touch with me. Later, I connected them with Dr Hutzler for his guidance on the accessible swimming pool, whom I met at a conference in Coimbatore.

Invitations from outside Chennai

Chairman of Sri Rajiv Gandhi College, Erode, Mr Rajan invited me to participate in their college anniversary day celebrations. The entire hall, packed with hundreds of students and other dignitaries, welcomed me with a standing ovation. On this occasion, the college conferred on me Swami Vivekananda Award with felicitations. I delivered my maiden speech in Tamil (partial). Many students interacted with me with inquisitiveness and admiration. That was my first talk outside Chennai. Mr Rajan treats me like his sister. Subsequently, he supported us by hosting a few wheelchair basketball events, namely two Tamil Nadu state-level championships and our 5th national championship.

Management of S. K. S. D. Mahila Kalasala, a very famous college in Tanuku, Andhra Pradesh, invited me as the chief guest for their sports and cultural day celebrations and as a distinguished guest for their college annual day celebrations. It was a great honour for me. Throughout the day I had interactive sessions with the students sharing my experiences. I could meet around 2,000 students. Secretary and correspondent of the College, Mr Ch. Subba Rao was very much interested in encouraging his students not only in studies but also in sports activities. With his efforts, they could get an in-door stadium with state-of-the-art facilities. They also wanted to have a swimming pool but were hesitating as there was an estimated deficit of ₹50 lakh to construct the pool. Inspired by my speech, he came out of the shackles of indecision and immediately announced his willingness to build a swimming pool in their college. I came back with a great satisfaction for their decision and for being able to play a humble role in motivating the students to achieve their goals in life with confidence.

Creating Awareness in Sathupally

I went to Sathupally on a vacation. To my surprise, there was a pool called Dolphin Swimming Pool constructed by Ganesh, my ex-student. He was then the president of the Rotary Club. The pool was maintained by Mr Nageswara Rao, a journalist at *Eenadu* (a Telugu Daily). The maintenance and standards of this pool were at par with any other pool in the big cities.

Mr Nageswara Rao, Ganesh and team planned a get-together with renowned dignitaries of our town along with print and electronic media. The short film *Yes, We Too Can!!!* was screened at the event, for which we received a tremendous response. People were astonished by the capabilities of the persons with disabilities shown in the film. After the meeting, I swam in the pool and showed them how it was possible for me to swim. Many kids and some of the guests also swam along with me.

Ganesh and his team members announced that they wouldn't charge any fee for the persons with disabilities for using the pool.

It was a wonderful experience for me to create awareness about the objectives of our movement 'Yes, We Too Can!!!' especially in my hometown. After seeing Venkatesh swimming in the film despite having no hands, they told me that they wanted to invite and honour him. They kept their word and later they also sent me a cheque to present to him. I arranged for the presentation of the cheque to Venkatesh by the SDAT member secretary, Mr Vijayakumar.

Andhra GO

My sister-in-law works in the Women and Child Welfare Department in Hyderabad. When I visited her, I met her superior Ms Chaya Ratan (IAS), who was also the head of Disability Welfare Department (DWD) at that time. She was a very committed and sincere officer. I met her to share my experiences with hydrotherapy and para swimming. She was already trying to arrange for issuance of a GO) on adaptive sports. Very soon the GO was issued, and she sent a copy to me through my sister-in-law. The GO provides many supportive measures for para sports such as giving concession in fee to use the government sporting facilities, making them accessible and organizing competitions.

I went to SDAT many times with a copy of Andhra GO to request for the issuance of a similar GO in Tamil Nadu as well. By that time, Mr Sahoo was transferred and another officer had joined there. I went to the DWD and some NGOs working for the persons with disabilities to explain these benefits. I used all my weekends to meet various relevant stakeholders. As I was not sure about my life span considering my health condition, I was very eager to do the best I could do in this aspect before I left this world.

When I went to the office of the state commissioner for persons with disabilities for the first time, I was surprised to see as it was on the first floor without an elevator. Later, they shifted their office to another place where it was on the ground floor. This enabled me to meet the commissioner and to request for his support to issue a GO.

I also used to go to the Secretariat to request the secretaries of both Sport department and DWD in this regard. I used to struggle a lot to park my car there in those days. Generally, they don't allow visitors to park inside. However, as I was the driver for my car, they gave me a special permission. But once inside, I had to park my car at a far-off place and come back to the concerned office in a wheelchair. So my dad had to accompany me to push the wheelchair; likewise, he came with me to so many other places. My parents helped me not only in my personal matters but also in my social activities. Later, we requested the concerned department at the Secretariat, and they allocated a parking slot for the persons with disabilities close to the main office.

As I frequently visited officials in both the departments to request for issuance of a similar GO, they added a new surname to my name—'Andhra GO' Madhavi. After seeing me in a wheelchair, the staff there would think that I had come to meet some DWD official. But when I asked sports officials, people used to get surprised. When I had gone to SDAT for the first time, the office subordinate there told me to go to the DWD even before I told him my reason for the visit. It was not easy for them to think/understand that a wheelchair user may come to the Sports department. My follow up for the issuance of GO continued.

Hydrotherapy Talks at Workplace

After knowing about my activities, our wholesale banking department head, Kwan, invited me to give a talk in their management team meeting. I explained to them the importance of hydrotherapy, how it saved me, and my efforts to create awareness about it. Kwan and his team appreciated my efforts and promised to support me in my endeavours.

Kwan gave me the opportunity of being a torchbearer in the opening of a sports programme at my workplace. I felt immensely happy that they invited me to a sports event in my office. Our corporate affairs team helped me in preparing presentations for my talks.

Later, I got an opportunity to address the senior leaders in our office with the initiative of Edwin and Gita. Hence, I could also create awareness about the benefits of hydrotherapy in my office.

While working on Project-1, I received a lot of encouragement from my boss Tim for my activities outside. After the project was completed, I came back to my trade finance work again. By working on this project and from my general experience so far, I was able to understand how to manage the work within the hours I spent at office. My seniors supported me in my efforts. Earlier, my job was everything for me. After starting my YWTC movement and swimming association activities, I started concentrating on these activities as well, beyond the office timings.

25

The Journey from a Participant to a Host

After coming to know that the IITM pool was under renovation, we thought of alternatives. Our intention was to have the pool and accommodation at one place if possible as it would reduce daily travel hassles. A 50-m pool was under the control of SDAT on Velachery Road, where I had participated in the corporate Olympiad. We came to know that IITM campus was very close to this pool if we came through one of its gates. We submitted a request at IITM to provide accommodation for our swimmers. They couldn't provide accommodation on working days, as all the rooms would be occupied by their students. They told us that they would try for accommodation during vacation days, but it would take time to confirm as they were required to check with various departments. Then we approached SDAT for their permission to conduct nationals at their pool with the dates during vacation time of IITM students. They had some hesitation initially to give permission due to the possible risk of drowning. In my initial interactions with many people from different organizations, I had observed that they all had so many doubts with regard to the risks involved in allowing the persons with disabilities into water. They had fears about what would be the consequences for them, if they allowed.

Finally, we got permission from SDAT. We informed Dr Dabas that we were trying to host the championship but could not confirm till we got the approval for accommodation. After a few months, we got the confirmation from IITM. It was a major relief for us. IITM campus was accessible to a great extent. We needed some modifications in and around the SDAT pool area. For that, we gave a request letter to SDAT to make the pool area accessible and followed up with them.

For any sports event, venue and accommodation are the major requirements. For a paralympic event, these are very important, considering the accessibility requirements. Our patron Mr Narsa Reddy agreed to support us in paying the fee at IITM for accommodation and food after getting their approval.

But still, there were so many other requirements. One of the major ones was volunteering. Hundreds of para swimmers would be attending. We needed many volunteers for receiving and taking them to the accommodation, bringing them to the venue and taking them back to accommodation daily, etc. I approached my corporate affairs team with the approvals from SDAT, IITM and Mr Narsa Reddy, and sought volunteering support and help with some other things such as transportation, publicity material designing and printing, etc. After some time, we got the approval.

My colleagues did a wonderful job during this time. We formed different committees for food, transport, hospitality, etc. We named the event Ripples. Sameer took the lead of this project at our office. Nagalakshmi, Vinod and Anitha from the corporate affairs team helped him in coordinating with all other committee heads. We invited a retired IPS officer with the help of Anand to guide us on the measures to be taken while hosting such a big event. His session was useful.

We went to IITM and saw all the hostels to verify the facilities available and noted down all that was required to be arranged such as buckets, mugs, locks and keys, mattresses, pillows and blankets. We planned for a helpdesk with volunteers at each hostel. We went to the pool and chose a spot for the food stalls. We also went to Chennai railway stations (Central and Egmore) and submitted request letters for their support while receiving the swimmers and to arrange a helpdesk. The officials were very supportive everywhere. My office arranged AC luxury buses to receive the swimmers and Innova cars for wheelchair users.

Pudhu Vaazhvu Project

One day, my sister Mythreyi's classmate from postgraduation, Mr Singaiah, who was working in a very senior position in the railways in Chennai, came to our house along with his wife, Mrs Rajeswari. She is an IFS officer, and both of them are very friendly. I met a female forest official for the first time in my life. I am always excited to see women in dynamic positions. Soon we became good friends. Whenever we go to their house, they treat us warmly. As and when my sister came, she used to join us to meet them.

Mrs Rajeswari told me about the Pudhu Vaazhvu Project (PVP), which is part of the Rural Development department. They were also working for the persons with disabilities. Till that time, I was only approaching the DWD and Sports department. But then I came to know that other departments also had projects related to empowerment of the persons with disabilities only because of Mrs Rajeswari.

We were able to finalize major requirements to host the event. Being a host state, we needed to have a good number of participants with solid skills; we were trying hard to identify them. At that time, with the help of Mrs Rajeswari, I met Ms Shajeevana, Assistant Project Director (APD), PVP. She extended wonderful support through her team in identifying persons with disabilities across Tamil Nadu who were interested to learn swimming and in arranging training for them. The project director was Ms Amudha. She is a very loving and caring official. Under her leadership, we got great support in encouraging more persons with disabilities from remote areas of Tamil Nadu to come and participate in the event. Victor and his team members Aroon, Saranya and Bhanu helped a lot on the field. With their support, we organized trials before the national championship.

Raising Funds

Major requirements were covered. But still, so many miscellaneous items were yet to be arranged. I was thinking a lot about how to get funds for the same. T. Nagar is the commercial hub of Chennai city. Our treasurer Preetha and I thought of going there and to try our luck in raising funds. We didn't have any idea about raising funds. The first shop we selected was a jewellery shop, thinking that they would have a lot of money. When we went there, they gave us a grand welcome, thinking that we were customers. They lifted my wheelchair as there were steps at the entrance. After going inside, we informed them that we wanted to meet their boss. They asked for the reason. When we told them the reason, there was a sea of change in their treatment. They told us that their boss was not available and just ignored us thereafter. We decided to leave the place. Their staff didn't even look at us. We requested some of the customers there to bring my wheelchair down the steps at the exit point.

We then went to a famous clothing showroom. They spoke very politely and told us that their budget was completed, and they could not extend any help. After that, we went to another clothing showroom; they treated us almost like beggars. We felt very bad. While coming back from that showroom, Rema Devi aunty's friend saw us in the elevator. As we had met her immediately after the ill-treatment from the showroom owners, we shared that humiliation with her. She felt very sad. Later, she told aunty to inform me not to go to the shops requesting for sponsorship. Uncle and she helped us for some of the remaining items through their contacts. Through uncle's contacts, we got help from Oriental Cuisines for lunch. Rotary officials supported two items. For some items we supported through our YWTC Trust and for some other items Anand helped through his contacts.

My colleague Lakshmi and her husband Mr Chithambaram introduced me to Mr Rajaji from a real estate company. Mr Rajaji contributed personally and through his friends for this event.

New Officials at SDAT and Sports Department

We came to know that both the SDAT member secretary and the sports secretary got transferred. It was a shock for us. Just before the championship, new officials had joined. We were still waiting to make the pool area accessible. We didn't know how supportive the new officials would be. One of my cousin's friends is an IAS officer. While speaking to him, I told him about our worries. He told us that Mr Rajaraman, new member secretary, was a very sincere and committed officer. He suggested that I meet him immediately. Next day, I tried for an appointment and met him along with my senior colleague at my office, Gita. We briefed him about everything and sought his support to make the pool area accessible. He promised to extend the required support.

Our event was in the first week of December; he had taken charge in November. Within a very short time, as promised, he arranged for a permanent ramp at the complex entrance and temporary ramps inside, and made the restrooms (for both men and women) accessible by arranging commodes, hand bars, etc. He also initiated the process for getting approvals to arrange an elevator at the SDAT office. This posting was an additional charge for him, apart from his other two existing assignments. Even then, things started moving very fast. Later, when I met my cousin's friend, I heard so many nice stories about the sincerity and commitment of Mr Rajaraman from him. He told me how the public used to call him even during midnights for any issues when he was the district collector, and how he used to attend immediately to those issues. I have great respect for him.

Sports secretary Mr Nasimuddin was also a very supportive official. During the tenure of these two officials, many supportive measures for adaptive sports were taken up.

Novice Association to Host a National Championship

Creating more awareness about hydrotherapy/swimming was our major aim through this championship. We called for a press meet. I requested the friends from the media who interviewed me earlier to cover our event. We requested railway officials to display a half-minute video of our event on their screens; they accepted our request. Chennai Central Station Manager Mr Govindasamy helped us a lot during that time. We also gave request letters to primary and higher education secretaries to send school and college students to our event.

At the last minute, we came to know that as the arrival date of the teams was 6 December (day of the demolition of Babri Masjid), there would be a lot of security at the railway station; our buses might not be allowed inside. In which case, the participants would be required to walk a long distance. Then we met a senior official in the security department and explained our situation to him. He understood our concerns and promised to extend all the required support.

Finally, it was the arrival day of the teams. Gita, Sameer and other volunteers went to the railway station in the morning around 3:00 am to receive the first batch of participants from West Bengal. One senior swimmer from the West Bengal team immediately sent me a message, appreciating our efforts greatly. As promised, the railway station and security officials extended wonderful support to our teams. Later participants said that they were overwhelmed with the warm welcome by our volunteers and the railway officials.

At IITM, we met each and every department to get all the required approvals. We got excellent support from IITM staff. Canteen staff also took care of covering both North and South Indian tastes. Participants expressed their happiness with the accessibility everywhere, tasty food and beautiful scenery at IITM. Our volunteers assisted the participants at each and every place. Lunch was arranged by Oriental Cuisines with many varieties and without any limitations to the quantity. Similarly, Mr Narsa Reddy made arrangements for snacks, fruits, energy drinks and lemon juice throughout the day on all the six days. The SDAT staff also extended amazing support.

We arranged for two ambulances and one fire engine for the safety of swimmers along with a medical helpdesk under the guidance of our medical director, Dr Ponraj. The NCC volunteers from Loyola College also helped us. With the support of the Rotary Club, we arranged spare wheelchairs for the swimmers who could not walk for longer distances. Good-quality medals and trophies were presented to the winners with the support of Mr Singaravel. Anand took care of bringing out a souvenir on our event with very useful articles in it.

We invited all the related government officials and our partners for the event. Sai, Preetha and I went personally to invite the guests to the event. Around 1,200 volunteers from our office supported this event on shifts. All the participants gave wonderful feedback on the arrangements made and the amazing volunteering support extended by my organization. Uthira aunty's husband Commodore (Retd) Ramachandran uncle became the master of ceremony (MC) for all our events from that time. He is very good at emceeing.

Technical part (rules, regulations and announcing the winners, etc.) was taken care of by Dr Dabas and his team. Our state won 17 medals from the contingent of 19 swimmers. Our team stood at the seventh position. In the 11th nationals, we had only four swimmers from Tamil Nadu.

We however could not get any support in inviting students as audience, except a few with the support from National Institute for Empowerment of Persons with Multiple Disabilities (NIEPMD). Media coverage for the event was also minimal. Although around 500 people comprising participants, coaches and other officials came from across India, unfortunately, the media did not find it interesting enough to cover. With the support of our partners, Mr Prabhu made a documentary film on our event.

Hosting this event helped us in changing the attitude of officials and parents of the children with disabilities towards swimming. It was a great learning experience for all of us.

We all heaved a sigh of relief!

For almost one year, I didn't sleep properly. I was always thinking about making arrangements and getting support for the smooth execution of the event.

It was really a great achievement for our association. In the very first year of its formation, we hosted a national championship. Generally, sports associations go step by step, namely conducting camps, organizing state-level championships and may then host a national. But to create more awareness about the benefits of this sport in our state, we had to take such an extreme step. But we had a grand success with support from all our partners, mainly because of the volunteering support from my organization. Participants gave quite an emotional feedback to us. They told us that we had succeeded in conducting a para sport event at par with the Olympic event by making excellent arrangements. Some of them told us that when their family members called them to find out how they were, they told them that they were more comfortable and felt more convenient here in Chennai than back home. We got so teary-eyed upon hearing such feedback.

With this experience, I realized that if our intentions are good, however difficult a task is, support would come from somewhere even in the last minute and the task would be accomplished successfully. This has proven to be so on many other occasions in my life as well.

Left: PVP—Ms Amudha honouring our swimmer. Ms Shajeevana is also in the pic. Right: Edwin Nevis, Gita, other leads—leaders from my office who navigated the wonderful volunteering

26

Happiness Makes Life Blossom

The things that one takes for granted may be a privilege to others.

Caring Community

When I was living in a rented house, our neighbours were very friendly. But as we were all busy, there was no time to speak much except greeting when we saw each other in the apartment complex. One day, when my father was doing something in the kitchen washbasin, the water tap broke and water started to come out with full force. Dad was trying to close it. In that process, as the water was gushing out with full force, a tile fixed to the edge of the sink fell on Dad's foot. His foot immediately swelled up like a balloon. I called the neighbours for help immediately. By the time they closed the water supply by switching off the main valve on the roof, our entire house was filled with water up to 3–4 inch deep. Mom had knee pain, dad's foot was swollen, and I, for sure, couldn't empty out the water. I was wondering how to manage the situation. I will never forget the support extended by our neighbours Satheesh, Prasanna, Sriram, Kaushalya, Subhashini and her mother on that day. The men attended to the tap in the kitchen. The women cleared the water from the house and offered breakfast and lunch to us on top of that. I realized the importance of the intention of our elders when they prayed to God for the welfare of their neighbours by lighting lamps every evening in olden days. We may have many relatives and well-wishers, but only neighbours can come to our rescue at the time of emergencies.

Love for Music

Since my childhood, I have loved music. But there were no opportunities to learn it in my village in those days. My father's friend Mr Kameswara Rao was a great violinist, and I wanted to learn how to play violin from him. But he told me that I didn't have enough physical energy to play the violin, as I was very lean and weak in those days. When we shifted to Chennai, my desire to learn music became even stronger as Chennai is known for its love and support to fine arts. Initially, I thought of learning to play an instrument. Due to PPS, my muscle strength came down drastically. I tried piano thinking that it would require less physical strength. But after playing it for a few days, my fingers started to hurt a lot and became numb due to the fast movements across the keyboard. I realized that for my condition, learning instrumental music was not possible. Then I shifted to learning vocal music. My music teacher was Mr Ranganathan. He has a great knowledge of Carnatic music. I attended his classes for six months. I felt music to be like yoga. We get great mental peace from it. Focus is improved. After moving forward in learning music lessons, I found it very difficult to hold the breath as only one of my lungs is functional, that too partially. Finally, I stopped learning that also. Now, I enjoy singing at home as per my mood.

Getting Around in Workplace

My office complex is very big. Sometimes I have to move between different buildings. Initially, I was walking with the help of a walker. Later, I started using a manual wheelchair to go to other buildings. But due to less strength in my hands, I could not propel the chair on my own. I had to depend on someone. So I decided to buy an automatic wheelchair.

Keeping in mind the availability of servicing facilities, I bought it from a local company for ₹75,000 in 2009. It brought a great positive change in my office life. I am able to move faster and with greater independence now. As the chair height is more now, my colleagues need not bend towards me to speak. We could also speak while moving. I started going to the canteen along with my colleagues for lunch. These small things gave me more happiness. My colleagues used to make fun of me asking for a ride on my chair. They also used to tell me that they were jealous of me as I was moving around the campus happily sitting in a chair with ease. Initially, I used the walker within the office and at home for shorter distances. But as I got a stress fracture in both my wrists due to brittle bones, a few years ago, I stopped walking with the walker. At home, I started using a manual wheelchair. The big challenge with the automatic wheelchair is transportation. Because of its huge size and heavy weight, it's very difficult to carry. If we get a relatively sleek model with less weight, it would be very easy to take it while travelling. I am looking for such an option at an affordable price.

Thriving in Corporate World

For the year 2011, I was honoured with the 'Woman of the Year' award from my office. It was one of the great moments in my professional life. Before joining this organization, I had faced a lot of discouragement from many people for leaving a secured job and facing a competitive life in the corporate world. This honour gave me great confidence in myself.

I became part of our CSR committee and worked particularly in the area of diversity and inclusion (D&I)[1] for many years. It gave

---

[1] Diversity refers to the traits and characteristics that make people unique while inclusion refers to the behaviours and social norms that ensure people feel welcome (Source: https://builtin.com/diversity-inclusion).

D&I is more than policies, programmes or headcounts. Equitable employers outpace their competitors by respecting the unique needs, perspectives and potential of all their team members. As a result, diverse and inclusive workplaces earn deeper trust and more commitment from their employees (Source: https://www.greatplacetowork.com/resources/blog/why-is-diversity-inclusion-in-the-workplace-important).

me a very good exposure in other areas of D&I, apart from the disability part.

Movie with My Colleagues

My colleague Najmuddin got promoted as a manager and decided to give us a treat at a mall. We all had a great time there. After lunch, they all decided to go for a movie. I told them that I would go home as I knew very well that theatres were not accessible for me. But Najmuddin and others insisted on me joining them. Although the theatre was not accessible, they lifted me with my wheelchair wherever steps were there and took me for the 3D movie called *Ice Age*. It was the first and last movie I watched in a theatre in Chennai till today. In a hurry, we forgot where we parked the car in that mall's vast parking lot. It took one hour for our colleague Sadiq to find my car and bring it to me. Overall, it was a hilarious experience. I am so happy that I have very friendly and caring colleagues.

The experiences I described above may appear very common to others, for example, watching a movie and having lunch with colleagues and winning an award in office, but for me, these are precious and very special.

27

Paving the Way for Future Champions

The crucial requirements to promote sports for the disabled from my experiences are to create awareness, gain technical expertise, availability of accessible infrastructure facilities and sports-related equipment, support from family, the government and other organizations, and recognition on par with Olympic sports. I would like to elaborate my experiences on them.

Awareness Creation

There is a dearth of awareness, especially in sports for people with disabilities. To create more awareness, I initially started by giving talks at various platforms such as schools, colleges and corporates. A key role player in creating awareness is media. I observed that the media would be interested more in writing about individuals' achievements than writing about the efforts of a group of people for a social cause. That might have been the reason for not getting good media coverage for most of our events. Luckily, as I became a national champion, more journalists came to me to take interviews. I used that opportunity to create more awareness on the benefits of hydrotherapy/swimming for the disabled. I also approached some of them on my own, seeking their support in this matter. In the process, I got a great opportunity to be part of a very popular Tamil TV programme 'Makkal Aarangam' (public platform), which was hosted by director Visu. Initially, they had thought of inviting me as a guest to be shown in the last five minutes of their episode. But Mr Visu was impressed with my story after interviewing me. He sent his videography team to shoot my lifestyle (e.g., driving from home to pool and office, swimming, my house, my parents, my educational qualification certificates, my work atmosphere and my medals). Till now, no one has covered my life in such a detailed manner. I was wondering why they were shooting in detail for just a five-minute interview. At the time of telecast only, I came to know that my interview was to be telecasted in two episodes, with the duration of 30 minutes each. Mr Visu wanted to give me a pleasant surprise with this. It really helped a lot in creating awareness. I received many emails telling me how inspiring my words were. One person wrote to me saying that he was about to commit suicide, but my interview stopped him from taking such a hasty step. I received many emails explaining how my story gave them confidence to overcome their struggles and brought a positive outlook in their lives. Wherever I went, people started recognizing me and came to me referring to those episodes. My well-wisher Deepak conducts classes for chartered accountancy students. He made it a point to show the recordings of these two episodes to all the batches of his students. By this time, it might have reached thousands of his students.

At some corporates, whenever I gave talks, the staff with disabilities would ask me if it would really be possible for them to take part in sports. The awareness is low in cities in general and is even less in villages in particular. To reach a wider audience, I approached National Film Development Corporation for their support to bring out a documentary film. Later, they helped us in making a documentary film during our trials.

Technical Expertise

When I wanted to learn swimming, the coach was unable to teach me as he didn't have any idea about how to train the disabled in swimming. I heard the same situation being faced by other persons with disabilities. The main reason for this was that many physical education graduates are graduating from the colleges without any training on adaptive sports. For every sport-related curriculum, if universities add a curriculum related to the same sport for the persons with disabilities as addendum, it would be helpful for all of us. More or less, the rules are the same for both Olympic and Paralympic sports for the same discipline. Only a few adaptations are required. We submitted a request to Sports University in Chennai and also to the Sports department of the Government of Tamil Nadu in this regard.

With the support of SDAT, during Mr Rajaraman's tenure, we arranged for a sensitization session for SDAT swimming coaches with the help of our medical director Dr Ponraj and technical director Mr Ananda Jothi, explaining the additional precautions they needed to take while training the disabled. We wanted to invite other coaches too, but it became a difficult task for us to find interested coaches. I observed that many people think that training the disabled in sports is like a charitable activity for which they might not get proper payment. This also might be one of the reasons for not getting trainers for the training programme from external sources. Among the SDAT coaches, Mr Vijaykumar showed a lot of interest in training our swimmers. He helped us a lot in this regard. Even after conducting sensitization programmes, only a few trainers came forward to train our swimmers.

Accessible Infrastructure Facilities

Another big challenge is accessible sporting facilities and accommodation. We have been struggling with this matter from the beginning. But wherever we organize events, we have been trying our level best to educate the local people on the accessibility part and making arrangements within the resources available for us. After reading *The Hindu* article on me, one person named Murali from the USA sent me a message. At that time, I had found a very good book on hydrotherapy on the Internet titled *Adapted Aquatics Programming: A Professional Guide*. But I could not find it here to buy. He bought that book and sent it to me through his parents. That book helped us in preparing the proposals for the government. While surfing through the Internet, I found a video on Israel Sports School for the Disabled. The facilities available there impressed me very much. I used that video in many of my presentations to educate people on how to construct accessible infrastructure facilities or modify the existing ones.

Dr Hutzler, scientific counsellor for Israel Sports Centre for the Disabled, guided us in preparing the proposal for the construction of a hydrotherapy pool to submit to SDAT. He shared with us the Americans with Disabilities Act (ADA)-related links. It was a great enlightenment for me going through those links. There are very comprehensive guidelines in them in making the sporting facilities and entertainment and leisure-related facilities accessible. I felt very happy for their concern for the persons with disabilities. We also included a temperature-controlling facility as some people cannot swim in cold water due to their health condition. And we included unisex toilets. I had personally experienced that when dad used to come with me, he could not come inside the ladies' toilet and I could not go inside gents' toilet. Unisex toilets would be helpful for people who come with a caregiver from the opposite gender. With the efforts of Mr Rajararaman and Mr Nasimuddin, Tamil Nadu government sanctioned a hydrotherapy pool. In 2018, its construction was completed and it was opened for the public. But wide publicity is required to encourage more people to use it.

One day, dad called me when I was in the office and told me that one letter from Tamil Nadu Sports department was delivered. I told him to open and verify it. It was the copy of the GO issued by the Government of Tamil Nadu. It was my dream to get a GO in Tamil Nadu, similar to the one issued by the united Andhra Pradesh government.

My dream had come true! This GO was issued with additional benefits when compared to the Andhra GO; persons with disabilities who were below 16 years of age could use SDAT facilities free of cost and those who were above 16 years of age could get 50 per cent concession in fee. SDAT facilities would be made accessible in a phased manner. SDAT would conduct competitions for the athletes with disabilities every year and had some more beneficial points. After hearing this news, I was elated. I had been following up on this for a long time. Finally, during the tenure of Mr Rajaraman and Mr Nasimuddin, that GO was issued. They are very dynamic and supportive officials.

I realized that though the government issues very useful orders for the benefit of the public, the main challenge lies in channelling that information to those who get benefit from them. I tried my level best to create awareness on this. I mentioned it in all my talks and media interviews. I wrote about it on my social media platforms. After starting the YWTC movement, I started blogging. Later, I also opened a Facebook account. When I decided to advocate for the needs of the persons with disabilities to participate in sports, I needed the support of social media platforms to share my views with others, which would be helpful for my efforts.

Once I got an opportunity to address government civil engineers. Whenever I faced problems with regard to accessibility, I used to think of bringing my bitter experience to the notice of the concerned engineer. On that day, I could share my feelings with them with great emotion: how we, the persons with disabilities, were facing so many challenges as they were not considering our needs while constructing buildings. I asked them what my biggest challenge as per their view was, but no one responded. Then I told them that inaccessible toilets had been my biggest challenge. We had alternatives for almost everything else, but for answering nature's calls, we didn't have any alternative but to use the toilet. Earlier, I used to feel very shy to tell others that I wanted to use the toilet. But in that meeting with the engineers (and after that too), I started speaking openly about toilets, accessibility, our challenges and ways to make our lives comfortable.

My talk at IITM turned out to be quite fruitful. While renovating their pool, they arranged for a ramp for the shallow pool. They made their restrooms near the pools accessible. For the deep pool, they planned to place a swimming pool lift. For the opening ceremony of their renovated pools, IITM director, Professor Bhaskar Ramamurthi, invited me. He gave me the honour to light the ceremonial lamp. I was immensely happy with their gesture and to see that accessible environment.

Availability of Sports-related Equipment

Whenever I got the opportunity to give talks at engineering colleges, I would explain to them how students from different disciplines (such as civil, mechanical and electronics) could, and in fact must, think about universal design to meet the requirements of people with different levels of abilities. Some of the students worked on some projects too. One of the students from Vellore Institute of Technology (VIT), Neelkanth, started working on a project to design a wheelchair which could be operated with oral instructions or with movements of the head. He met me after my talk at VIT to discuss some points. He worked very hard on that project and completed the prototype at a very affordable price. Due to the overstrain involved in bringing it out, I remember he was hospitalized for some time as well. Later, he got a job and could not work on it further.

This episode made me realize that there are many brilliant students who want to work with great passion on some assistive devices, but later, their work would be available in their college records only. For students, it's their project work and for colleges it's a record. Unless it's manufactured and launched in the market, all the great efforts of students go waste. When I got an opportunity to speak at University Industry Conclave, I raised this point. I requested the manufacturers to encourage students to work on assistive devices and bring them into the market at affordable prices. I also made it clear to them that such assistive devices that they bring into the market would be of use not only for persons with disabilities but also for the elderly people.

Hence, the percentage of demography would be increased, and they would have demands from more people. After my talk, some of the industrialists responded positively, saying that if anyone approaches them with a good project, they would consider funding it. But I don't think any further progress happened in this matter.

During that time, I came to know Santosh through one of my ex-colleagues, who was working in the USA in a company that manufactured assistive devices. He came to Chennai to meet me. It was a great learning experience to listen to his experiences in that field. I was amazed when I came to know about the projects he worked for his mom to make her life more comfortable in the kitchen and for his grandpa to read books in his old age. Till that time, I hadn't seen any engineering student designing any item for the comfort of his/her family members.

After speaking to him, I realized that assistive devices' manufacturing would only be possible with the support of grants from the government or big NGOs. Unless industrialists find a business cause in it, they don't usually come forward to invest in these devices. But even today, I strongly feel that the persons with disabilities and the elderly population can jointly become a considerably large market. Whatever devices I am using today not only make me comfortable but also my parents. He also explained to me how they would price the product very low without giving much importance to its appearance. Only the purpose of the product is important. We both, jointly, gave a talk at VIT. It was a great experience. As an end user of those assistive devices, I explained to them how comfortable I was after using them, for example, walker, modified scooter, car and automatic wheelchair. He explained to them the work that they were doing, and how it could be done. Our talk was very well received by the students.

Later, we both went to NIEPMD. Director Ms Neeradha showed us their plan for constructing a hydrotherapy pool. We shared our suggestions with her. I saw such an accessible place for the first time. Elevator buttons were within the wheelchair user's reach, all the floors had elevators and ramp facilities. Those ramps were made in such a way that propelling the wheelchairs on them was very easy, as the slope was not steep.

IITM students also came out with a swimming pool lift prototype. We used it in one or two of our state-level championships. But unfortunately, that lift didn't come out as a finished product in the market yet.

Support from Family, the Government and Other Organizations

Support from the family is crucial in encouraging sports for the disabled. Generally, parents think that their children are already vulnerable due to disability, and their participation in sports would further worsen their condition. I appeal to the parents of children with disabilities to encourage their children to participate in sports and share their experiences, which would help in motivating other parents too.

As almost all the infrastructure facilities are with the government, their support is crucial. From my interactions with the concerned officials, I have observed that the sports departments of some states feel that they have to be concerned only with Olympic sports. They also feel that paralympic sports should be supported mainly by the Social Justice department or DWDs. Over a period of time, I could see a little improvement in this area. Coordination between various government departments would help us a lot.

Support from corporates and international NGOs also plays an important role. I have observed many corporates saying that sports are not in their CSR agenda. Some of the officials told me that they might consider proposals from health- or education-related projects but not sports. I have been trying my best to convince them that sports is a part of education and health. But I still face challenges in this area.

Left: Hydrotherapy pool constructed by Tamil Nadu government at our request Right: Prototype of swimming pool lift designed by the students of Professor Sujatha, IITM, demonstrating to Mr Rajaraman

Recognition on a par with Olympic Sports

When we started our efforts to support sports for the disabled in Tamil Nadu, there were no clear guidelines on the recognition part of the winners of paralympic sports. We gave a detailed request in this matter to the Government of Tamil Nadu by providing the supporting data on how equal recognition is being accorded for paralympic sports at international level, at the Central government level in India, and also in other states like Haryana. While preparing this proposal, my friend Sadhana (MD of a company) and her colleague Benedict helped me in submitting it in a professional way. They also accompanied me to meet the sports secretary, Mr Nasimuddin, when I went to submit that proposal. Later, when Mariappan from Tamil Nadu won the gold medal at Paralympics, he got equal remuneration from the Tamil Nadu government, at par with Olympic gold medal winners.

To address the challenges for adaptive sports, the crucial step is to create awareness. Increased awareness leads to an inclusive environment in sports.

28

Year 2013: Can You Play Basketball on a Wheelchair?

This year I was introduced to two amazing adaptive sports, blind cricket and wheelchair basketball. We were able to send our very-well-prepared state team to the nationals. I could also share the joy when a blind person experienced how it felt to drive for the first time.

Varied Experiences I Had with Journalists

I faced a few embarrassing situations with my interviews in various print and electronic media. Some journalists write the articles accurately, keeping all the points I tell them intact. But others change some facts altogether, for instance, my age at the time of the polio attack. I was affected by polio at the age of seven months in the year 1970. But some wrote seven years. And an article even mentioned that I was affected by polio in 2007.

One may treat these mistakes as negligible, as they are not hurting anyone. But for an article, though I had said that I could not go to college due to their inaccessible infrastructure, the reporter wrote the reason to be my friends not supporting me. After reading that article, one of my friends' husband asked her why she didn't support her friend who was in need. She called and told me about this incident. I apologized to her and informed her about what had happened. The reporter might have thought that this new story might get me more sympathy. But, in fact, it actually put me in an embarrassing situation.

I thought that if it's electronic media, such embarrassing situations might not arise as I address the audience directly. But in one interview, I explained the teamwork we put in to achieve something and they edited the clip in such a way that it looked like I was the only one who did the entire thing by myself. I was upset for the information that had been manipulated. It definitely would have also hurt the feelings of others who worked so diligently and tirelessly alongside me.

To avoid such situations, I started asking reporters to share the draft of their stories with me before publishing so that I could do a fact-check. Some shared, while others told me it was not possible due to their policies. Although the media helps us in creating awareness, there are some downsides with misinformation, which I think are rectifiable.

Blind Cricket

A group of college students named AUGA invited me to a school for the blind children on the eve of the Republic Day celebrations. I came to know that those school kids played cricket, volleyball, etc. But many people are hardly aware of this and look at blind people or disabled people only from a narrow lens of support for livelihood or education. I wanted to promote awareness about the abilities of blind children/people among sighted people and so I requested the AUGA members to arrange a cricket match through our trust. Considering my request, they arranged for the match. It was the first time for me to see a cricket match played by blind players. They used a ball with ball bearings, which rattles for audible tracking. Accordingly, they do batting and fielding. To make the bowler understand where the stumps are, batsman will make a sound with the bat. I had a great time mingling with them and presented pen drives to them as gifts as per their choice. But I felt sorry about the state of facilities available there and thereafter in my talks, I brought it to light. Later, I came to know that some corporates had started working for the betterment of conditions in that school.

Blind Car Rally

I participated in a blind car rally as a driver for the first time. In the rally, a blind person acts as a co-driver navigating the driver through the instructions given in Braille regarding the route map with landmarks in that route and speed/time/distance. It was aimed to make the blind person to experience the feel of driving a car. Among the 100 drivers who participated in the rally, I was the only one with a disability. Organizers started the rally with my car. IPS officer Mr Sylendra Babu started it and actor Karthee was the guest of honour. Karthee is so simple and humble. When he came to greet me, I didn't know who he was, as I didn't use to watch any Tamil movies at that time. In that rally, the blind person played a key role in driving the car. We all know that the formula for distance is speed multiplied by time. In the instructions, only two out of these three parameters would be given. We need to calculate the third one and drive accordingly to reach the destination by following the given route. My parents and Neelkanth came along with me and were in the back seat. Neelkanth did the calculations. Directions told by my blind companion were accurate. As we were able to see, in our over-enthusiasm, we tried to use our brains without meticulously following the blind person's instructions and deviated from the correct route. Our detour added 15 km (~9.3 mi). On the way, there were a few stalls with volunteers in them. We needed to go and sign there. Based on the time it took between stalls, they could infer if we followed their instructions or not. Finally, we completed the distance and reached the starting point.

Festivals at Our Native Place

Mom very much likes to celebrate Deepavali and Sankranthi festivals at our home in Sathupally. On those occasions, all her children visit our home with their families to celebrate together. It brings her immense happiness. However, after moving to Chennai, due to my health initially and my social activities later, we could not celebrate these festivals in our hometown. Once, for my birthday, we happened to be there in Sathupally. All my siblings, except for my brother, joined us along with their families. We planned to celebrate both the festivals on my birthday to give the satisfaction and enjoyment to my mom which she missed for the last few years. We got the cow dung from our milk man. Early in the morning, my sisters cleaned the front yard, sprinkled cow dung water, drew beautiful rangolis in front of our home and decorated them with colours and gobbemmas. In the evening, we celebrated Deepavali by lighting diyas and bursting crackers. Among all these festivities, we celebrated my birthday by cutting a cake. Our neighbours were puzzled when they saw our untimely celebrations. They might have thought that we were crazy. It was an awesome and a nostalgic experience.

Acting in a Short Film

My colleagues decided to make a short film based on my life story for a competition in my organization. The entire team was from my department. We were not allowed to bring any external technical assistance. My colleague Rani played my younger self. Raman was the director. I played my role. My other colleagues played in other roles. While others were acting, I was playing my own role. At that time, I could not understand the concept of acting—to portray someone else's character. My coach's role was played by a colleague who didn't know swimming. Whenever he gave me instructions about swimming during the shoot, I would burst into laughter. Similarly, when they shot the scene with the doctor, I could not control my laugh. My colleagues struggled a lot with me to shoot the film as they were also unable to control laughter as it's contagious. At that time, I realized how difficult the job of acting was. While speaking to the person in my father's role, I didn't get any emotions as I could not imagine any other person in my dad's place. So they gave up on me and shot the video mostly from my back without showing my facial expressions. Later, when I saw the film, I was surprised to see the effective performance of my co-actors, though I was laughing sitting in front of them while shooting those scenes. When I told this to mom (I could not show the film to my family, as it could only be shown within our organization), she advised me to try for perfection in whatever I did, even if it was new to me. I felt too bad. Had I acted well, our short film would have received first prize instead of third. I thought of trying to act in a better way next time. But I didn't get any opportunity to act after that.

State-level Championship

We planned for the first state-level swimming championship in 2013 with the support of SDAT, PVP, our patron Mr Narsa Reddy and some other well-wishers, to be conducted at SDAT Aquatic Complex in Chennai. As my organization took care of most of the arrangements, we didn't struggle much. During trials in 2012, we observed that most of the participants didn't have the financial capacity even to purchase the basic gear such as swimsuits, caps and goggles. From then, we tried to arrange gear for participants in our events every year. The PVP officials helped in bringing participants from across the state. They started to support our swimming events when Ms Amuda was the head. They continued to extend their support when other officials took charge. The new head of this project, Ms Mythili, also supported us a lot. During the event, IITM students displayed the prototype of the swimming pool lift under the guidance of Associate Professor Sujatha. My colleagues volunteered for this event with great passion. They told me that they were inspired by the positive attitude of our swimmers, and that their personal problems which looked very big hitherto now appeared to be trivial.

A total of 160 para swimmers (144 males and 16 females) took part in the 2-day event representing 30 districts of Tamil Nadu. From this championship, we selected the participants for the 13th nationals to be held in Bengaluru.

Briefing Session

With the support of the SDAT and PVP officials, we could organize training sessions and camps for the selected candidates for the 13th nationals.

We arranged a briefing session on the coaching camp to prepare our swimmers for the forthcoming national event to be conducted in Basavanagudi, Bengaluru. Our technical director Mr Ananda Jothi demonstrated fitness exercises to our swimmers. He showed a different set of exercises depending on the abilities of the swimmers. It was very helpful for all of us. With the support of my organization, we could distribute protein powder packs and theraband (resistance band) to all the swimmers participating in the national event.

We conducted training sessions every weekend for three months for the participants in their respective districts. Later, with the consent of all the swimmers, we arranged for a coaching camp in Dindigul for three weeks. It was the first time in Tamil Nadu that such intensive coaching was provided to para swimmers. We took the initiative with the intention of encouraging our swimmers by providing intensive training and bringing laurels to our state.

Friendship That Helped Our Cause

I participated in one of NASSCOM[1] conferences as a panellist in a D&I-related panel discussion. Amar from R. R. Donnelley was the moderator, and Archana from Cognizant was one of my co-panellists. I met them for the first time and didn't know then that our friendship

---

[1] NASSCOM: The National Association of Software and Service Companies is an Indian non-governmental trade association and advocacy group focused mainly on information technology and business process outsourcing industry.

would be helpful for our para sports activities. After knowing about my involvement in adaptive sports, they both showed interest in supporting me in these activities.

Training Camp

District collector Mr Venkatachalam was very supportive and took personal interest in arranging accommodation for players, and the staff from the Sports department helped a lot for the smooth conduct of the camp. Under the guidance of our coach, Mr Vijayakumar, we conducted the camp in Dindigul. I arranged for physiotherapy with the support of my trust and protein powder packs with the support of my office. My childhood classmate Prasad, who is in the pharma industry, provided the required medicines for our players. Some prominent people in Dindigul visited our camp and motivated the participants with their encouraging words. In those days, preparing the participants for the nationals by a state association was recognized as a great initiative, considering the minimal support received for such events. As promised, Archana took the initiative to connect me with Cognizant volunteer leads Sankara and Saranya. They coordinated with their volunteers and helped us in Dindigul during our camp. We were satisfied that we did our bit in preparing our participants for the nationals.

Visit to Madurai, Rameswaram and Palani

While going to Dindigul camp, I applied for additional leaves for two days so that I could go to Madurai and nearby places along with my parents. One of our swimmers, Abdul Salam, is from Madurai. He helped us a lot in finding an accessible hotel and on-site seeing. Madurai is famous for Arulmigu Meenakshi Sundareshwarar Temple. It's a very old temple with beautiful architecture. We got a good darshan of Goddess Meenakshi and felt very peaceful. Later, we went to Abdul's house to meet his family members. My colleague Raman is also from Madurai. He told some nice things about Madurai which we should not miss, for instance, eating street food in the evening, trying *jigarthanda* (a type of cool drink) and tasting halwa (sweet dish) at a specific place. We did all those things with the help of Abdul. We didn't miss the street food, even though it was raining. It was a nice experience. The only thing we missed on our list was to buy jasmines; Madurai jasmines are very famous. While coming from Dindigul, we went to Palani, where Lord Murugan Temple is situated. Although all those temples were not fully accessible, staff in those temples were very supportive and helped us in having good darshan. We took a cable car ride for the first time, and it was an amazing experience.

With Abdul's guidance, we could see Rameswaram Temple also. Seeing the ocean at the feet of Lord Shiva was an unforgettable moment. We went to Dhanushkodi where two seas meet. But we could not go near the meeting point, as it was difficult to travel in sand in our vehicle.

After coming back from Rameswaram, we invited my niece Pavani with her husband Prasad for dinner. She had shifted to Chennai after her wedding, as Prasad was working in Chennai. We felt very happy to have their company. But soon they moved to Hyderabad due to his transfer.

13th National Championship

With all the preparation, 39 swimmers participated in the championship from Tamil Nadu. Our team was placed at the 5th position by winning 26 medals, consisting of 5 gold, 9 silver and 12 bronze. In the 12th nationals, our team was placed at the 7th position. Year by year, we could see improvement in the number of participants, number of medals and in our rank at the nationals. As most of the participants were from PVP, they took care of the transport for the swimmers to participate in the nationals.

Societal Stereotypes: The Biggest Barrier in Accessing Basic Amenities

Due to an event in Andhra Club, where I go regularly for swimming, the pool was closed. My neighbours informed me about a pool that was near my house. My father went there and enquired about the timings and charges. At that time, they told him that they didn't allow persons with disabilities for swimming in their pool. Then my father explained to the employee that I knew swimming, and that I was a former national para swimming champion. She promised to check with her boss and get back. After hearing that, I decided not to leave this matter, as that was nothing but discrimination towards persons with disabilities. Hence, I followed up with her daily. I got the contact number of one of the owners from a friend. After making a few calls, she finally agreed to let me go to the pool. When I went there, the employee checked with another owner, and the owner instructed her not to allow me. Even after a lot of arguments, they didn't allow me. When I asked them to give their response in writing, then they asked me to come back on the next day with a medical certificate stating that I could swim and also to bring my championship certificate.

Will any doctor give such a certificate? Doctors generally will tell whether swimming is safe for her/his health condition or not. How can other para swimmers bring championship certificates? In the absence of these certificates, how can they access the pool?

The next morning, that owner called me and said that they denied me to use their pool as they had fears about the drowning of persons with disabilities. And later through her friends, she came to know about me. She apologized and requested me to use their pool. I told her to come for our events and see how efficiently our para swimmers could swim. I also told her that we could offer training for their coach on how to train kids with disabilities in swimming. I didn't go to that pool again. She didn't call me either.

Learning a New Language

My colleagues Srinivas and Sankar started teaching me sign language after seeing my struggles to communicate with them. They used to teach me sign language in a very fun-filled way. I found many advantages of learning sign language apart from communicating with persons with hearing impairment. We can speak with our friends without disturbing others and also without much effort we can communicate with people from some distance.

Under our D&I programme, we started conducting sessions for staff in sign language with the intention to create an office environment which would be more inclusive. Sankar and other colleagues used to take the sessions. Being one of the lead members of our CSR committee, one day I was coordinating for the session. I introduced Sankar to the audience and advised them to take my help wherever needed to understand what Sankar was teaching (though I am not an expert in sign language, I can manage to some extent). But to my surprise, no audience approached me for help though they were freshers for learning that language. Sankar made the session so lively and the participants were laughing throughout the session with the jokes cracked by Sankar through his body language.

Until I interacted with Srinivas and Sankar, I used to think that, among all the disabilities, hearing impairment was not much of a disadvantage as they could see and walk to any place independently. But after interacting with them, I quickly realized that the reality is different. They feel lonely even when they are sitting among many people, as most of the people hesitate to speak to them due to lack of knowledge in sign language. As their disability is not visible, people tend to get angry with them for not responding to their queries. In many programmes, they may not be able to understand what the speakers were telling. Also at school level, there are many gaps due to lack of sign language-based education. It affects kids a lot while learning a language, especially English, which adversely impacts access to higher education and employment. After coming to know their challenges, through our D&I committee, we took up many initiatives to make our office environment more friendly for them and some CSR initiatives with deaf children in schools. If we are sincere in making our society more inclusive, we must interact with the people from diverse backgrounds. Otherwise, it will be difficult to understand their needs and feelings.

Introduction to Wheelchair Basketball

In December 2013, I was invited for an international conference by a UK-based NGO, along with their partners. Rajasekharan, co-founder of V-shesh (an organization working for the skill development and recruitment of persons with disabilities) had referred my name to them. But I didn't know him personally at that time. After seeing my profile, they understood that I was interested in the promotion of adaptive sports. They contacted me and expressed their desire to promote wheelchair basketball in India, and that they were looking for like-minded local partners. They asked me if I would be interested in partnering with them. I told them to allow me some time to think over it. I didn't know much about basketball. I searched online and watched some wheelchair basketball videos.

Until then, I was working only to promote swimming, which is an individual sport. Wheelchair basketball is a team game. So naturally, players with different levels of abilities can complement each other and strengthen their team. Through the videos I watched, I understood that it is a very dynamic sport. I felt that it would be a great opportunity to inculcate leadership skills and team spirit among persons with disabilities through this sport and give an opportunity to the youngsters with disabilities to showcase their energy and dynamism. In our society, it is very difficult for the disabled to get the opportunity to take the lead in any aspect. It's mainly because of the lack of confidence from society towards people like us. Due to this perspective, we, disabled people, also may not get the confidence to lead. Since my childhood, I got a lot of 'advice' from my well-wishers to not do many things, suggesting it would be difficult for me. Fortunately, as my parents have always had confidence in me, I could do all the things I have been doing till now. I decided to support this initiative through our trust. I checked with my trust members, and we sent our acceptance for their proposal. At that time, I didn't know what a big task it was going to be.

Manoj is the founder of that NGO, and he informed me that coach Jaspal Dhani would conduct the camp. They requested me to arrange for a training camp when they would arrive in Chennai. Within a week's time, I made the arrangements for a one-day camp. SDAT gave us permission to organize the event at J. N. Indoor Stadium, Chennai. There were two outdoor basketball courts. As they hesitated to allow us to use the indoor court for fear that their indoor wooden court would get damaged due to wheelchair movement, they permitted us to use the outdoor court only. Cognizant helped in providing food for the participants and volunteered for the camp. With the support of local NGOs working for persons with disabilities, we could bring in some participants. Some of our swimmers also participated in it. Manoj and team brought a few sports wheelchairs. With those chairs, we conducted the camp. I also tried to play sitting in that chair. Due to its shape, it's very easy to move the chair in 360-degree angle. All the participants felt incredibly happy. Volunteers and journalists also tried to shoot after seeing the court. I observed that when anyone comes to the court, they try to play, remembering their school/college days. It's the magic of sports.

In the camp, the UK NGO also introduced boccia to the participants with severe disabilities. I feel that boccia is the ultimate example for inclusion. Persons with disabilities, however severe their disability level may be, can participate in that sport. I met Rajasekharan for the first time. Whenever I think about that event, I wonder how we managed to arrange it in just a week's time. Thanks a ton to SDAT, Cognizant and other NGOs.

Manoj and I met Mr Rajaraman. Manoj shared his knowledge on the accessibility part. We requested Mr Rajaraman to make J. N. Indoor Stadium accessible for wheelchair users so that we could host our events in it. At that time, he suggested another facility, which was under construction, to make it a centre for paralympic sports. He connected us with the concerned engineers. We both went there. Manoj suggested some changes that were required to make the facility accessible. Manoj also requested the SDAT officials to have sports wheelchairs at their stadium for the use of our players.

At that time, a shocking news was revealed—Mr Rajaraman got transferred to another department. During his tenure, so many developments took place in support of adaptive sports. He is a very dynamic and honest officer with great compassion for persons with disabilities. He made decisions very fast. Like a small kid, I became very emotional. After he left, the proposal for the centre of excellence for sports for the disabled didn't move forward.

I heard from some other people that his wife, Ms Kalyani, used to work for many social causes. Earlier, she had worked for kids with intellectual disabilities. I wanted to meet her to request to join us in promoting adaptive sports. But I couldn't get the chance to do so.

By that time, we had formed the trust and simultaneously supported the state association for para swimming in organizing many events for swimming at state and national levels with the support of like-minded people. Hence, I felt that we were pretty comfortable in taking up another sport, considering the experience we had gained. However, every new task would have its own challenges—we learn from both the successes and the failures equally.

29

Year 2014: As the Wheels of Change Turned

I wanted to share the benefits and spread the joy I experienced through wheelchair basketball among my fellow persons with disabilities living throughout the country. So I, with the support of some like-minded people, formed a national-level federation. We went around the country organizing many camps to increase the awareness on adaptive sports and train the interested candidates and organized an inter-state championship.

International Seminar on Disability Sports and Social Inclusion

In February, we organized an international seminar at ITC Grand Chola, inviting diverse stakeholders such as sports officials, DWD officials, corporate officials,[1] doctors, media officials, sports associations' leaders, para sportspersons, physical education teachers, educationalists, international coaches, disability rights activists and

---

[1] Some of the officials are from Confederation of Indian Industry (CII) and NASSCOM.

NGOs. The event focused on the difference sports can make in the lives of persons with disabilities, as well as how these can promote social inclusion, self-esteem and motivation.

Organizing a disability-related event in such an eminent 5-star hotel did take a lot of people by surprise as it was least expected. My view was that when companies can hold their conferences at such venues, why not adaptive sports-related events. This would certainly bring attention to and change the outlook of people and key stakeholders towards serious professionalism and commitment of parasport players. It was indeed a very happy moment for me to see our players enjoying the ambience. It was also good to see the hotel set-up with accessible infrastructure such as a stage ramp and suitable fixtures to make the toilet accessible, as it is very rare. Usually, in most of the places, they used to either carry me along with my wheelchair on to the dais or request me to talk from the place where I sit, which used to make me think seriously about organizers' commitment to accessibility and inclusion.

A lot of groundwork was put in to make this event successful. First, we had to select the topics, then to find suitable speakers, to coordinate with them, to arrange conference calls with the panellists and moderators, and finally to invite the participants. This seminar set the tone for building a network of like-minded allies paving the way for establishment of WBFI.

We invited Kalyani Rajaraman, who I knew is very passionate for social causes. I met her for the first time when I invited her for the seminar, yet we connected very well and became good friends in the first meeting itself. She accepted my invitation and graced the occasion. At that time, we didn't know we would become associates and work together to promote wheelchair basketball. We were fortunate to meet many new people in the seminar, and many of them have been extending their support since then. Some of them are supporting financially, some others are volunteering their time and energy, some are spreading the word, some are inspiring us and the players, and some are keeping us in their prayers.

Anand introduced me to Aram, a wheelchair basketball player from the Netherlands who was visiting India. Both his legs were affected by polio. During the conversation, I came to know that he does a 10-km wheelchair ride every morning just like how others go for walking for fitness. Again, after a small break, he would go to gym and later to the court to practise wheelchair basketball. His body above the hips was very fit. Until then, I never saw such a strong wheelchair user. To the extent of my experience and knowledge, everyone used to speak about rehabilitation for the persons with disabilities, but no one talked about improving fitness. I also wondered about his intake of food and other habits. Till that time, I only saw persons with disabilities consuming very less to maintain weight. He spent some time with us at the court and gave us some tips on how to dribble, shoot and move on sports wheelchairs.

Swimming Events

We received a lot of support from the organization I work for. After starting my activities with regard to promoting adaptive sports, my senior colleagues/bosses Saibal, Aarti, Sadhish, Ashok, Guna, Srini, Ram, Govind and Sridhar encouraged me by volunteering for our events or by interacting with our players to inspire them or by motivating our staff to volunteer for our events.

With their support and with the help from a few others, we conducted the 2nd state-level championship with more than 200 para swimmers. We also guided an affiliate[2] to independently organize events. Our coach Mr Vijayakumar took the initiative and helped them to conduct the event successfully. Later, we arranged a two-week camp for the selected swimmers for the nationals. In all, 59 para swimmers represented Tamil Nadu at the 14th National Para Swimming

---

[2] Madurai District Paraswimming Association, an affiliate to our Paralympic Swimming Association of Tamilnadu (PSATN), and they organized the 1st South Zone Paraswimming Championship.

Championship. Tamil Nadu attained the 4th position with 34 medals. All our association members were extremely happy for the consistent progress our state swimmers were making every year.

Positive Difference That Was Brought by Swimming

It is always surprising to see new positive changes day after day that swimming brings into the lives of our swimmers. The swimmers, whom I saw were very hesitant in the beginning, lacking self-confidence or at least not exhibiting the same, slowly started to open up and speak to the officials and media reporters very confidently. Several of them started to recognize the improvement in their health. I like to share a couple of these stories.

When I saw Perumal for the first time, he was covering his hand with a towel. He met with an accident and lost his hand. He hesitated to show his hand to others, mainly out of apprehensions that people would judge him as less capable seeing the deformity. During the national championship, he slowly gained confidence and comfort with the cohort of other players and officials, and I saw him moving around without the towel. I asked him why he was not covering his hand. He told me that after seeing so many other persons with disabilities who had accepted and come to terms with their disability and were confident of themselves without hiding their disabilities, he thought that there was no point in hiding his disability. Accepting ourselves with whatever challenges we have is the first step to lead our lives with confidence and cheerfulness. He went on to win many medals at the national level. Today, he is the owner of a small business (that has 4 tea shops) and employs around 25 people in his business. He proudly displays all the medal-receiving photos and paper cuttings in his shops. Whoever comes to his tea shop looks at him with great admiration. He has become a role model for many.

Velmurugan, another swimmer, has won many state- and national-level medals. With the support of these achievements, he got admission in the National Institute for Sports (NIS) and became an NIS-certified coach. He also got international certification as coach. He has started to train wheelchair basketball players. He is now financially independent and settled in life. He bought a house, which was his long-cherished dream, and also an agricultural land with his job. He is very grateful to swimming which has brought great positive changes in his life.

Not only our swimmers but also people who supported us are equally happy. Some of the senior officials from government and corporates told me that supporting our sporting events was one of the most satisfying experiences in their careers. Volunteers also expressed their happiness for having such a great experience. They mentioned that volunteering for our events helped them change their perception towards life in a very positive way.

One such volunteer is our coach Vijayakumar. He shared his experiences with me. He is an ex-serviceman. He loves to take up challenges. When he came to know about para swimming through us, he found it quite challenging and wanted to take it up. He started training Abdul Salam and Perumal. He felt that it was not easy to train para swimmers considering their physical challenges. Slowly, he learnt the required skills by giving training to some of our para swimmers and with the guidance extended by our medical director Dr Ponraj and technical director Ananda Jothi. He guided and trained our swimmers in all our coaching camps. He also encouraged them to become coaches later. He mentioned that training para swimmers gave him great satisfaction. He was recognized by the district collectors and from his department, SDAT.

Bringing Together Olympic and Paralympic Players to Inclusion in Sports

Mr Troy Justice, NBA Senior Director, visited Chennai. We came to know about it through our well-wisher Jayashankar Menon, a former national basketball team captain. Jay used to take sessions for our players during weekends. We invited Troy to meet and interact with our players. He accepted our invitation and spent some time with our players and shared his valuable tips with us. Being beginners in this sport, interacting with an expert like Troy was a wonderful experience for us. Basketball coaches from across India and running basketball players also participated in this session. On that day, I could see how sports bring people together, whether it is Olympics or Paralympics.

Seven-day Wheelchair Basketball Training Camp

In July, we organized a seven-day wheelchair basketball training camp at J. N. Indoor Stadium, Chennai, under the guidance of coach Mark Walker from Australia and Manoj Soma. For the first time, we could enter an indoor wooden stadium. It was a great experience for us. Until then, we were practising only in outdoor stadiums. As per the suggestion of Manoj earlier, we informally started a club with the name Chennai Eagles. He advised us to register it but we could not. PVP officials helped us in bringing participants (both male and female) from different parts of Tamil Nadu. Cognizant, RRD and my office colleagues volunteered for the camp. We arranged volunteers to translate as players were not comfortable with English. Wooden ramps were arranged at the stadium entrance and in toilets. Accommodation was also given at the stadium.

On the first day, players were hesitant to speak up. They told me that for the first time in their life they saw such an international standard stadium, sports wheelchair and a foreign coach. Coach Mark Walker started taking his lessons not only on the court but also off the court. He taught them some basic player etiquettes as well, for instance, to go to the restroom to wash hands before going for lunch, to take the plate, move in a queue to get food keeping the plate in their lap, put the plate in the dustbin after eating and then wash hands.

In India, many people are ready to help the persons with disabilities. Generally, if we go to any function, someone will bring food for us.

There will be no need for us to stand in the queue to get food. Given this context, players were initially struggling with the routine of having to do many things by themselves. From the second day onwards, they started following it sincerely. I was observing all these things with a big surprise. In the court, whenever the coach whistled, in the beginning, players used to continue to play without understanding the meaning of it. Coach started giving them punishment for not stopping the play after hearing the whistle and for not going to the coach immediately. Punishment was like pushing the wheelchair front and back 20 times at the edge of the court. I was concerned that players might feel bad. But they felt happy for being punished like any other person. We, persons with disabilities, don't like to get special treatment. After the punishment, players learnt to stop playing immediately and rush to the coach without any delay. Players didn't take the help of translators much. The coach and players started interacting with each other mostly through body language.

I could see a sea change in their attitude in just seven days. Their faces were glowing with beautiful smiles and confidence. They were shouting to call their teammates by name and were learning leadership skills. I realized how sports could teach in a joyous way the very important lessons of life within a short time. We didn't even know that we were learning such important and necessary lessons. I really wonder how anyone can say that sports are not a part of education and how much time it would generally take to teach these lessons in a classroom atmosphere. It was enlightening for me. Although we read such things in books, learning them by personally experiencing them is altogether a different perspective.

Basketball coaches and a volunteer from Cognizant, Thayumana, participated in the camp and learnt tips. We invited Corporation Commissioner, Mr Vikram, for that camp and explained the need for making the infrastructure facilities accessible. He was very much impressed with our presentation. He called his engineers and ordered them to follow our suggestions to make J. J. Stadium, which was under his control, accessible. Later, Manoj, Anand and

I went there and provided our suggestions. After that, they arranged ramps at the entrance of the stadium and made one toilet wheelchair accessible.

British Deputy High Commissioner (BDHC) Mr Bharat Joshi's office is just beside my office. I sought his appointment and met him at his office to invite him for our camp. He accepted my invitation graciously. We had Mr Joshi and Mr Narsa Reddy for the closing ceremony. We usually request the guests to sit in a wheelchair and play with us for some time. It helps the guests to understand the challenges and experience the fun of playing basketball sitting in a wheelchair. Many guests used to think that specifications of court size, basket height or ball size may be less compared to running basketball. But both are the same. After attending our events, they used to understand that this is quite more challenging than 'running' basketball.

After seeing the benefits of the camp, we thought that it should not be stopped with Chennai and should reach the entire country. So we thought that it would be nice to have a national federation. We had a meeting with all the well-wishers at Anand's institute before Manoj left India. I invited Kalyani too. After having all the discussions, we formed WBFI, with me as president, Kalyani as secretary general, Preetha as treasurer, Shanthy as joint secretary, Anand as technical director, Rajasekharan and player Jagannathan as EC members and players Dinesh and Arul as members. We gave much importance to having women and the persons with disabilities as office-bearers and members to the maximum extent possible. Other non-disabled members in the executive committee also had great passion to work for the persons with disabilities and also gain knowledge in the field of disability. We framed our bye-laws and got it registered.

We used Anand's institute's address for our office address. Anand gave us some space to keep our files in his office. We used to have our meetings in his office. Our members informed me that they could contribute in doing the work related to our federation in their respective areas of specializations. But with regard to raising funds, they suggested that I take care and promised to extend support wherever it was possible for them. I accepted it without even knowing the challenges involved in it.

My First Air travel

My niece Pavani was blessed with a baby girl Prathulya in August 2014. To see the baby, we planned to go to Hyderabad. Till that time, we used to travel by train. But due to the deterioration in my energy levels, I felt it very difficult to enter into the train. Earlier I used to hold the rods at the entrance and try to sit on the stool that I take along with me. I also used to go to the toilets using a walker in train journeys. In one such journey, while I was walking, I could not control and fell down. Later, I tried to avoid going to toilets in trains by holding nature calls hours together. As I found it difficult to manage long journeys in trains, to go to Hyderabad we booked tickets in a flight. In my childhood, watching airplanes in the sky was super fun and exciting. I got a window seat. I enjoyed watching clouds being so close to me. But the seating arrangement in economy class was very narrow. From that time, all my long journeys have been only by air. For short distances, I go by car. In that way, I am avoiding buses and trains, as accessibility is a big challenge.

Partner from the Inception

When the International Committee of the Red Cross (ICRC) Physical Rehabilitation Project Manager Roberto and his colleague Anil came to Chennai, Kalyani and I met them. We explained to them all our efforts so far in arranging training camps and our wish to promote this sport across the country. They were very much impressed with our sincere efforts. I was personally very much impressed with their concern to make me feel comfortable in each and every aspect like in selecting the hotel and the table reserved for us. I think we had our meeting in an auspicious moment. Partnership between ICRC and WBFI, which began in 2014, has been growing from strength to strength since then.

Efforts Culminated in the First Nationals

WBFI has organized camps at six different places, and I have been supporting WBFI and swimming activities through our trust with the limited funding we have from my relatives, friends and ex-students.

We put a lot of effort to get the contacts in different parts of the country and coordinate with them to arrange camps. Due to lack of funding, we could not go to those places in advance. Hence, we had to explain all the things over the phone and through emails only. One can imagine the difficulties involved in organizing camps with new local partners that too for a new sport with so many accessibility-related requirements and without any personal pre-event visits.

Kalyani, Anand and I went to different camps. I went to Delhi along with Anand. That was the first time I travelled without being accompanied by any of my family members. Dad told Anand several times to take care of me. Airlines staff took care of all the things. As Anand was with me, I also didn't feel that I was travelling alone. After reaching Delhi, ICRC arranged a vehicle for us to reach Indian Spinal Injury Centre (ISIC). It was a very accessible place. They gave me a room in their guest house and also appointed a person to take care of my needs. They have their own hospital. They have a hydrotherapy pool as well. They provide all rehabilitation services. We arranged a camp in Amarjyoti School as well. They support kids with disabilities in studies and sports. In the evening, we conducted a roundtable conference with all the stakeholders at ISIC. Through our friends, we could invite many guests. All the coaches also participated in it. It was a great get-together. Coaches from abroad shared their experiences in promoting the sport.

I went to the Pune camp with Jess Markt. The Paraplegic Rehabilitation Centre (PRC) is in Pune. Army officials arranged this rehab centre for their ex-staff who were injured on duty and became wheelchair users. They encourage their residents to participate in all types of sports.

Local organizers received us at the airport and took us to the hotel. They appointed a girl to be with me. She came from an agency which arranges caretakers for people with ailments. For her, all the people sitting in wheelchairs were patients. While coming from PRC in the evening, she told me that she was surprised to see all the patients playing very fast. I could not understand what she was saying in the first instance. When I enquired where she was working, only then I realized why she was thinking our players to be patients. I tried my level best to make her understand that all the people sitting in wheelchairs were not patients. But I doubt whether I was successful in my effort or not.

PRC is like a world for the persons with disabilities. All the facilities there were very much accessible. I felt like I came to a different world. Generally, wherever I go I have to think about so many things related to accessibility. But at PRC, I did not have to worry about anything. They have a swimming pool and a basketball court as well.

While returning to Chennai, at the Pune airport, Jess kept our luggage in a trolley and some other small things in his lap. He started pushing his wheelchair and trolley. After going some distance, he looked back for me. I was far away from him. I could not push my wheelchair. It was heavier. He came back and started pushing my wheelchair from the back. He managed to push my chair to lessen my strain, pushing his chair and trolley all at a time. Some people offered us help. But he rejected it very politely. I was in a pleasant shock observing all these as they were very new to me. I never knew that a person sitting in a wheelchair could be this fit to efficiently manage multiple things simultaneously. It's a pleasant memory for me.

A day after reaching Chennai, we started our camp. Kalyani, Mark and Manoj completed their camp at Bengaluru and came to Chennai.

At Bengaluru, Paralympic Committee of India officials helped us in arranging the camp. My office supported in arranging the camp there. They also sent volunteers. We organized another camp at Vellore CMC rehabilitation centre.

We also arranged a roundtable conference in Chennai. Again, with so much effort, we could gather information on the experts from different fields related to sports and invited representatives from every field and got their RSVPs. Dr Sumanth Raman, a very well-known sports commentator, moderated the discussion. He also spoke in the international seminar arranged by us earlier.

We invited all the teams who had undergone training in five states to have our first national championship. Simultaneously, we also organized a corporate championship. We wanted to create awareness about this sport among corporates too. We trained running basketball players of four corporates in playing wheelchair basketball and arranged a championship for them. Those participants told us that they enjoyed playing basketball sitting in a wheelchair, though it was quite challenging.

Five states' men's teams and three women teams with all state players participated in this championship. Maharashtra won the championship, and Cognizant won the corporate championship. Honourable Governor of Tamil Nadu Mr Rosaiah graced the closing ceremony. The event went very well. On our request, the SDAT member secretary made arrangements for the accommodation with accessible toilets.

We were extremely tired after making the arrangements for eight camps, two roundtable conferences and one national championship simultaneously within a few days' time. But it gave us great confidence. Till that time, I was coordinating for the events in Tamil Nadu. For the first time, I got a great exposure to coordinate with people across India and with coaches from abroad. ICRC and Manoj helped us in bringing coaches from abroad. Later, as Manoj concentrated on other activities in some other countries, he could not continue to work with us.

Daily Quotes

One day, in my office canteen, I met Ramdas, who worked in a different department. It seems that he had heard a lot about me. He appreciated me for my efforts to support fellow persons with disabilities to take up sports. At that time, he told me that he used to share nice quotes with some of our colleagues every day. He told me if I was interested, he would include my name in the mailing list. From that time onwards till date, I receive emails from him every morning with a very good quote. I start my office work only after reading his quote. The quotes sent by him would uplift my mood whenever it is off. Even after retirement, he continues to practise this very religiously, without fail. He won't even expect a thank you in return.

Kerala Visit with Parents and Siblings' Families

We went on a trip to Kerala, God's Own Country, a very beautiful state about which I had heard a lot. It was a long pending wish to visit it. I went with my parents, siblings and their families. We went to Munnar, Alleppy, Kumarakom and Guruvayur and had a wonderful time there. We stayed in a boathouse for one night and one day. It was an amazing experience. It was my dream to spend time on a boat on a full-moon night. During the day, we all sat on the top floor of the boathouse and played many games and watched the beautiful scenery. Munnar[3] is a very beautiful hill station. We all enjoyed that trip a lot.

Visit to Ujjain

When we went for the 14th National Para Swimming Championship to Indore, we went to Ujjain as it was nearby. Since my childhood,

---

[3] Munnar: The name Munnar is derived from the combination of Tamil words *mun* and *aar*, which means three rivers that are flowing in that area.

I have read many stories about the kings in Ujjain and the great Sanskrit poet Kalidasa. The moment we entered that place, I got goosebumps. It was a very different feeling. It's a great place on both spiritual and historical sides. We went to many temples in that place including Lord Shiva's temple and Goddess Bhadrakali temple.

30

Year 2015: Growing My Network, Learning the Ropes from Experts and Chennai Floods

Year 2015 was an eventful year for us with so many vivid experiences such as participating in an international governance meet (IWBF Asia Oceania Zone [AOZ]-level conference) held in Japan, organizing a national championship outside Chennai, growing my network through various talks and facing the impact of devastating Chennai floods.

Developing Technical Expertise in Wheelchair Basketball

I attended India's country strategy stakeholder workshop of the Leprosy Mission Trust India in Delhi. My sister Anantham accompanied me. I had a nice interaction with people from different organizations and different countries working for people with leprosy and people with disabilities. I brought to their notice the importance of promoting adaptive sports. After my talk, they all asked me many questions about the achievements and challenges in promoting adaptive sports.

As we didn't have enough funding for our WBFI, we were not able to travel to other places to approach sports officials and other stakeholders in different places in the country. Hence, whenever anyone invites me for any talk, I always try to use the opportunity. I used the Delhi visit to meet the then Director General (DG) of the Sports Authority of India (SAI), Mr Injeti Srinivas. I met him along with ICRC officials and explained all the efforts made by us to promote para swimming and wheelchair basketball. He was very impressed with all our efforts. I requested him for his permission to arrange the 2nd nationals at Indira Gandhi Indoor Stadium, Delhi. He advised me to go and see the stadium, and we visited it. It's very much accessible with ramps at all the entrances and with accessible toilets. The stadium has very good wooden courts.

Sports wheelchairs which we use to play wheelchair basketball are meant for indoor wooden courts. And also playing on indoor courts gives protection to the players from severe injuries when compared to the cement courts. In our country, there are only a few indoor basketball courts. Most of the owners of these facilities think that wheelchairs would damage their court. It's always a big challenge for us to convince them. Luckily, as SAI officials were very supportive, we didn't have any challenges in that aspect.

Unfortunately, accessible accommodation was not available in that stadium. We decided to try for accommodation at other places. Our intention was to arrange the events every year in different places to create awareness about wheelchair basketball across India.

On the way to the airport, our car driver showed us Qutub Minar. I saw ramps there. Hence, my sister Anantham could take me to all the places there. Thanks to all the disability rights activists for their tireless efforts to make the environment more inclusive.

While returning to Chennai, on the flight, I had a conversation with the person sitting next to me. During the conversation, I shared my story with him and our efforts to promote swimming and wheelchair basketball. He was very impressed with all our activities. I came to know that he was Mr Ishari Ganesh, the chancellor of Vels University. He promised to extend his support to us. Later, he kept his promise and supported the courses we conducted for our wheelchair basketball coaches/classifiers/referees. We usually see such incidents in movies, but it happened in my life. As we are very ambitious to have many useful programmes for our players without having even the minimum resources, to make them successful, I always think about ways to bring support for our events.

With the support of our partner ICRC, we planned to conduct courses for coaches/classifiers/referees of wheelchair basketball. As this sport is new in India, we wanted to develop technical expertise in India. ICRC accepted to bring coach Jess Markt and take care of all the arrangements for him. Our federation was required to find the participants and arrange the venue, accommodation, food, etc. We could reserve the SDAT court and accommodation. Vels University chancellor (whom I met in the flight) supported us for SDAT stadium-related expenses and food. The main challenge was to find interested participants for the courses. We approached the Basketball Federation of India officials, our well-wishers like Jayashankar Menon and our volunteer coaches. We also shared the notification on our social media. Anand helped in finding classification course participants. A few participants from Nepal also requested us to allow them as they didn't have any such programme in their country. Local players also participated during these courses. Our friend Amar from R. R. Donnelley, an MNC, also participated in the referee course. ARR Media Works made documentary films on these courses. Watching those informative videos with the demonstration by our Indian players for the first time was a proud experience for all of us.

Participation in a Conference Outside India

After getting affiliation with International Wheelchair Basketball Federation (IWBF), we received an invitation to participate at our zonal-level conference which was to be held in Chiba, Japan. We would love to participate in it as we would get a chance to witness the performance of other teams in our zone, learn the best practices other federations were following, meet and update the IWBF officials about our efforts to promote the sport in India and seek their support and guidance. But to get support for the events itself is very difficult and, now, finding support for a foreign travel would be a more challenging task. We tried with many people, but no one was able to extend support. Finally, with the support of my well-wishers, we supported this travel through our YWTC Trust, as we very well knew that this participation would bring more support for our country. Our EC decided to send Kalyani and me to participate in this conference.

As we had limited funding for this journey, we tried to get an economic hotel with the support of our member Raja's friends, instead of staying in the hotel arranged by the organizers. Generally, I travel with my stool to all the places as I am not sure about the accessibility part of the toilets. But Raja requested his friends to buy a stool and send it to the hotel where we were going to stay to avoid carrying the stool all the way to Chiba.

With a layover at Hong Kong, we reached Japan. As the toilets in the flight would be narrow, I used to avail toilet facilities in the airports only. I saw the train station within the airport, for the first time in my life. We didn't book any taxi as it would be expensive and also going by public transport would give more exposure to the country and their culture. We confidently took that decision as we heard a lot about how accessible Japan is for wheelchair users.

We went to the Metro officials after buying the ticket. After seeing me in a wheelchair, one staff member brought something with him and asked us to follow him. As most of them didn't speak English, we conversed with each other through gestures only. We didn't know what item he was carrying in his hands. He took us to a place and was waiting. Later, the train arrived and stopped right in front of us. He opened the item he was having with him. It was a detachable and foldable ramp. With that, he connected the platform with the coach. He brought me inside and left us there. We were very much amazed with the facility and support from their staff.

Later, we were worried on how to manage at the destination as they didn't know that we needed support. But by the time we reached the destination, there was a person ready with the ramp again and helped us to come out. We were surprised by their efficient communication between stations. At that time also, we feared that the train might start before we deboarded. Later, we came to know that the information of passengers with disabilities on board would be available with the driver. Till those passengers deboarded, the train wouldn't start. I felt so happy for their concern. Their staff helped us to push my wheelchair. At that time, I asked them to tell where our hotel was by showing the hotel reservation email. He took us through an elevator which directly led to the hotel. I was surprised as I did not expect that the Metro station and hotel would be in the same (connected) building.

Some more surprises were awaiting us at the hotel, both positive and negative. The hotel staff told us that due to some confusion, the one and only accessible room in that hotel was available for us for only two nights. It was booked on someone else's name for the third day. So we had to adjust and move to another room on the third day. The entrance of the room was narrow, and my wheelchair would not fit through the door. With the support of a stool which was sent by Raja's friend, I went inside. We suggested to the hotel to arrange for a small wheelchair that could pass through the doors. In that room, the toilet and bathroom had sensors. When we went inside, the lights turned on automatically. The bathtub in the room had handles to hold. We couldn't take shower outside the tub. I sat on the stool and took shower, and with the support of the handles, I came out. Alarms were there at many places in the room. In case the person fell at any place, they could press the button to alert the staff.

Meeting IWBF Officials

After taking rest for some time, we went to the stadium. We met IWBF officials and introduced ourselves to them. Till that time, we were contacting them only through emails. They felt very happy to meet the representatives from WBFI in person. IWBF Secretary General Ms Maureen had a detailed discussion with us. We explained all our activities, progress, potential and challenges to her. We sought guidance and support from IWBF to promote wheelchair basketball in a more professional way in India. She promised to guide us. We interacted with the teams and their officials. Other IWBF officials also spoke to us. We observed the matches for some time. We were very much excited to see such a big stadium with good accessibility.

It was a feast for our eyes to see tough competitive matches. We were astonished to see the very good level of fitness maintained by those players. We wondered when our Indian team would participate in such a championship. It was a great pleasure for us to meet our coach Jess there. He brought the Afghanistan team to participate in that championship. It was their maiden participation at such a competition, and they were very enthusiastic. We introduced ourselves to every team and tried to learn some points from their coaches, officials and players.

We went around the stadium. We observed that the parking slots were given for each country's team to park their teams' sports wheelchairs. Teams which were not playing locked their chairs in their parking slot. While entering the stadium at the registration desk, they gave us a souvenir on the championship. It contained all the details about the teams and the schedule. We also observed the facilities for wheelchair maintenance and medical support. We noted down all the good points we observed there. Every match started on time. Overall, it was a great learning experience for us.

We asked the people in the stall for water. They showed us a place where we could buy water. We were surprised. Because in India, we are habituated to supply everything at free of cost in the events related to persons with disabilities. But there we had to pay to avail any facility. When I went to the restroom there, I accidentally pressed the alarm. Immediately their staff came running and tried to break the door. Luckily, Kalyani was waiting outside. So with great effort she conveyed to them through gestures that it happened by mistake, as she knew our challenges. All the instructions on the buttons were in Japanese, and we were unable to understand.

Later in the evening, we went to a place which was the highest building from where one could see the Chiba port. Kalyani and I had a nice time there. She helped me a lot to push the wheelchair. As my wheelchair was heavy, I found it very difficult to push it. After coming down, we realized that we left our handbag on the top floor. After I sat in the taxi, Kalyani went inside. By that time, they were closing it. She requested and went to the top floor. Fortunately, our bag was there. Down in the car I was worried as our passports and money were in that bag. And I was also scared that the taxi might leave before Kalyani's arrival (as I remembered the general tendencies told by my dad regarding the safety of women). After a few minutes, Kalyani came there gasping.

It was night by the time we reached the hotel. Surprisingly, they had arranged a small wheelchair as suggested by us to enter the room. Kalyani had brought ready-to-eat food items from India to save money and also as we were not sure about the type of food that we would get there.

Next morning, we went to the hotel to attend the conference, my maiden experience of participating in such an event. While speakers were presenting, I saw that some people were cross-talking.

I wondered why they were doing so. Later I came to know that they were the translators who were translating the speech into their respective languages. During the break, we interacted with IWBF President Ulf Mehrens, other officials and the representatives of the national federations from other countries. We invited IWBF officials for our forthcoming 2nd national championship to be held in Delhi and requested them to guide us on the technical part of conducting such events. They graciously accepted our request. The Thailand Federation president showed interest in sending their players to our country if we could arrange local accommodation and food for their players. He was ready to take care of their travel expenses. We thought of inviting them to an event.

We were hungry but didn't want to try in that expensive hotel. So we decided to go to a '7-Eleven' store and buy bread. We started walking (I mean Kalyani on foot helping me in pushing my chair). We asked a person on the road for the store location. He told us that it was very near. But we walked a long distance to reach there. On the way, two people came to us. After seeing us, they understood that we are Indians. They told us that they had been to India for some project. They spoke in English, and one of them also spoke in Tamil. We felt very happy. We bought bread and went to a railway station to go to a temple. The railway staff there also helped us in a similar way. There was no direct train to that temple. We had to change in between. The staff took us from one station to the other where we could catch our next train to the temple and handed over us to their staff. To go via steps, there was a box-like arrangement (open at the top). If we went into that box with the wheelchair, they would close the door for our safety and operate it with a remote. I enjoyed that experience a lot.

We went to the temple just before its closing time. But I could not go inside as we could not find fast access to the accessible entrance. I told Kalyani to go and get darshan. She could visit it just in the nick of time. We however had a lot of fun outside and met our Indian Navy officials. Apparently, their ship had reached Chiba seaport. We took photos with them.

While returning to the hotel, after entering the train at the first station, we were trying to take photos in the train. To get a better pose, I unlocked the break and tried to move to a better place. Within no time, I fell down. We didn't realize how fast the train was moving till that time. Immediately, Kalyani and all other passengers helped me to sit back in the chair. After that, we went to another station to catch the train to our hotel. At that time, we realized that Kalyani's spectacles were missing. We requested the staff to go back to the first station. They took us there. We went there to file a complaint. It was really a big challenge to explain to them the story in sign language. One of the staff at the hotel where we stayed knew a little bit of English. Hence, we requested them to call that person by giving his visiting card. They called him. We spoke to him and requested him to convey the matter to the railway officials. Finally, they registered our complaint and after investigation they informed us that they could not find any such item. We came back to the hotel in a sad mood. Later, when I was trying to get up from the wheelchair, I saw the spectacles in the wheelchair itself. They might have fallen in the chair when I fell down in the train. We both heaved a sigh of relief and started laughing remembering all our challenges in making them understand our complaint. In that journey, it's an unforgettable memory for us.

Next day was our return flight. We shifted to another room as informed by the hotel staff. As it was not an accessible room, there were no handles to the bathtub. As I could not take bath in that tub, I skipped the bath. Before going to the airport, we thought of having at least one meal at the hotel. We went to a big hotel complex. When we asked for vegetarian food, the staff called for a huddle to understand what vegetarian food is. We tried our level best to make them understand. Finally, they found one Chinese restaurant that served vegetarian dishes and accompanied us to reach there. We observed that Japanese are very friendly and supportive. If we ask for any help, they wouldn't leave until they finish it. Even if we tell them not to bother, they wouldn't listen to us. Particularly for persons with disabilities, everyone will come forward to help if we seek support. I didn't feel any fear there, though we were new to that place and without any knowledge of the local language. We developed great respect for the Japanese after seeing their courteous behaviour.

We tried to take a bus ride to the airport, thinking that it would be accessible. But it was not. They lifted and made me sit in my seat in the bus. I didn't feel comfortable with it. Had we known about it, we would have booked a taxi. But I got the opportunity to observe their bus driver's patience and the technical facilities available in that bus.

We flew in through one airport and flew out from another. Both the airports are very big. It was a great learning for us in all aspects.

2nd National Championship in Delhi and the Chennai Floods

After meeting the SAI DG in Delhi, we started working on the conduct of the 2nd nationals in Delhi. We got permission to arrange the event at SAI stadium free of cost. The DG and other officials were very supportive. For us, the next biggest challenge was to arrange for accessible accommodation for our players. We tried with local NGOs and Social Justice department officials. But all those accommodations were available for only a few people. Our requirement was for around 160 people. We also tried with nearby hotels, but they were expensive. Moreover, the hotels were not accessible. Our coach Varun suggested a hotel, which was 15 km (~9.3 mi) away. ICRC officials helped us a lot to go and verify the accessibility in those accommodations. It was a 4-star hotel and was accessible to a great extent. Finally, with the support of ICRC officials and coach Varun, we could finalize that hotel at a very reasonable cost. ICRC officials had a session with the hotel staff to sensitize them about disability. They sent us all the details such as the width of the doors at rest rooms, slant angle of ramps and elevator entrance door width to share with our teams, so that they could come prepared to stay in that place.

We could finalize two major things. But so many other things were still required to be arranged. As our partner Cognizant had an office in Gurgaon, we requested them to extend volunteering support. They happily accepted it. Next one was transport. We approached Delhi Metro officials with a request to provide us a few accessible buses. They accepted. Some items were supported by our local partners ISIC, Amarjyoti, etc. Raising funds for transport, food, transport of wheelchairs from Chennai to Delhi and return, etc., became a big challenge. We struggled a lot. In the final moment, when I approached my friend Veeru Murugappan, whom I met during one talk, he arranged for some monetary help. We made arrangements for an ambulance, medical help desk, wheelchair maintenance, etc.

We came to know from IWBF that five senior officials were planning to come for our event. As the classification officer Toufic was among them, we planned to have a course on classification. Neeraj helped us in inviting the participants for the course.

We worked restlessly in fulfilling the tasks, for instance, getting applications from the teams, teams' arrival and departure details, number of regular wheelchairs and sports wheelchairs to arrange transport and to make some other arrangements. SAI officials deputed their basketball coaches to help us.

For wheelchair basketball, sports wheelchairs are the prime requirement. Cost of these chairs varies. It goes up to lakhs of rupees when we go for high-performance customized sports wheelchairs. We couldn't go for such expensive chairs. To begin with, we needed to have a basic model chair at a reasonable cost. Fortunately, Motivation UK has been manufacturing sports wheelchairs at a very reasonable cost (around ₹40,000 per chair) with good quality. We could spread this sport to new places only because of those chairs. Otherwise, buying chairs spending lakhs of rupees to spread this sport would be a very big challenge in a country like India where most of the parents think that sport is only a futile activity. For a federation like us, having sports wheelchairs to arrange the events and to store them is also a very big challenge. Unless we get a place to keep the chairs in the proper way, all the chairs would get damaged. As these chairs are not available in India, we had to import them from another country. Sometimes as it takes time to import, donors may go back as they want to utilize the amount immediately.

We ordered for medals and trophies in Chennai itself as the cost would be less. R. R. Donnelley has been extending support for designing our publicity material from the beginning. We planned to bring out a souvenir on our championship. We saw it at the Asia Oceania Zone Championship held at Chiba. Kalyani worked a lot on this. I worked on bringing messages from the officials and our well-wishers and some other details. Kalyani worked with R. R. Donnelley's team and technical commissioner and coordinated with state teams to get all the teams' details and fixtures. It came out very well. It was released by SAI DG in the opening ceremony.

Just before our trip to Delhi, there were continuous rains in Chennai. Due to the rains, it used to take three hours for me to reach home from the office which was 7 km away. Generally, if I go on a long trip, I go along with my parents. I don't want to leave them alone in Chennai. I booked tickets for them at personal expense. Kalyani and I wanted to go first to Delhi to make arrangements. Shanthy had left already. Our coach Thayu and Anand had planned to come the next day. The vendor told me that he could deliver them the next day at the earliest. So I told him to deliver them to Anand. By the time we started, it was raining heavily. In that heavy rain, medal vendor Chetan came and delivered the medals on the same day after we sat in a taxi. At that time, we didn't know that had he waited to deliver to Anand, we would have missed those medals. On the way to the airport, we saw a car floating in the water. All the roads were overflowing with water. With great effort, our taxi driver took us to the airport. Our flight was the last one that left Chennai airport. Later, the airport was shut down due to heavy rains and floods in Chennai.

Whenever I remember that incident, my heartbeat would stop for a few seconds. Had we not gone to Delhi, how the situation would have been in Chennai! For almost 10 days, Chennaites faced so many challenges due to power cuts and floods. Several people died due to floods. One of our well-wishers, who addressed our swimmers during one of our camps, also died in those floods along with his wife. The situation was very scary. I could not call my neighbours and staff to know whether they were safe, as no phones were working. Many of our well-wishers from other places called us to enquire about our safety, thinking that we were in Chennai. Anand and coach Thayu could not come, as no transport was available from Chennai. As players from Chennai and Shanthy started early, luckily, they could reach Delhi.

If any event happens in Chennai, I take my automatic wheelchair to the venue so that I move independently. But I could not bring the automatic wheelchair to Delhi. I feel comfortable moving in a sports wheelchair rather than a regular wheelchair. But as we had only a few sports wheelchairs, even those would not be available for most of the time. We invited all the officials and other supporters. The hotel was on the border of the states Uttar Pradesh (UP) and Delhi, and we came to know that the hotel came under UP and for movement of buses between two states, special permission was required. I was at the stadium to take care of the arrangements there, and Kalyani had gone for such approvals and for other work outside. As our other members were unable to come, we three strained a lot. Kalyani had to manage all the work where mobility was required. ICRC officials also helped us a lot.

IWBF officials reached Delhi. The secretary general took care of the technical part. Rarely do we see such an energetic person. Even at the age of 70 years, she used to work actively from morning to late night. Every night she used to arrange meetings after dinner to discuss the arrangements for the next day. We might be tired, but we never saw tiresomeness on her face. First time she introduced us to

3-on-3 matches.[1] As we had very few female players, she introduced it for female players. Mr Abraham Poulose, a senior referee, assisted her with regard to technical matters. After that, we appointed him as the technical commissioner for all our championships. He took care of that part meticulously.

Toufic took care of the classification course part and guided the participants to classify our players while matches were happening. Classification is grouping of players according to their functional abilities. In wheelchair basketball sport, points start from 1 to 4.5 (in increments of 0.5). Total points of five players should not exceed 14 points at any point of time. In that way, it would be a fair play between both the teams. For the opening ceremony, Mr Srinivas, SAI DG, Mr Bharat Joshi, BDHC, Chennai and other guests were present. All the guests spoke in a very supportive manner. The closing ceremony was graced by the Minister for Social Justice, Government of India, and other dignitaries.

Second National Championship—Souvenir Release by DG, SAI Mr Srinivas. BDHC Mr Bharat Joshi, officials from IWBF, ICRC, Motivation UK, Amar Jyoti School and Kalyani were present

[1] The regular basketball matches have two teams, with each team comprising five players. The 3-on-3 matches have three members in each team.

Disability rights activist Mr Javed Abidi also graced the event. He felt very happy to see the performance of our players. He said that when he saw wheelchair basketball played by US players, he thought whether it would be possible for our Indian persons with disabilities. He said that he felt immensely happy to see his dream come true. Volunteering support from Cognizant won the hearts of all the participants. I sincerely feel that the success of all our events mainly depended on the selfless support from the volunteers. Maharashtra, Punjab and Tamil Nadu stood at 1st, 2nd and 3rd positions, respectively. We learnt many things from Maureen and other IWBF officials. They were very much impressed with our efforts and with the enthusiasm of our players. They told us that they were working on a project with the support of Agitos Foundation with the intention to encourage developing countries like India (with regard to wheelchair basketball) in developing technical expertise. They told us if we were able to bring participants from across India and make arrangements for accommodation, venue, food, etc., they would start their project with India. We discussed with our members and accepted their proposal.

We are used to taking up very challenging tasks without having any confirmed support, either in swimming or in wheelchair basketball, considering the enormous benefits derived from these efforts to our players. Later, by putting many sincere efforts and with the support of many well-wishers, we have been completing the tasks successfully at the end. But it gives us a lot of mental strain. With regard to team games, as we all know, a lot of coordination is required and it is more expensive too. Team game for wheelchair users would be more challenging, considering inaccessible infrastructure facilities and transport facilities in our country. Some people told me that it was foolish to take up such tasks without having confirmed support. But for this type of task, we cannot expect people to come forward and pour support as there was minimal awareness on the benefits of adaptive sports in our country. I don't mind if someone calls me a fool. Sometimes only fools can take up Herculean tasks that are otherwise deemed impossible.

The Taj Mahal Visit

As our flights were postponed due to floods in Chennai, we had to stay back for two more days. We went to the Taj Mahal along with IWBF Secretary General Maureen. It was a dream for me to see the Taj Mahal. The journey was also an unforgettable one. We started early in the morning. As we were new to Delhi, we experienced the fog completely blocking visibility on roads for the first time. We could not understand how the driver could drive the car in that poor visibility. On the way, we even saw an accident. We were nervous throughout the journey but finally reached safely. It was a fantastic and pleasant feeling to see such a marvellous monument. We took some photos. But I could not go inside. People need to wear shoe covers to go inside to protect the monument, which is facing structural erosion. In such a situation, how could they allow a wheelchair. I sent my parents and Maureen inside. Generally, my parents wouldn't leave me alone in such a situation. But I insisted that they go as Maureen was also there. Maureen also felt bad to leave me behind and go inside.

From there, on the way back, we went to Lord Krishna's temple at Mathura (birthplace of Lord Krishna). I wanted to stay there for some more time. But we had to leave as Maureen needed to catch her flight. To my surprise, the temple was very much accessible, and the staff there were also very supportive. They were in a mood to show me all the places in the temple. Unfortunately, we could spend only a little time there. If possible, I want to go there once again and spend some time leisurely in that peaceful atmosphere in future.

Next evening, we left for Chennai. Upon arrival, we saw the after-effects of the floods, as quite a few places were still immersed in water. We also heard some tragic stories where the water flowed into houses suddenly at midnight when people were sleeping and had very little time to realize and escape. All these stories were heartbreaking but, at the same time, it was heartening to see humanity on rise as people from all backgrounds came forward to help their fellow beings selflessly. I could not physically help the needy but did my part in contributing financially to those who helped them directly.

Learning a New Sport: Rifle Shooting

I participated in a national conference on CSR and sports as a panellist in a panel discussion on 'expectations of sports federations' along with other Olympic sports federations, which was held in Delhi. The conference was organized by SAI, Federation of Indian Chambers of Commerce and Industry (FICCI) and Vision Foundation.

I discussed with the Artificial Limbs Manufacturing Corporation of India (ALIMCO) chairman the need for manufacturing sports wheelchairs in India. Even today we are importing sports wheelchairs from other countries. He told me that unless we place an order for at least 500 chairs, it would be difficult for them to take up the task. It's impossible for us to give an order for 500 chairs even today.

It was an opportunity for me to bring to the notice of all related stakeholders the requirements of paralympic sports. I explained to them the challenges we faced in arranging accessible accommodation for our players during the 2nd nationals in the capital of the country. I sought the support of all the participants to provide support in whatever way possible for them.

Mr Vipen Vig, a shooting sports solution specialist, immediately promised to support persons with disabilities in learning shooting. I shared this information on my Facebook and advised interested people to approach me. I received messages from some people expressing their interest to learn shooting. I connected with them all through a WhatsApp group. As my schedule was already packed with swimming and wheelchair basketball activities, I asked the interested people to take the lead in this initiative. Later, Mr Vipen arranged a camp in Delhi for them. This is a very good example of the positive side of social media.

Later in 2016, we conducted a shooting camp in Chennai. I also participated in the camp and learnt rifle shooting. On the last day, they conducted a test in which I got the highest points. Coaches told me that I would have a good possibility to go to international level if I practise sincerely. But due to my job and responsibilities as a sports administrator, I could not take it forward, though I liked it very much. Later, some of the participants from these camps went to national- and international-level competitions and won medals.

Car Modifications: When Existing Support Takes a Step Back

At that time, I was trying to change my car as it became very old. When I approached the same company, they told me that they had only auto-gear vehicles and were not ready to do any other modifications like earlier. And if we arrange for the modifications after buying the car, they said that they couldn't give warranty. I felt that it was not fair. I sent an email to them saying either they needed to modify or allow their authorised dealers or manufacturing engineers or any organization approved by the government to modify. Otherwise, they needed to extend warranty if we go with outsiders for modification in the absence of any arrangement from them in this regard. But every time they gave a standard reply saying that they had the auto-gear option and disregarded all my other questions/suggestions.

I met the senior official in the Social Justice department in Delhi, shared the correspondence with the car-manufacturing company with him and sought his support. But no further progress could be made in this matter. I also could not follow up on this. Later, I bought a car in 2016 from Hyundai company, who agreed to provide warranty if we went with a government-approved organization for modification.

31

Year 2016: Honouring of My Mother

The new year started with some nice experiences. One day, at the swimming pool, one lady official from an MNC came to me and told me that she was inspired from one of my talks and decided to take part in water sports. She was taking her first swimming class that day. I felt very happy. In our busy schedule, many people feel that they don't have enough time to do any physical activity. But I feel that everyone should take up some activity to maintain their physical fitness, irrespective of their age.

Once I met Archana's mother, who was 65 years old. She said that she heard a lot about me from her daughter. Inspired by my story, she started to go for a walk regularly. And she eventually felt better. She showed me my photo on her phone that she uses to motivate herself whenever she goes off track. To improve her health condition further, she was thinking of learning swimming.

Actually, whenever I come across such inspired people, I get motivated to continue my efforts more.

A R Rahman takes a selfie with the paralympic gold medalist swimmer Madhavi Latha

Selfie with A R Rahman

Meeting the Legendary Music Director Mr A. R. Rahman

I was invited to the Adding Smiles Ambassadors Awards function to receive the 'Built Tough' award. There, I got the opportunity to meet the legendary music director Mr A. R. Rahman, who attended to receive another award. As it would reach a bigger audience, I requested for his support in creating awareness about adaptive sports in my speech. He accepted my request and took a selfie with us and posted on all his social media platforms.

Interview at Radio Station

RJ Sulabha invited me to Radio One 94.3 FM station for an interview. I shared with her my childhood memories about small-sized people being inside the radio. On that day, the naughty child in me thought that I became the lilliput of my childhood innocent imagination by giving a talk from radio.

Mother's Day: Well-deserved Appreciation to My Mom

Every year, Krishna Sweets MD Mr Murali honours mothers of celebrities on the eve of Mother's Day. In 2016, he invited me and

Honouring of Mom (Mr Murali on left in white dress)

my mother along with other family members. Till now, many people have invited me for many programmes. But only the Krishna Sweets team followed all our customs in each and every step. The way they invited, received and honoured us—everything was with great respect and regard and in a very traditional way. It was an unforgettable day for me. I remember the days in my childhood when people passed comments to my parents that my situation was the result of their sins from previous births. But on that day, after I explained in detail how my parents helped me at each and every stage, all the participants and their mothers praised my mom and dad very much. I became so emotional. Thanks to Mr Murali and Krishna Sweets team for recognizing my strength—my parents—and giving my mom the well-deserved appreciation.

Arrangements for the National-level Technical Camp

The next morning, we left for Hyderabad to celebrate my parents' 60th marriage anniversary at my brother's house. Generally, dad doesn't like any celebrations. But we convinced him to celebrate just with our siblings' families. We had a great time.

I used this personal travel also for the purpose of our sport activities. After providing our consent to IWBF officials to arrange a wheelchair basketball national technical camp in India, we were trying to find the venue for this camp. Anyway, as I went to Hyderabad, I wanted to try to find a venue there. I went to the Secretariat along with my nephew Prasanth and met Sports Secretary Mr B. Venkateshwarlu. I explained him our activities and sought his help to arrange the camp in Hyderabad. He was very much positive and advised me to meet the MD of Sports Authority of Telangana State (SATS) and see the basketball court. Later, I met Mr Dinakar Babu, MD, SATS. As their office was upstairs, he came down to meet me. He and his team were very supportive. As suggested by them, I went to Kotla Vijaya Bhaskar Reddy (KVBR) Indoor Basketball Stadium. Mr Ravindra, Stadium Officer, showed me the entire stadium. It was very accessible except for arranging hand bars in bathrooms. There was provision for a medical help desk, and rooms were available for conducting classes for three courses simultaneously. I found it very much suitable for our programme. My heart was filled with overjoy. I never expected that we could find the venue for our camp that easily.

The next requirement was accommodation. Cognizant volunteers came along with me. We went to some nearby hotels. None of them were accessible and were expensive too. Someone suggested that we could consider the National Training Institute, which was situated very close to the stadium. I wanted to go there but couldn't as it was already late and I had to catch an early morning flight to Chennai the next day. Hence, I told the volunteers that I would contact the institute from Chennai and requested them to follow up with the institute later.

Kalyani took care of the accommodation part. Finally, that institute agreed to provide accommodation. However, as it was not accessible, we sought help from Cognizant. Through their vendors, they made that place accessible for wheelchair users. We went back and forth over phone calls with the carpenters to make them understand our requirements. Later, when we went for the event, I was surprised to see the great work done by the carpenters. Rooms were on both sides, and the passageway between those rooms was low lying. We needed to take stairs to access the passageway and again to go in/out of the rooms. Carpenters raised the platform on the passageway with big wooden planks. At both the ends of the passageway, ramps were arranged. With that, the players could happily go to their rooms without any hassle. It was a wooded campus and was like a beautiful forest. Cognizant accepted to take care of local transport for our players. Accommodation was just across the street from the stadium. But we had to go around for 1 km due to the ongoing Metro construction work. Max Cure hospitals arranged a medical help desk and an ambulance. Staff at the stadium and at the accommodation place helped us a lot. ICRC partnered with us for this event.

We could find interested participants from across the country with the support of Basketball Federation of India and some other well-wishers. From each state, we invited a few players who had participated in the previous nationals. At that time, we were trying hard to find participants to represent India in U23 Men's World Championship Qualifiers to be held in Thailand. We gave announcements on our social media platforms and shared the information with NGOs working for persons with disabilities across the country through our contacts.

I told my sister-in-law, Venkata Laxmi, who is working in the Women and child Welfare department to refer some under-23 boys. She could find five boys in the age group of around 17–19 years. She went to their houses in person twice to convince their parents in the hot summer. They were all from lower-middle-class families. Their parents rejected her proposal right away, saying that their children were already in a bad condition due to their disability. Further they said that if they get any injury while participating in sporting events, their condition would become even worse. I asked her to put me on the phone with them so that I could try and convince them. But it seemed that they were not ready to listen. We quit. This is a classic example of how parents' fears could become an obstacle for the bright future of their children. I can understand their feelings very well as my parents also had similar concerns earlier. We cannot expect the change in one day.

Inspired by my 'Yes, We Too Can!!! movement, my sister-in-law arranged early intervention treatment for kids with disabilities as a pilot project for six months. Later, many parents expressed their happiness on the positive changes they observed in their children's health and mobility. They also promised to continue physiotherapy.

IWBF Secretary General Maureen, Technical Commission Chairman Norbert, Classification Officer Toufic and a coach from the UK reached Hyderabad. Sessions went very well. I also participated in the classification course to understand it in a better way. We had a panel discussion with government officials and sport science experts. Maureen moderated it.

In the opening ceremony, the sports secretary promised to provide sports wheelchairs to Telangana players. Later, he kept his promise.

We invited the Thailand team to play an exhibition match with our national team. They accepted our invitation. That was the first international match in wheelchair basketball played in India. Everyone was surprised with the faster movements of the Thai players. Their participation helped us a lot in making all the stakeholders understand the importance of high-performance sports wheelchairs and consistent practice.

For this camp, coaches, classifiers, referees and players came from all over India. Since we got participants through different sources, they didn't know each other. Hence, we called for a meeting with all of them and suggested they form a group with their concerned state participants from all the courses. We asked them to use this camp to know each other and to start thinking about forming a state association for their respective states. We also promised to provide all the guidance required to them. While preparing WBFI bye-laws, in line with it, we prepared draft bye-laws for the state associations too with the intention to guide the people who want to form wheelchair basketball state associations, which could be used as a reference document.

My First TEDx Talk

My first TEDx talk was at SRM Engineering College (TEDx SRM-Ramapuram). It was a different experience, as there was a maximum limit of 18 minutes for each talk. My student Aruna came all the way from Hyderabad just to listen to my speech in person. I felt very happy with her nice gesture.

Meeting Legend Sri Milkha Singh

I was invited as a speaker for Pune International Sports Expo. I had the wonderful opportunity of being honoured by Sri Milkha Singh. He is very supportive. Later, he gave a video statement in support of our U23 players on my request.

I took this opportunity to meet our players at PRC and the Director (Col) Mukherjee. I could also meet many sports science experts there. I met Shiny Surendran, a famous nutritionist. Our friendship has been continuing since then. She has been helping our players by assessing their diet requirements and by providing her valuable advice since then.

Mom and Dad's Health (2016)

One day, my mom got a severe fever and body pains. She took paracetamol.[1] But by the next day, her condition became more severe. At that time, swine flu and dengue were spreading fast. We got scared and took her to the hospital. They asked us to admit her till the test results were out. Dad had to run around between medical shops and different departments of the hospital. He also got fever and body pains by the evening. Even in that stage, they both didn't want to leave me alone. Dad stayed with me at home, and we requested the staff at

---
[1] Paracetamol is a common painkiller used to treat aches and pain.

the hospital to take care of mom for that night. I informed my brother and sister-in-law. They immediately started by train as flight tickets were not available. My neighbour, Thyagaraju uncle, came to help us. Dad's fever was so severe that he was not fully in a conscious state. When uncle[2] asked dad what he wanted for dinner, he told uncle not to worry about him and requested to arrange dinner for me. Dad also told him that if I didn't eat anything, he couldn't sleep. I could not control my tears. Whatever difficult situation they were in, they always thought about me and my comfort only. By next morning, my brother and sister-in-law reached, and it was a great relief for me. Later, test results showed that mom got chicken guinea and dad got a viral fever. We also admitted dad in the hospital. I never saw them admitted in the hospital. After a few days, they both recovered. But mom got knee pain from that time. I will never forget the tension I had till my brother and sister-in-law came. I felt sad for not being able to serve them when they were in need. God is great for giving me such loving and affectionate parents.

Our neighbours sold their house. The new owner gave it for rent. Lakshmi and her daughter Poornima became our immediate neighbours. They are very friendly and supportive. If mom or I fell sick, dad could take care of us. But if dad fell sick, we used to struggle a lot, as he was the only person with better mobility in our house. Mom with her knee pain used to find it very difficult to go to the market, though it was just beside our apartment gate. After Lakshmi became our neighbour, in all such occasions she helped us a lot. She even helped in taking dad to the hospital. Even today, we keep in touch, though we are in different places. Our other neighbours Prasad and Uma also used to help us on such occasions.

New Treasurer for WBFI

As Preetha became busy with her profession, we had to find another treasurer for WBFI. By that time, we felt that it was better to have

---

[2] Uncle: It is a polite way to address others who are equivalent in age to that of your parents' age. Usually, We do not address someone older than us by their name as we consider it impolite; we use aunty or uncle instead.

WBFI Executive Committee Members (till 2020)

Madhavi Latha P — President | Kalyani Rajaraman — Secretary General | Shanthy Ramachandran — Joint Secretary | Vishal Kothari — Treasurer

Ananda Jothi — Technical Director | Rajasekharan P — E C Memeber | Jagannathan D — E C Memeber

WBFI Executive Committee Members (till 2020)

a chartered accountant as the treasurer, considering the accounting work involved for a national federation and the knowledge required to manage the transactions. We approached our well-wisher Deepak CA. He referred Vishal Kothari, CA, his student, to us. Vishal joined us as a professional member and became the treasurer. It's an amazement to see such a youngster with that much social responsibility. It's a great support for WBFI. As we all know, having a sincere, committed and knowledgeable treasurer with integrity is a great boon to any not-for-profit organization.

First State Para Swimming Meet Held outside Chennai

We arranged all three state championships in Chennai, mainly with the support from my office, our patron Mr Narsa Reddy and PVP. For the first time, our Theni District Association came forward to host the state championship. Our coach Mr Vijayakumar took the initiative and got support from local NGOs and local business units. District Collector Mr Venkatachalam (who supported us in Dindigul and got transferred to Theni) helped us a lot in arranging that event.

Our Vice-president Uthira aunty and uncle went by their car. Anand, Sai and I went in Anand's vehicle. I enjoyed that journey very much. Wherever seasonal fruits were available, Anand stopped the vehicle and bought a few. We enjoyed the journey eating those tasty fruits and cracking jokes. I remembered my childhood days.

Theni is a very beautiful place. It's surrounded by hills. Everywhere we can see greenery. The clouds in the mid of the blue sky looked as if they were within our reach. The weather was also very pleasant.

Before entering Theni itself, we saw big hoardings of our event. We felt very happy. We could not make such arrangements earlier. In Theni, local people extended great support with admiration for our swimmers. Thanks a ton to all of them. At the pool, they arranged ramps. The event went very well with very good support from district officials. We didn't know that the event would be the last championship organized by us. Later, due to International Paralympic Committee (IPC) guidelines, the Paralympic Committee of India decided to take care of the four sports which were directly under their control, namely athletics, swimming, powerlifting and shooting. Therefore, they told us to dissolve the separate state associations for swimming. As per their instructions, we dissolved our state association with heavy hearts. Before dissolving, we bought two swimming pool lifts and gave to SDAT to keep at Aquatic Complex in Chennai and Theni swimming pools. The remaining amount was given to Tamil Nadu Para Sports Association.

Overall, I have won around 30 medals in swimming at state and national levels. After that, I concentrated mainly on WBFI activities and didn't participate in any swimming competitions. However, I have been continuing my efforts to promote swimming as an individual through my various presentations.

Offsite with Colleagues

For one of my office-related offsite programmes, I went to a 5-star resort in Chennai. Throughout the day, we were busy with our sessions. In the late evening, we went for dinner. Sitting just beside the sea and having food in a very jovial atmosphere with our colleagues was a wonderful experience. I always love to go near the sea. I enjoyed the cool breeze and the nearness to the sea very much. After dinner, I went to my room. My room was in a different building, as there were no accessible rooms in the building my colleagues stayed in. Generally, accessibility comes with an extra cost. But our trade department head Sadhish gives much importance to the accessibility part. So he made sure that I got an accessible room, though it was very expensive. On the way to my room, I enjoyed the lighting in the night, trees and cool breeze a lot. After dropping me off, the hotel staff asked me to call them if I needed any help. My colleagues asked me whether I needed company. I told them that I could manage by myself. I am habituated to staying alone after I started organizing sporting events. From outside, the cottage looked like a hut and inside it was a luxurious hotel. It had all the accessible facilities there, including shower chair. Curtains could be operated through a remote control. All sides had glass doors covered with curtains. If we opened curtains, we felt as if we were outside. I was very much excited.

On that night, the sea was not visible in the darkness. I woke up at 4:00 am the next morning and took a shower. When I opened the back-side door, I saw a closed place. If we wanted, we could take a bath outside as well, watching the moon and the clouds. By 5:00 am, I was ready and called the hotel staff. The staff took me for a ride of the entire resort on a battery vehicle. Being a nature lover, I enjoyed the beauty of nature in the early morning and took some photos. After coming back, I saw a swing cradle outside my room. I sat there enjoying the nice aroma of my green tea. From there, I could see the sea very well. I met colleagues at the breakfast area. When I told them what I did, they all got surprised. Most of them woke up late, as we went to bed late in the night. After lunch, we left the place. It was a great experience.

My Second Car

After 13 years of buying my first car, I bought my second car, a Hyundai Xcent. It took a few months for me to complete all the formalities like earlier. But Hyundai officials helped me a lot at every stage. I didn't struggle much. This time, an external person, Shankar, modified my car. His organization is approved by the Tamil Nadu government to do modifications. Although I had experience in driving, as the new car had power-steering and more quick acceleration, it took me some time to drive with confidence. Again for a few days, my dad came with me to the office till he was confident that I could drive alone.

Our Experience with a Crowdfunding Platform

With great effort we could find around 20 players under the age of 23 years from across the country. We wanted to organize two training camps for them and later we wanted to send them for U23 World Championship Qualifiers. For that, first of all, we needed to pay registration fees. At that time, we realized we could get support for events in India with a lot of effort. But many organizations were not ready to help with registration fees. We tried a lot. But no support was forthcoming for us.

At that time, someone suggested us to go for crowdfunding. We checked with one entity. They showed a lot of interest and met us in person too. We clearly explained our two requirements to them—first one was registration fee payment and the second one was to make all other arrangements. We also informed them about the deadline to pay the fee. They told us that it was our responsibility to raise 40 per cent of the required total amount in the initial one week or ten days from the starting date, and then the rest would be taken care of by them. We started sharing the link among our contacts and tried our level best to raise the 40 per cent of the amount. But we could only raise a meagre amount.

At that time, I requested one of my journalist friends who works in a popular English daily to write an article about our requirements. She interviewed me and wrote a nice article. Following this, one real estate company owner called me in the early morning. He told me that he was ready to support us with around ₹3 lakh and told me to share the bank account details. I shared this news with our crowdfunding-related group on WhatsApp and informed that I would tell the donor to credit in the crowdfunding link so that they would take into account that amount towards our 40 per cent share. They all congratulated us. We got a great relief as the last date was within two days to make the payment of registration fee.

After crediting the amount into that link, I requested the crowdfunding entity officials to transfer the amount so far collected to our account after deducting their charges. That official replied to me saying that it was not possible as per their rules. He also told me that it was clearly mentioned on their website and asked me whether I had not verified it. I asked them why they didn't alert me about this rule before crediting the amount, even after telling them our requirements daily from the beginning. I felt very bad about it. In spite of requesting a lot to relax their rules as missing the deadline would lose the whole point in raising the funds, he didn't accept it. Later, I had gone through their rules. One rule says that if the donor wants to take back the funds, they could do it within three days. When I asked about it, he told me it was possible. In spite of knowing this possibility, he didn't suggest it till I asked. We requested our donor to take the amount back and give it to us. But for all that to happen, it would take 10 days according to that crowdfunding platform person. As the deadline was fast approaching, I was in tension. It was during Deepavali festival. I was anxious and couldn't celebrate the festival. After seeing my mental state, my ex-student Aruna told me that she would adjust the amount temporarily to meet the deadline.

It was a great learning experience for us. Many a time, while taking any insurance policy, etc., we may sign the document without reading all the terms and conditions. But only when we go for claims, we come to know many conditions in that fine print that are not in our favour. In this case, they spoke so friendly to us and told us so many things but not this point. Finally, it was our mistake that without asking all the relevant questions and getting clarity, we entered into an agreement.

Attempts to Conduct the Nationals in Other States

Our intention was to organize the nationals every year in a different state to create more awareness about this sport across India. We put our sincere efforts to make this happen. But as we could not get the required support, just three weeks before the anticipated date, we had to finalise the venue as Chennai as all our efforts to conduct elsewhere were failed. It was the only possible option, as we are all based in Chennai. The event was a success with the support of all the partners.

Ordeal of Arranging Flight Tickets for Our Players

We decided to arrange for two camps with two weeks' duration each for our U23 players. Sathyabama University came forward to help us again in organizing the camp for our players. Toufic, our AOZ classification officer, came to train our players. When he arrived in Chennai, I invited him to my office to address my colleagues. Our staff felt very happy to meet such an enthusiastic and active person. After lunch, he went to some nearby places in his manual wheelchair just for a ride. I could not even imagine doing such a thing. Later, I realized that their wheelchairs were very expensive and were light-weight. Till that time, I didn't know that manual wheelchairs also had expensive models which cost lakhs of rupees. He used to scold me for taking support from others to push the chair. But still, I am using a heavy-weight, less-expensive chair.

Toufic came from Lebanon to help us voluntarily. Cognizant volunteers helped us in finding accessible accommodation for him in a nearby service apartment and also arranged for his transport. Our coaches Mr Periera and Thayu also learnt many points from him, along with the players. Apart from learning skills, players got motivated a lot, particularly from coaches who were also wheelchair users like them. Our supporter, South India Shelters, mainly helped for this participation besides Sathyabama University.

The next big task was buying flight tickets to Thailand. Till then, all our struggles were related to accessibility and funding. When we got some confirmed promises for funding, we started checking with airlines. When they came to know that the passengers are with disabilities, they asked us many details and later told us to wait for some time. Sometimes it even took two months. We approached all the budget airlines which were having services to Thailand. We did lots of correspondence with those airlines. Finally, they told us that they could allow only four wheelchair users in one flight. We couldn't send the team early as we had to pay for their stay and food there. Again, we tried with different airlines and finalized the flights which arrived there with a little difference of time. It was a very challenging task to figure out the number of players in each flight, the destination airports and transportation between them and with the extra luggage. We had to give our personal and sports wheelchairs dimensions, weight, quantity, etc. After putting a lot of effort, finally we completed booking tickets in two airlines. But destination airports were different. Depending on the capacity of the flight, the number of wheelchair users allowed in it would be decided. Small flights would allow around four people, and more for big flights. Generally, in budget airlines, we can get only a few seats for wheelchair users. The price matters here.

Finally, all the issues were sorted out, and we were all excited to represent India at the international stage.

32

Year 2017: Making History on the Global Stage

The year 2017 had taken many turns from representing India at an international stage to the loss of a very dear friend Preetha and a beloved swimmer Mayure. A close friend moved out to the capital city, which helped to stretch the wings of our federation. I had an opportunity to meet many legendary sports personalities.

Maiden Opportunity for Young Indian Players to Perform at a Global Stage

Global Adjustments Foundation team took a session for our team members, as most of them were going abroad for the first time in their lives. They explained how to behave in a foreign country and taught some Thai words as well. It was a useful session. Dr Ponraj interacted with our players and provided his valuable suggestions on preventing injuries and strengthening muscles.

Twelve players, two coaches, Mr Pereira and Mr Thayu, team physio Anand, Shanthy and I were part of the Indian team. Ashkar and

Ambareesh came as participants for the classification course.[1] After going to the airport, when we unloaded all our luggage, it turned out to be a big lot. The airlines helped us a lot at the Chennai airport. As we knew, it would be difficult to use the toilet in the flight, we all used the toilet before entering into the flight. Our team travelled by two different flights. Thank God, it was only around four hours of travel. At that time, we had no idea of what to do in case we had to use the toilet urgently. In Thailand, the airline staff brought us out of the flight and left us there. We had to take our luggage and go out of the airport by ourselves. Among us, Thayu was the only non-disabled person in our flight. Whoever were sitting in a wheelchair kept some luggage in their lap. Those who could walk with artificial legs pushed the trolley. Had we taken a picture, it would have shown very well what a team effort is. We all supported each other in the manner possible for us and could finally come out. After coming out, volunteers were waiting for us with accessible buses. The buses had the lift facility, and we were all excited to board the bus using that facility. We reached the hotel. There, they replaced the bathroom doors with curtains, so that the wheelchairs could easily go inside. It was a good idea to make toilets accessible with less cost.

Shanthy and I shared a room. Although we knew each other for a long time, then only we got a chance to know each other very well. We both had severe polio attacks, but our perspectives to deal with it were different. Shanthy gave very much importance to her polio treatment. As she is from Kerala, which is known for Ayurvedic treatment, she followed that treatment religiously along with physiotherapy from the very first year of her polio attack. So she could get more improvement. She is able to walk with the help of callipers (only for legs) without crutches. With regard to marriage, her parents were also reluctant as they had doubts that she might not be happy if she got married. But she could convince them in this matter, as she strongly felt that she could not lead her life alone. She wanted to have her own

---

[1] Generally, along with the main event, they organize courses for classification and referees since it is easy to have practical experience for the participants.

family. Finally, her parents could find a nice gentleman as her husband. She is blessed with twins, a boy and a girl. She is working as a gazetted officer in a Central government organization. She is leading her life happily with her family as per her wish. She is a very bold woman.

We went to the stadium the next day. The arrangements there were good. Thai government officials had extended wonderful support to conduct that event. The government arranged a mobile toilet (a modified bus with lift facility) outside the stadium. Inside the toilet, there were very good facilities such as Western commode and washbasin.

In the opening ceremony, all the speeches were completed in just 6–7 minutes. It was a great surprise for me. Generally, in our events, we would allocate at least one hour or more for the ceremony. But there, it was completed in just a few minutes.

The opening match was between India and Australia. On hearing that news, I got scared since I knew Australia was a very strong team. But as they knew that it was a maiden match for our Indian U23 men's team at the international level, they played in a very friendly manner. Hence, our team could do a respectable score of 25 against their score of 86. But I observed a notable thing among our players. Although they were first-timers and their sports wheelchairs were of basic model, they didn't lose heart to play with highly experienced teams. Even when the difference in scores was huge between the two teams, our players did not give up till the last minute and fought boldly. With this exposure, they could understand the very need of vigorous practice to play at the international level.

Unfortunately, one of our players Gulzar fell sick due to a urinary tract infection. Thai government officials asked us to send him to the room after consulting the doctor. They asked him to wear a mask and also asked us to wear a mask when we meet him. Our team physio Anand used to take him to the hospital daily. They said that until their doctor certifies that he was fit to travel, we could not bring him back to India. But luckily, by the time the championship was over, he became normal. He could only play one match on the first day. He was a very enthusiastic boy. Unfortunately, we lost him recently due to his health issues.

Our well-wisher ARR Media Works founder Rajarajan came to Thailand and made a film on our team's first-ever participation at the international level. AOZ Secretary General Don Perriman said to our players, 'You should be very proud of the fact that you were the first-ever team from India to compete at an IWBF tournament, and that future Indian teams will look at you as the pioneers of the game in your country.'

During the tournament, we could interact with other country officials and coaches. Australia Wheelchair Basketball Project Head Leigh promised to help us in training our players and coaches. Indonesian official Rodney invited us for the Bali Cup International Tournament. Many coaches and officials showed interest in the development of wheelchair basketball in India and promised us to help.

One day, after our matches, we requested the organizers to take our team outside for shopping on a bus. They accepted our request. We had a nice time with our players at the shopping mall and bought some souvenirs for our friends. Almost all our players travelled abroad for the first time. They enjoyed their stay there very much.

While coming back, at the airport, we had a tough time. Although we were sitting at the airline counter for two hours, they didn't issue our boarding passes. The flight was about to start in a few minutes. Then I lost my temper. I blasted those staff. Then their senior official came and expedited the process of issuance of our boarding passes. He also allotted 5–6 attendants to help us in our luggage check-in and get us through the security check. Within a few minutes, they brought us to the flight. Due to this, the flight got delayed, and we were the last ones to board the flight. After reaching Chennai, we could get great support from the airline staff. But for that particular airline, service in Thailand was very poor.

Buying an Apartment in Chennai

As we decided to settle in Chennai, mom insisted on me buying a flat. The same struggles faced by me in Hyderabad repeated here as well. Finding an accessible flat itself was a challenging task. Adding to that, I had a new requirement—a swimming pool. I started looking for flats with pools. Either I had to go to the outskirts of the city or buy an old flat within the city to have the cost within my budget. At that time, Kalyani told us that there was an apartment for sale in their complex. We liked it for two reasons. First that Kalyani would be our neighbour and second that it had a swimming pool. It was expensive, although it was not a brand new flat. I decided to sell the plot given to me by my parents in Sathupally. Apart from that, I took a loan. At that time, due to demonetization,[2] the prices went drastically down. But as I had already entered into the agreement, our flat cost wouldn't change. No real estate transactions took place at that time. I was in a big dilemma whether to go ahead with the transaction or not. Finally, I decided to go for it.

After registration, we did housewarming in a simple manner. Having a pool in our own complex was a great advantage for me. I could save around three hours in transit, and I had the flexibility. I could go to the pool as per my convenience. I felt very happy. As the pool maintenance is very much important for me, I worked in the apartment association as EC member for some time. Instead of asking others, I thought that it would be good to take the lead. Our neighbours are very friendly and cooperative.

---

[2] On 8 November 2016, the Government of India announced the demonetization of all ₹500 and ₹1,000 banknotes of the Mahatma Gandhi series. It also announced the issuance of new ₹500 and ₹2,000 banknotes in exchange for the demonetized banknotes. Prime Minister Narendra Modi claimed that the action would curtail the shadow economy and reduce the use of illicit and counterfeit cash to fund illegal activity and terrorism (Source: Wikipedia).

My Journey with Toastmasters

One day, one of my colleagues told me about the Toastmasters Club in our office and that we could attend as guests for their session. From the name Toastmasters, generally new people assume it to be a cooking-related club. I didn't have any idea about it either, but my colleagues gave me a brief idea. So just out of curiosity, I attended the session. I found it very interesting. Toastmasters is a USA-based international not-for-profit organization. It is aimed at improving communication and leadership skills of their members. Across the globe, the format of their sessions is standard. There will be three segments in each session. Part 1 is called 'Prepared Speeches where members would prepare in advance and deliver their speeches. Mentors would guide the mentees on how to prepare for the speeches and encourage them to take up other leadership tasks. Part 2 is called 'Table Topics: Impromptu Speeches', where the speaker has to speak on the given topic extempore. It improves creative thinking. Guests can participate in this segment. Part 3 is 'Evaluation', where the senior Toastmasters would evaluate the speech in a sandwich method, starting with positive remarks, and then on to areas of improvement, and then closing with encouraging remarks.

On the first day, I participated in the 'Table Topics' segment. I liked it very much. It was like a lab where we could do experiments and improve our communication skills with learned and encouraging audiences. Later, we would get very useful evaluations also. It's a member-driven organization. Every activity needs to be done by its members. Taking up these activities would help us in improving leadership skills.

Later, I joined the Toastmasters Club in my office. My colleague Aruna who was also my mentor in Toastmasters encouraged me to become its vice-president (PR). After taking up the role, I started working on creating awareness about our club and the benefit of joining that club. I became the president of the club later. My tenure was for one year. Our VP (Education) Govind and I tried to arrange many educational sessions for our members. Personally, I completed certifications in competent communicator, competent leader and advanced leadership bronze (ALB). Joining this club helped me improve on various aspects. I could communicate more effectively and confidently. It also provided me an opportunity to meet several people and increase my network. I received the Hall of Fame award for excellence in Membership Building at Toastmasters International District 82 Semi Annual Conference.

Our Trade department head, Sadhish, and senior leaders from other departments helped us a lot in membership building.

We attended sessions at other clubs and competitions at various levels. I was surprised to see the performance of VIT students in those competitions. Joining the Toastmasters at a young age would help students a lot. One day, my team member Manoj brought his friend Kamesh to me. Kamesh was desperate to improve his communication skills. He was planning to join a spoken English course. I advised him to join in Toastmasters. I always get surprised seeing his progress in delivering speeches. Later, he shifted to our Bengaluru office. There, he initiated the Toastmasters Club. As its president, he developed it a lot. Now he has become the area director. Toastmasters' journey helped him in improving his communication and leadership skills. This is a classic example of how zeal and hard work lead to great progress in a person's life.

Mayure, Our Beloved Little Swimmer

In 2012, when we hosted the 12th National Para Swimming Championship, we tried a lot to identify swimmers from Tamil Nadu. At that time, we met Mayure. She was a very sharp girl. She had muscular dystrophy. Earlier, her parents used to struggle a lot to make her do physical exercises. After starting swimming, Mayure used to be after her mother to take her to swimming. I still remember how happy she was when she became the national champion in her category. Whenever I got the opportunity to give media interviews, I tried to invite our players too. To give an interview, I went to a TV studio along with our swimmers Mayure and Balasubramaniam. They both spoke very confidently in that interview. Mayure told that she wanted to become a genetic engineer to find solutions for the diseases caused by genetic disorders. Her intention behind that desire was that like her, others should not suffer.

She was very mature in her thinking and very clear in communicating—a very lovely girl. Unfortunately, we lost her at a very young age (in her teen years).

Being a Selection Committee Member for Rajiv Gandhi Khel Ratna and Arjuna Awards

I was selected as one of the members for Rajiv Gandhi Khel Ratna and Arjuna Awards selection committee in 2017 by the Sports department, Ministry of Youth Affairs and Sports, Government of India. It was a great honour for me. Legendary cricketer Mr Virendra Sehwag and sprint queen Ms P. T. Usha were among my co-committee members. It was an immense pleasure to meet such great sports personalities during our committee meeting. That year, paralympic athlete Devendra Jhajharia was conferred with Rajiv Gandhi Khel Ratna Award.

During the conversation with our committee members, I requested Mr Virendra Sehwag to help us in creating awareness about wheelchair basketball sport. He immediately responded positively and told me that he could come for one of our events if the venue was convenient for his journey. He is the first celebrity who gave his direct contact details to me. I met sports-related journalists also there. Later, he kept his promise and graced our 4th nationals held in Hyderabad.

Sports officials arranged accommodation for me at Asoka hotel. It was an accessible room with an exceptionally spacious bathroom and bedroom. I took photos and kept on my social media pages. Wherever I find accessible places or assistive equipment, my joy knows no bounds.

Athlete's Conclave and Pro Kabaddi Event

If the accommodation and the event we need to attend are at the airport itself, how nice it would be?

I had this comfortable experience with accessible accommodation when I attended the Athletes' Conclave organized by Gosports Foundation in Bengaluru. It is a very useful initiative by them. I got the opportunity to share our experiences in wheelchair basketball. I met Mr Anish Dayal, an advocate at the Supreme Court, who mainly handles sports-related cases. Inspired by our activities, he came forward to be our federation's legal adviser. He kept his promise and guided us till he became a high court judge.

In that conclave, I met great sportspersons, Mr Rahul Dravid and Mr Abhinav Bindra.

One day, when our players were practising at J. N. Indoor Stadium, Chennai, the organizers of Pro Kabaddi League 2017 event spoke to our players and coach. Later, they contacted me and informed me that they wanted to invite us for their event, which Bharat Ratna Sachin Tendulkar was also attending. They wanted to introduce us to him. As promised, they arranged a brief meeting with Mr Sachin. He spoke with our players and coaches and inspired everyone with his encouraging words. Our players, coaches and EC members were extremely happy to meet such a legendary person. Later pro-kabaddi players from Tamil Nadu, Pune and Gujarat met our players and congratulated them for their achievements in wheelchair basketball sport.

Surprisingly, I met three legends from cricket in the same year.

Losing my Friend Preetha: A Rude Shock

As my mother was struggling with knee pain, Anand suggested we take her to a naturopathy centre, as she was not very comfortable doing exercises. At that time, Preetha told that she would also want to come with us. It was a 15-day programme. As direct flights were not available, we booked train tickets. Anand and Preetha met us at the railway station. Anand and dad helped me get into the train. Preetha and I thought of not discussing anything about our professions. For two weeks, we wanted to forget all other things.

That centre is on the riverbank and is a very beautiful place. I liked the place, but it was not much accessible. We were mostly given fruits and vegetables. All the food items that they served us were without oil and salt. As we were unable to move easily due to the inaccessible environment there, for me and mom, they used to come to the room for therapy. Dad and Preetha used to go to the concerned places for therapy. All outdoor walking paths were filled with gravel, as it would work like acupuncture therapy for feet. They had a battery-driven vehicle. For me to go outside, that battery car was the only source, as it was difficult to propel the wheelchair on the gravel path.

We used to wake up at 4:00 am to do yoga and meditation. I went to the meditation hall a couple of times. But it was a big struggle for dad. The staff there were very cooperative. But what I observed was that they thought that wheelchair users could not do anything. In their view, it would be better for wheelchair users to be at home and if possible be confined to bed. If anyone spoke to me in a sympathetic way with this attitude, then Preetha used to immediately get angry at them and reply with an irritated voice. She used to tell them about me, like my qualifications, my designation, my driving abilities, my sports career, etc. After hearing her, they used to look at me with admiration. Daily, that had become a routine for us.

Preetha and I started to feel like students living in a hostel but along with our beloved parents. People there used to think that we both were sisters and came along with our parents. Preetha and I decided to meet the head of that institute and explain to him how that place could be made accessible for persons with disabilities with a few modifications. We also wanted to explain to him the need for the persons with disabilities also to undergo such therapies.

On 4 July, we woke up early in the morning and practised yoga for some time. Later, we went for a swim in the river (it's in a protected place). It was the first time for both of us to swim in a river. Preetha went for therapies back to back. She left the room for yoga in the evening. But before going to the yoga hall, she came back thrice to our room to say something or take something. We didn't know that it was going to be the last time that we saw her alive. In the evening, their staff came to our room and started to ask us about her. They were all in tension. We could not understand what happened. Initially, they told us that while doing yoga, Preetha had fallen down. We were worried about injuries or fractures that she might have got. But later we came to know that she was no more. It was an unbelievable bitter shock for us. Anand came there immediately after getting the news. We all went in a very joyful mood, but we came back with heavy hearts. It took me six months to come out of that sorrow. Even now, whenever I think about her, I remember her beautiful smiling face which I saw for the last time. It's a great loss for all of us.

Development of Our Female Players

When I attended a function at BDHC's Office, I met Australian Consul-General Mr Sean Kelly. He told me that he wanted to speak to us about our initiatives for female players. Later, they partnered with us along with 'Motivation India' to send 10 of our female players and 2 coaches for a 10-day training camp in Thailand. Almost all those girls travelled abroad for the first time in their life. That journey gave them a lot of exposure. One of the girls, Malathi, told us that earlier her family and relatives used to treat her with sympathy, but after this participation they started admiring her. She was the first person in her family to go abroad. Later she grew into an influential person with a good network and brought support for her co-players multiple times. So many such nice stories!

Participation at 4th Bali International Tournament

Rodney invited us to Indonesia to participate in the 4th Bali International Tournament. We decided to send both our men and women teams. To prepare them for the tournament, we invited coach Bradness from Australia (whose team won one gold and two silver medals at Paralympics level) in partnership with Australian Consulate. Our players were inspired very much after interacting with Brad.

Later, we arranged another camp before the tournament at PRC, Kirkee, Pune, for boys and at Satyabama University for girls. Only for the women's team we could have the support confirmed. So we started our efforts vigorously to find support for the men's team. In spite of putting many efforts, the result was negative. Then I approached our CEO at that time, Mr Kwan, and explained to him our helpless situation. He responded positively. Finally, we booked flight tickets for both the teams.

In Bali, the event was arranged in a school. As they didn't have accessible buses, they arranged buses for players and an additional vehicle to carry wheelchairs. Their volunteers, our coaches, doctors and physios helped the players to get into the bus. They tried their level best to find accessible accommodation. The rooms were accessible, but the rest rooms were not fully accessible.

Dr Ponraj and his wife accompanied us as team doctors. So this time when our players had health issues, we could manage without going to the hospital. They not only extended medical support but also volunteered for helping the players wherever required.

Both our teams won bronze medals. In the history of Indian wheelchair basketball, those were the first medals at the international level. We were all extremely happy.

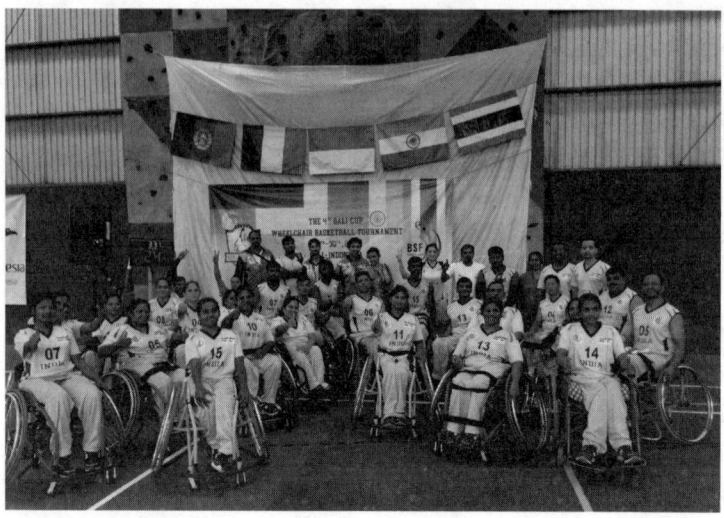

Bali International Tournament—First medal at International level for our men and women teams

Kalyani Moved to Delhi

After I bought an apartment in Chennai, I felt very happy as my friend Kalyani was living in the same complex. But after a few months, due to her husband's transfer, she moved to Delhi. Personally, I felt sad as I would miss meeting her in person often, but with regard to WBFI, I felt happy. As we didn't have sufficient funds to travel and create awareness, we depended on my talks at various places and used those trips to meet the concerned local officials. When someone invited me for any talk, they would take care of my logistics. In that way, we avoided all those expenses. Now as she moved to Delhi, it became easy for us to spread the sport to northern states and also to interact with sports officials in the Government of India.

President and secretary general are very important positions for any national federation. Coordination between these two individuals is very crucial for the better performance of the federation. I observed that even between good friends differences surface due to ego clashes. On different issues, we both had differences of opinion and debates. But we both know very well that both of us are sincerely concerned for the empowerment/benefits of our players. Hence, finally whoever is convinced that the other person's decision would be more useful for the players, we would respect it without any ego issues. Once I told Kalyani that as long as our egos wouldn't become more important than our players' well-being, we would remain good friends and could work together. I am happy that till date we remain good friends.

Spreading the Game to New States

Every year we made it a point to spread the sport to new states by planning to conduct an introductory camp there. Generally, sports-related infrastructure facilities are mostly with the government only. We first approach the sports department in that particular state for their permission to arrange the camp in their indoor stadium. We also seek their support to make the stadium accessible for the camp and to depute their basketball coach for our camp to learn the techniques of wheelchair basketball. Responses vary from state to state. Some state governments are very supportive and some are not. We also approach local NGOs working for persons with disabilities and the Social Welfare department (DWD) in that state to create awareness about this sport and also to identify participants for the camp. We also try to work with the media officials to get their support in spreading awareness. During the camp, we would identify the passionate people to take the lead in promoting this sport in that state and encourage them to start a state association to take this initiative forward. We generally follow this format. After moving to Delhi, Kalyani could concentrate more on spreading this sport to northern states. Our partners ICRC and Star Health Insurance helped us a lot in spreading this sport to new states.

4th National Wheelchair Basketball Championship

As the Telangana government is very much supportive of conducting our National Wheelchair Basketball Technical Camp, we requested for their support to organize the 4th nationals. We got their approval. But this time, accommodation at the national institute was not available as they had some other events. Our volunteers from Cognizant went to many hotels near the stadium and gave us the details. I went to Hyderabad to finalize the hotels. All the hotels had one step to the bathroom. Only difference between the hotels is in the height of the step. We could not find a single hotel without a step to the bathroom. Some hotels agreed to arrange ramps outside and in dining areas, etc. They told us that they could provide a chair and a staff to assist to go inside the bathroom. Finally, we finalized the hotels who promised to make these changes. ICRC supported us in this regard.

We shared all the details with the state associations to convey to players about the facilities available at the hotel. We tried to get an accessible bus from the Telangana government. However, as the cost was more, we could book only one accessible bus. Much of the staff from Cognizant and my office volunteered. ICRC official Angel, stadium officer Mr Ravindra and staff also supported us a lot in conducting this event. A senior Cognizant official visited the stadium. At that time, he humorously told me that he could see his staff being more active in the stadium than in the office. It was true. I observed that everyone (guests, reporters, volunteers, etc) who came to the stadium became very active. It might be because they remember their childhood/college days and also might be inspired after seeing our players' dynamic performance. Most of my friends told me that they never thought people sitting in wheelchairs could play with great energy and spirits. Many of my friends from corporates started to look at the abilities of our players rather than looking at their disabilities. There was a big change in their perception towards the disabled people after watching their performance in the stadium.

Hyderabad is famous for paradise biryani and kurbani ka meetha (a very tasty sweet with dates), among other things. As I had worked there earlier, I knew about it very well. I strongly wanted our players to try them. But as we had exhausted all our sources for the event,

I found it very difficult to get the required support to arrange these delicacies. I shared this wish on my social media. Santosh, the electronic engineer who worked on assistive devices, came for the event with his wife. After knowing my wish, he immediately came forward to contribute a major amount for the same. Aruna took care of the remaining part and also placed an order for both the items. It was a great satisfaction to see the happiness of players while tasting those delicious items. I wholeheartedly extend my thanks to Santosh and Aruna.

As a part of the arrangements for the championship, one day I went to Jubilee Hills Police Station to present the request letter to arrange security for our event, as Mr Sehwag had accepted to grace our event. The police station was very modern unlike the ones that were shown in movies. It looked like a corporate office. However, as the elevator was not available, I could not go inside. The concerned official came down to meet me. He accepted our request and also told me that they had plans to have an elevator soon. They spoke in a very polite way. It was a pleasant surprise for me to see such level of facilities in a police station.

Our partners Australian Consul-General, ICRC officials and Telangana government officials graced the event. Mr Virender Sehwag honoured us with his presence for the closing ceremony as he had promised earlier. His presence inspired our players a lot. With great patience, he posed for photos with each team separately. The audience were very eager to meet him and took selfies with him. Our volunteers also had to do the bouncer job. Finally, with the help of the police, we could bring him out safely and send him in the car to the airport. At that time, I realized that it's not an easy task to manage the crowd when we invite celebrities. We could get better media coverage for our event due to his presence. Mr Sehwag also spoke with the media about all our challenges and the need for promoting adaptive sports. Thanks a ton to him for keeping his promise and for traveling all the way from Delhi to Hyderabad for our event. After the event, social media platforms were flooded with the photos shared by our players with Mr Sehwag. Many of them had met such a sports celebrity for the first time in their lives.

Year by year, we could see a very good improvement in the number of participating teams and in their performance. Through our YWTC Trust, we started giving cash prizes to the teams who stood in the first three positions, with equal amounts for both the genders. We introduced this practice in this event, and it has been continuing since then.

33

Year 2018: Making India's Voice Heard at the International Level

This year, I met the US Consulate Cultural Affairs Officer Ms Kathleen, who helped us in getting a great opportunity to learn more about the sport for our wheelchair basketball fraternity. Our teams participated in two international events, and we organized a camp to develop beginners and advanced players.

Participation at Asian Para Games (AOZ—Central and East) Qualifiers

We decided to send our men and women teams for the Asia Para Games Qualifiers. Again, our challenges resurfaced. With the support of Satyabama University, we organized selection camps for men and women separately. UK coach Jaspal Dhani along with our Indian coaches, Mr Pereira, Lee and Thayu, trained our players during these selection camps. SAI officials supported us by hosting a training camp for the selected players at their Aurangabad training centre. We invited coach Thomas Kyle from Australia to train our players. He had also travelled with our teams to Thailand. He is excellent in video analysis of the sport. This analysis helped our players to understand their mistakes and learn proper skills. They also enjoyed watching their own performance in video clippings.

Initially, our players were allowed to play only on the outdoor court because their indoor court was a synthetic one, and movement of chairs on that court wouldn't be as easy as that on a wooden one. As it was very sunny outside, we requested them to allow the practice session inside. Finally, we got their approval. I went to start the camp and returned the next day after making all the necessary arrangements. Incharge of that centre and other officials were very supportive. They provided nutritious food for our players. Later, Kalyani went there to monitor the camp.

After attending the camp, our teams went to Thailand to participate in the qualifiers. Since U23 Men's World Championship Qualifiers, we have participated in many AOZ events in Thailand. I was glad to see the amazing support from Thailand government and other local organizations in hosting these events. We could see a great improvement in their teams' performance. From what we heard from their teams, we understood that around 50 top players from their country would be trained throughout the year with the support of the government and during this period they would also get stipend. They invite other countries' teams to their country to play with them. They also send their players to other countries. As they are the hosting country for many such events, their teams would automatically get the opportunity to participate without going through the qualifying process. Due to this international exposure, there is an amazing improvement in their performance. This progress in Thailand teams' performance is a classic example of how consistent support from the government helps the players.

My ex-boss Shyamala introduced Chandrakala from Hanon Automotive Systems to me when they were looking for a speaker for the Women's Day celebrations. She helped us through her organization and her friends for many of our events. We became very good friends. Their support was crucial for participation in those qualifiers in which our men's team won a match against Indonesia. That was the first win for India at an IWBF event. We all felt very happy.

The closing dinner was on a ship. We went for a short cruise. It was an unforgettable memory. Our players Rekha (youngest) and Varun (tallest) became the centre of attraction in that celebration. Rekha was the baby of that championship, being the youngest player of all. Opponent team players also liked her very much.

Initiative of Bhavia Joshi

BDHC Bharat Joshi's wife Bhakti and daughters Bhavia and Bhavini became very good friends of mine. To support our efforts in creating awareness about our sport, Bhavia arranged an exhibition match in her school. It was between our wheelchair basketball players and the running basketball players who came to her school to participate in an international tournament. It was a great experience for our players.

Later, with her initiative, her school invited me to address their students. I felt very happy to see her concern for the fellow beings at such a young age. When I went there, I was amazed to see all the facilities and greenery. It is an international school and has international-standard sports facilities.

Mom's Knee Surgery

Mom had been suffering with knee pain for a very long time. But she was reluctant to get surgery and was trying to push it as long as she could. Unable to bear the pain anymore, she finally accepted it. We decided to get the surgery done at NIMS, Hyderabad, as my niece Dr Padmsri was doing her MD Radiology there. My sister Nirmala and my brother-in-law came to Chennai to stay with me till my parents came back. We thought of going for surgery for both the knees at the same time. However, considering her age and health condition, doctors suggested to go with one knee at a time. Padmasri took special care of mom during that time. After going through the pain and other challenges, mom didn't opt for the surgery to the other knee. Due to that, she could not get complete benefits of the surgery.

Aruna and the Raging Sun: An Inclusive Arts Performance Show

Internationally acclaimed performance companies Graeae (UK) and La Fura dels Baus (Spain) planned to present their performance show in Chennai. Bharat Joshi introduced us to the officials of these companies. They met me and expressed their interest to involve our players in their show. Their representative, Patrick, coordinated with us for this event. Even my colleagues participated in this event. I accompanied my colleagues and our players for their audition. With great patience, the organizers made the candidates understand their requirements. It was an entirely new experience. They brought very big cranes. Many persons with disabilities participated in that show. Those performances were around 50 m above the ground. They took very good precautions for the safety of the participants. Before the show, they announced the location of accessible toilets, medical help desk and drinking water. They made comfortable arrangements in the gallery for the persons with disabilities. Thousands of audience attended the event. After the show, we left that place without any hassle in spite of the presence of a huge crowd. I never saw such a spectacular performance by persons with disabilities. The performers had got just a few weeks of training. Even then they could perform well without any fear in the air.

Attempt to Host an International Event, Though Unsuccessful yet a Confidence Booster

IWBF sent a message to all their affiliated members to check if anyone would be interested to host the U25 Women World Championship. They said that they could not take up the entire cost but would provide partial support to the host country. We had been trying our level best to create awareness about this sport. We thought that hosting a world championship would be an opportunity to attract the attention of all the stakeholders. We came to know that very few teams would participate in it. So it would be easy to host the event. Encouraging young female players is a big challenge not only in India but also across the world. That's why the expected number of teams was less. Being the host country, our team would definitely get the opportunity to participate in it.

Considering the great support we got from Telangana state for our previous events, we wanted to approach them. I went to Hyderabad for a family event. At that time, I stayed there for two more days and approached the concerned officials. I met the sports secretary and discussed this event with him. He was very positive. As we needed two courts for the world championship, we sought permission to host in Gachibowli Stadium. He advised me to go and see the stadium myself. By that time, our EC member Raja had reached Hyderabad. We both went to the stadium. It was accessible to a great extent. However, some modifications were needed to make it fully accessible. Raja is an expert in conducting an audit for accessibility. I offered my suggestions with my knowledge from practical experience. And then we prepared the list of changes that were needed.

From there we went to some nearby hotels in search of accessible accommodation as the stadium didn't have any. But the rooms in most of the hotels were not accessible. I was also checking the possibility to make the rooms accessible like the way they did in Thailand at a lower cost. Finally, we found a 5-star hotel in which, with some minor changes, the rooms could be made accessible to a great extent.

We checked with the hotel officials. They were interested as it was for hosting the world championship. They promised to consider our requests positively, if the event was confirmed.

We submitted a letter to the sports secretary in Hyderabad, requesting their support for us to host the world championship. He provided a letter which stated the items list that they would provide support for—stadium, transportation, etc. With that letter, we approached the Government of India for their support and permission to bid to host the championship.

Simultaneously, we tried to identify more female players and to train them for the championship. We organized a camp for U25 female players in Chennai. Lee and Suvarna were the coaches. Many senior female leaders from different organizations met our players including Saundarya, founder of Avtar, Sanjula from Wellsfargo Bank and Archana from United Way. It was great inspiration for our players to meet such dynamic female leaders. Volunteers from Cognizant and my office supported the players. My colleagues Narayanan, Vikrant and their team supported the players by presenting balls and providing snacks. R. R. Donnelley officials invited our players and arranged a talk with their senior leaders. They explained to them how they could get jobs in the corporate world. Players were very much motivated to work in such places. One day, Cognizant volunteers took our players to a shopping mall and to the beach. I went with them, and we had a lot of fun. They played many games in the mall. At the beach, the volunteers with great effort carried the players in wheelchairs to the water. They all enjoyed and played with water.

One of our players, Inshah, had come from Jammu and Kashmir (J&K). She is a Muslim and one of the days in her stay happened to be a festival. She requested us to send her to a mosque. On the way to the stadium, I saw a mosque. I checked with the officials there. They shared the contact details of the closest mosque which allowed women. I contacted them. With the support of our volunteers, we could send her in. As their prayer place was on the ground floor, she could manage without any difficulty.

After the camps, for the next few days I used to miss our players very much. I always see myself in our players. If they are able to enjoy and learn new things, I feel as if I were doing those things at that age.

We followed up with the Government of India for their approval. But we could not get it before the last date for bidding to host the U25 Women's World Championship. Although we failed in that attempt, we realized that there was an opportunity to host such a championship even in India if we had permission from the government and sufficient support. Until then, I was doubtful whether the environment in India was accessible enough to host such championships.

Efforts to Strengthen State Associations

We planned for a two-day symposium for our state associations, as we strongly wanted to work on their capacity development. Kalyani and I spoke about the organization structure for para sports in general and wheelchair basketball in particular from international level to club level and sports code. Our treasurer Vishal explained the best accounting practices, Raja shared his knowledge about the accessibility and the ways to achieve it, and Anand and Charu from ICRC briefed regarding the fitness and the screening process of players. We also invited speakers from relevant fields to give them a fair idea of legal matters, fundraising, etc. Ms Deepthi, a senior official from GoSports Foundation, graced the opening ceremony of the symposium. We requested the state associations to share the best practices they were following in their respective states. It was a good opportunity to learn from others' experiences. We recognized the states that were taking initiatives very actively for the promotion of the sport by presenting mementos. ICRC officials supported this initiative not only in making arrangements but also in taking sessions. Pranav, my colleague Sharanya and my nephew Sachin volunteered for this event.

5th National Wheelchair Basketball Championship

Year after year, the number of teams to participate in the nationals was increasing. Organizing the event was becoming a Herculean task for us due to lack of funding and accessible accommodation. Our players used to eagerly wait for the nationals throughout the year. We never wanted to disappoint them. We tried in so many states to organize the nationals, but none of our efforts were fruitful. At that time, Mr Makkal Rajan, correspondent of Rajiv Gandhi Polytechnic College (RGPC), came forward to host the 5th nationals in Erode, Tamil Nadu. In 2011, when I had become the national para swimming champion, he had invited me to address their college students. I had known him since then. He had also extended his support in conducting our Tamil Nadu state-level championships twice in Erode. With that experience, they came forward to host the nationals. SDAT officials provided approval to host the event in their Erode Stadium. Our partner ICRC also supported. We approached the district collector to facilitate two accessible toilets. He arranged them with the support of some business entities.

Mr Rajan arranged a temporary covering to the outdoor basketball court. Accommodation was in hotels. Our TN players went to those hotels to verify the accessibility part. Many local leaders, officials, doctors and artists came to watch our matches. RGPC students and Cognizant volunteers helped the players. By that time, Deepak took charge from Archana at Cognizant with regard to their outreach activities. He also started extending wonderful support to us.

We take all the available sports chairs with us to the camps and nationals. Many teams don't have their personal sports wheelchairs. For such teams, we lend our chairs and collect them after the match for the use of the teams that play the next matches. All the process of collecting the chairs and giving them to the new team and then to get ready for the next match by tying straps, etc., requires a lot of time. Starting the match on time with all these issues was a very challenging task. With the efforts we are putting forth to create awareness about this sport in the country, we sincerely hope our players will get the support to buy their own sports wheelchairs in the near future.

The closing ceremony was graced by the chief minister of Puducherry and other dignitaries.

Within a very short time, Mr Rajan and team had made the arrangements for hosting the national championship successfully.

Our Participation at IWBF World Congress Held in Hamburg

Kalyani and I participated in the World Congress held in Hamburg, Germany, during the World Championship. Again, as usual, with a lot of efforts, we could make arrangements for our trip.

Organizers sent a person to receive us at the airport. Her name was Sabine Becker. I fell in love with her driving expertise of a Mercedes Benz vehicle. I enquired her about different features of the vehicle. She explained all the details very politely. Later, we got to know that she was a senior HR professional in Germany's renowned airlines. She had applied for two weeks' leaves in her office to volunteer for the Wheelchair Basketball World Championship. She could drive any type of vehicle. All other drivers were professionals in government or corporates. Vehicles were arranged by Mercedes Benz. Whoever registered as volunteers began to learn English to interact with the teams during this championship. Arrangements had been going on for the last few years. All the volunteers were feeling proud about hosting this event in their country.

This was the congress in which we got the opportunity to vote as it was the first world congress after getting IWBF affiliation. It was a very useful platform to interact with the teams from across the world. It was an amazing experience to watch the matches in the world championship. When they discussed the insurance coverage for their tournaments, we tried to check with their insurance company to extend a similar coverage for us in India. But as they didn't have branches in India, they could not entertain our request.

We took a ride in a local bus in Germany. It was a nice experience. We could not go sightseeing as we stayed there for only for a short while.

Surprisingly, Sabine, who received us on our arrival, dropped us back at the airport at the time of our departure. For our commute to the stadium and back to our room during our stay, different volunteers came by to drive us.

At their airports, they take the wheelchair users into the flight in the end. In contrast to that, in India, wheelchair users are taken in first. As we weren't aware of this practice, we were in full tension till we boarded the flight. We went to Hamburg via Turkey. All those airports are very big. The wheelchairs have a footboard on the back side. Their staff would stand on it and use the remote to move the wheelchair. Using manual wheelchairs in such big airports would be a challenge. In one of the airports, Kalyani went inside to call the airline staff to take me inside. After she went in, someone came to me with the wheelchair. I thought Kalyani sent him. After I went inside, I could not find her. Just imagine my situation—they could not speak in English; I could not speak their language; her phone was not reachable. In that big airport, if we miss each other, unable to converse in the local language, how can we manage to find each other? I called Kalyani's name loudly thinking that she would listen to me if she was nearby. Everyone around me turned towards me. But I didn't mind about it. Luckily, Kalyani heard my voice and came to me. Thank God, finally we could meet. Now when I think about this incident, my fears look silly, but I was really worried at that time.

Dad's Health

Dad was not feeling well. So we shortened our initially planned trip to Hamburg and came back immediately after participating in the conference. My nephew Dr Prasanth stayed with us for more than a month during that challenging time and took care of dad. Having a doctor in house will always be a great luxury. If mom and dad are doing good, I can go anywhere and can do any difficult work. I feel tense whenever my parents are not doing well. When my boss Subhashini enquired about dad's health, I could not control my tears. After seeing this, my colleague Rani told me that she thought that I was a strong woman and enquired why I became so emotional. I told her that my parents are my strength and at the same time they are also my weakness. I could not even think about getting separated from them. They were getting old, and my health was also not very good. Sometimes I will be scared thinking that among the three of us, who would be leaving the world first and how the remaining would manage in their absence. Each and every activity of my parents in a day would revolve around me only. They would feel my absence very much whenever I travel. My feelings are also the same. That's why I always used to take them along with me for any long trip. But for foreign travels, they were not much interested. Hence, I could not convince and take them with me. During such trips, I ensure having a video call daily and update them on how I was doing and vice versa.

After observing my feelings, Subhashini suggested that I be strong to face any consequence in life as we all need to leave this world one day.

By God's grace, dad's health condition improved. I always pray to God for the well-being of my parents. If they are fine, I will definitely be fine.

Working Out at Work

In our office, a gym was opened for staff, using the services of an external vendor. I saw the communication long back. But I didn't think about using it. One day, when I was looking into the internal communications, I saw a message about the gym again. I wondered why I shouldn't use this facility. It was on the ground floor without any steps. I met the instructor. She had come across a staff member with a disability expressing interest to use the gym for the first time. She told me that she would check with her bosses and get back to me. Later, I spoke to them and to our property team. A senior official from that vendor's organization met me, discussed my requirements and gave the required guidelines to the instructor who was also a physiotherapist. My organization added some equipment to the gym such as medicine balls and less weight dumbbells. From that time onwards, I started using the gym, after completing the office work for the day. Instructor Raji supported me a lot in doing the exercises. I could make new friends in the gym. It was an awesome experience.

Development Camp

We organized a development camp for our male players in partnership with ICRC and R. R. Donnelley. Both beginners and advanced players from across India participated in it, including all our Indian coaches. We invited coaches Joe Higgins from Canada and senior player Fonzie from Hong Kong to conduct the camp. Joe was a highly experienced coach. He used to take theory sessions to our coaches apart from practicals. As Fonzie was a senior player, our players could interact with him comfortably, treating him as one among them. Joe used to make us dance daily in the sessions. He gave importance to not only learn sport skills but also enjoy the participation simultaneously. We invited US Consul General Mr Robert, Ms Kathleen and other consulate officials, SDAT member secretary and leaders from all our partner organizations. R. R. Donnelley volunteers and some of my colleagues supported the event.

We organized sessions for our players on various topics related to personality development. Whenever players attend these camps, we use the opportunity to have such sessions.

During the camp, a young player got a fever. For two days, we took him to the hospital. But as he was a young kid, we thought that he would feel better if he was with his family. We sent him back on a flight to Delhi. He recovered soon thereafter. While having camps for junior level, we had to be more cautious.

Participation of Our Men's Team at 2018 Hanna Lahoud Wheelchair Basketball Cup

With the support of our partner R. R. Donnelley, we organized a camp for our national team under the guidance of coach Jaspal along with our Indian coaches Sharad and Thayu. Initially, we started the camp at J. J. Stadium, but as the wooden floor was having some issues, we had to move the camp to J. N. Indoor Stadium. BDHC Mr Jeremy, our TN sports secretary and many other dignitaries visited the camp and inspired our players. R. R. Donnelley volunteers helped us a lot.

Kalyani accompanied the team along with coaches and physios to the Lebanon tournament. Our team won the bronze medal. The Indian embassy head met our team there. The Indian team was announced as the best team for behaviour and politeness on court and off court and keeping the gym, room and cafeteria clean. It was specifically mentioned that our team did not waste food. They separated the portion of food that they would eat and packed the remaining food and returned it back on all days. Hats off to the entire team. Our players praised a lot the arrangements made by ICRC officials there. We struggled a lot as usual to make this participation possible. While going to Lebanon, in the last minute, the airlines officials told us that due to the capacity of the flight, they could not take all the players in one flight. Finally, two of our players went on the next day. While coming back, luckily, as the capacity of the flight was more, the entire team could travel by the same flight. Every time, though we plan well in advance, we were unable to avoid this last-minute hassle due to many factors that were not in our control.

As I didn't go with the team, I utilized the opportunity to receive our team. I went to the airport in the wee hours with my parents to welcome and felicitate our medal-winning team. It was a nice experience to receive them and make them cut the cake. After seeing our celebrations, some of the passengers at the airport came to us and greeted our players and took photos.

Each and every experience so far has taught me something. Some of them were surprising and wonderful, and others were bitter and painful. But with infinite possibilities in life, there will always be many more to experience and learn from.

34

Year 2019: The Year of Many Firsts

Year 2019 gave me the opportunity to do many things for the first time in life, for instance, going to the USA on a sports visitor programme, introducing the unique idea of a mentorship programme with corporate leaders for our players, swimming in the sea and visiting the banks of the holy Ganges.

Introducing the Sport to Some New States

In the first quarter of 2019, we arranged four camps with the support of our partner Star Health Insurance. With this, we were able to reach out to 23 states. One of these camps was in Puducherry. Within a very short time, the players there could pick up a lot of techniques. Fortunately, they had a very good coach, Bala. They formed the state association and got support from the state government to get the sports wheelchairs. Their team won the best emerging team award in the 6th nationals. Everyone praised their determination and perseverance.

We tried a lot to arrange a camp in West Bengal. In spite of our numerous efforts, we couldn't organize it.

Hiatus Hernia, Me and Yoga

When I went to Kolhapur in 2011 to participate in the 11th nationals, I started taking Pantacid[1] tablets, as my stomach was upset. I continued taking it regularly as I used to feel the acidity. I did not think much about its side effects. In 2018, when my doctor nieces and nephews came to know about my regular intake of Pantacid, they told me to avoid it as it was not good for bones. But whenever I stopped it, I used to face a severe acidity problem. I consulted Dr Ravi Shankar, my ex-tenant, who is a surgeon in gastroenterology. He suggested that I go for an endoscopy, and I went for it. The doctor found that I had hiatus hernia. I had never heard about it till then. It's a condition in which a part of the stomach pushes up through the diaphragm muscle into the chest cavity. It's common for many people. But in my case, as only one of my lungs was working, that too partially, I needed to be more careful as the corrective surgery would be highly risky. After I came to know about it, I could not help but think about the consequences if the condition further aggravated. I was not sure whether I could continue my exercises or not. Dr Ravi Shankar told me to continue all my exercises, as they were not very strenuous. He also suggested pranayama to me. All my doctor friends unanimously suggested yoga as a countermeasure for this condition. Through Kalyani, I came to know Dr N. Chandrasekhar (popularly known as Dr NC), a yoga therapist.

Until then, I had seen only those yoga trainers who had a set of standard asanas and who used to make people do those asanas in a group. I had no idea whether they could pay individual attention to me and suggest asanas adapting to my health condition. After meeting Dr NC, I understood that 'yoga is for all.' He prescribed asanas as per my condition, albeit with some necessary modifications. I also started meditation parallelly under his guidance. Suddenly, great enlightenment dawned on me about the greatness of yoga. I felt so bad for not starting it earlier. As I am a swimmer, I started to do experiments in

---

[1] Pantacid is a medicine which reduces the amount of acid produced in your stomach.

water with yoga asanas. In our complex, a group of women used to practise yoga near the pool every morning. Dr Rina was one among them who regularly practised yoga for one and a half hours without a break every day. I tried to practise in the water what she was doing on the ground. Within a few days, I was able to do many asanas in water. I found that I could do many asanas in water more easily than on the ground.

Meditation is a great practice, and everyone should start it from their childhood itself. It gives us more calmness and mental stability and strength. I have read many books on yoga written by Dr NC. Through our trust, we also made a documentary film on *Yoga for All* with the support of ARR Media Works and Dr NC. Shanthy, a few players and I did asanas in water for that film.

Interviews of Dr NC and me were taken by a TV channel on the eve of International Yoga Day to popularize aqua yoga. Later, in their social media platforms, I saw some comments under the video link that said to not publish such unrealistic and misleading things. They probably thought that it would be impossible for a person like me with severe disability to do such things. They probably also thought that it was detrimental for persons with disabilities. Such people were not just from India but also from all over the world, and this happened just recently, not many years ago. This tells us that still a lot more needs to be done to create public awareness to remove misconceptions about disability.

In this way, each health issue is giving me an opportunity to understand life from a new perspective.

Aqua Dance

Many persons with disabilities may want to dance but hesitate to do it due to the physical challenges or lack of support. As I found that it was easy to make movements in water, I requested my colleague Gopal who is a choreographer to train us in aqua dance. He is a very good dancer. But he never tried to dance in water. He did some research on it and came forward to train us. My colleagues Sharanya, Raktim, WBFI Joint Secretary Shanthy, players Malathi and others joined for these sessions. We enjoyed dancing in water. But later, as we all got busy, we could not keep it up.

Trip to the USA

On 30 June 2018, when I attended an event arranged by the British Council, I met Ms Kathleen, an official from the US Consulate, Chennai. When she came to know about our wheelchair basketball activities, she was very much impressed and expressed her interest to see our practice sessions. In the month of July in the same year, she came to one of our practice sessions during a weekend and played along with us. We spoke about our efforts to promote this sport in India and the challenges we were facing. Kathleen explained about the opportunities available for exchange programmes with the USA. She introduced me to the US Consul-General Mr Robert G. Burgess who was very supportive and evinced keen interest in our activities. Finally, with the initiation of Ms Kathleen and with the support of US Consul-General, Chennai, a team of 15 people from wheelchair basketball family (administrators, coaches/aspiring coaches, physical educator and physiotherapist/classifier) across India were selected for a two-week sports visitor programme for coaches and administrators of wheelchair basketball in India to be held from 16 to 30 March in the USA by the US Department of State (DOS), along with their programme partner FHI 360.

Preparation for the Tour

Not only for me but also for all the other participants with disabilities, the biggest challenge was to sit continuously for long hours. When we brought this issue to the notice of the concerned official Chitra, she got required approvals to book executive class flight tickets for the persons with disabilities in our team.

My First Long-hour Flight Journey

I was worried about the long duration of our flight. But since our seating was in executive class, I found it quite comfortable. The area management in the executive class was very efficient and was done without compromising on comfort.

Whenever I am travelling, my main concern is using a toilet. I was very happy as I could use the toilet in the flight comfortably. Airlines staff were very supportive. Whenever I wanted to use the toilet, they supported me with great patience. We had a short layover at New York during which my nieces along with their families visited me at the airport. They brought Indian food. I spent some quality time with them while relishing the Indian food. After a 20-hour-long flight (due to some technical issues, our flight was rerouted), we finally reached Cleveland. The two-week programme was held in three places, first week at Cleveland and Akron in Ohio and the next week in Washington, DC.

Jackie (Ms Jacquelyn Piansay) received us at the airport, and Sara (Ms Sara Owens) welcomed us at the Crowne Plaza Cleveland hotel. The two-week sports visitor programme was very productive.

This particular trip was a huge learning curve for all of us. During our trip, we attended various workshops including on mental and physical health, mindset of a successful athlete and public speaking. I would love to describe them in detail, but it would require another book to accommodate that knowledge. But there are a few really important events I would like to highlight. Let's dive right into them.

On 19 March, we met Ms Melanie Hogan, Executive Director, LEAP (Linking Employment, Abilities and Potential). LEAP is a federally recognized centre for independent living. It aims to be an agent of positive change, working to advance participation and equality in the society for people with disabilities in Northeast Ohio. I was really glad to know that there's a centre which enables persons with disabilities to live an independent life. Generally, in the life of a person with disability, most of the people shower sympathy. But not everyone needs sympathy, all they need is a direction to lead an independent life. The concept of independent living for persons with disabilities needs more attention, and the society should start working towards it.

We went to Quicken Loans Arena in the evening to watch an NBA match between Cleveland Cavaliers and the Milwaukee Bucks. This was the first time in my life to watch an NBA match in person. It seems that the arena needs to be booked years in advance for any event. Hundreds of events happen every year in this arena. It was a wonderful experience to see such a big arena with so many facilities. We could watch a very nice match. The Cleveland Cavaliers won the match. The stadium was fully packed with the audience.

When we went to the Adult Division 1 Games at City of Tallmadge Recreation Center, we met Ms Sarah Castle, the then President of National Wheelchair Basketball Association (NWBA) of the USA. Ms Sarah was a highly experienced player, former secretary, vice-president and president of NWBA (she served as the president till 2019). She was a champion in paralympic games in both swimming and wheelchair basketball.

She patiently answered all our queries regarding how they were managing the accommodation for the players while conducting an event. There are various competitions across the country conducted by different clubs. Based on the points they get, a certain number of teams would be selected for the national-level championship. Otherwise, it would be a very difficult task to invite all the teams for the national championship. Also, they have three levels of championships: for beginners, for middle level and for the advanced level.

Female players have more opportunities than male players. They can also play in men's teams. One point would be reduced for female players in classification when they play in a men's teams (e.g., if a female player's classification point is 3, her classification point would be 2 when she plays in a men's team). As the team total points should not exceed 14, it would be an advantage for the men's team to have a very good female player in their team.

They even have insurance for their tournaments. But in India, we approached many insurance companies to extend their coverage for our events. But we didn't get a positive response from them.

We also learned that every player and coach would pay registration fees annually to NWBA and register their names with them.

We requested her to send their men and women teams from Division 3 (which consists of players at the beginning level) for the international tournament we had planned for August 2019. She responded positively and said that if there was a possibility, she would definitely send them.

We got the opportunity to watch the semi-final match between Milwaukee and Arizona wheelchair basketball teams. Milwaukees won the match. It was a festival for the eyes to watch their amazing performance. But the number of audience was very low.

We had a meeting with NWBA coaches. We discussed many points to know about their functioning and how they overcome their challenges related to promoting wheelchair basketball. It was a very useful interaction. We met Michael Frogley, one of the best wheelchair basketball coaches in the world. Later, he guided us on many matters when we sought his help.

Another inspiring personality with whom we had the good fortune to meet was Ms Ann Cody, Senior Foreign Affairs Officer, Bureau of Democracy, Human Rights and Labour. Ms Ann started her sports career in wheelchair basketball and later moved to athletics and won multiple paralympic medals. Her contribution to promoting disability rights is phenomenal.

We met Ms Ann Cody at the US DOS office on our final day of the programme. She gave insights into DOS exchange programmes and their other activities. Kalyani and I enquired the possibility of working with US sports wheelchair manufacturers to encourage Indian manufacturers to partner with them. DOS officials explained the facilities available for the alumni and even mentioned the 2020 exchange programmes for young players and coaches. They advised us to be in touch with the concerned alumni official and the Department of Commerce officials (concerning US manufacturers) at the US Consulate in India to apply for these programmes.

On our final day, each one of us had to present our proposal for a project at the FHI office. I presented the proposal on our dream project, that is, 1st Indian wheelchair basketball international tournament. However, we could not accomplish it due to lack of funding. We sincerely hope it becomes a reality soon. As said before, these are just the tip of the iceberg of experiences we gained through our participation.

As a part of their programme schedule, we did a bit of sightseeing on the first day in Washington, DC. We visited the White House, Abraham Lincoln Memorial and the National Museum of African American History and Culture. Apart from their beautiful architecture, it was exciting to know their culture and traditions.

On the penultimate day of the tour, we had a wonderful time with Mr and Mrs Jagannadha S. Bhamidipati. Jagannadha is the brother of my ex-student Aruna. They took us on a city tour at night. A city's true beauty can only be seen at night. Watching monuments in DC during night time was an awesome experience. We had tasty tamarind rice brought by them, stopping near Martin Luther King memorial, on the side of the road. It is an unforgettable memory!

I am really thankful to both of them for making it possible.

Accessibility Leading to Inclusion

Our team members were invited for a dinner by local US families. During my visit to a family, I was thrilled to see the home adaptations made for their son who was a wheelchair user. A few examples for those adaptations are sensors for lights, fans TV, etc., and a small lift for pool in their house. They were sweet, and I was touched by their hospitality.

There were a few points I loved in general in the USA. While taking a tour around different cities, I found almost every public toilet with special provisions for the disabled people, which was mandatory. I even saw a ramp at a few places which were mobile and easy to install. These features help the wheelchair users to have more freedom to explore. The National Museum of African American History and Culture was also pretty accessible. Table reservations especially for wheelchair users were available at a restaurant in the museum. Along with these features, there was one particular aspect which caught my attention, the emergency signboards. There was an emergency board with instructions for wheelchair users in case of an emergency; this is something rare to see, or we can even call it 'once in a blue moon' event. It was a humbling experience visiting the museum. The hotel we stayed in Cleveland had a temperature-controlled swimming pool and a hot whirlpool which was a new experience altogether.

One special incident happened in Cleveland. I am a religious person, and I love visiting temples. According to Hindu customs, before or after offering prayers, a person generally rings the bell in the temple. It is considered as a good omen. But I never got that opportunity (at least not without other people's support). We visited the Greater Cleveland Shiva Vishnu Temple. For the first time in my life, I could ring the bell all by myself sitting in my wheelchair. Yeah, it may sound pretty normal, but to me it was nothing short of extraordinary.

During my stay in the USA, I noticed through my observations and interactions that there were a few things which were similar to our country such as the popularity (as per the number of audience) for wheelchair basketball matches was quite less compared to their running basketball matches. In hotels, only a few rooms were accessible. Most of the gyms did not have accessible equipment. And, finally, quite a few corporates in the USA had apprehensions to recruit persons with disabilities.

Meeting My Nieces' and Nephew's Families in the USA

After this programme, I stayed back for just two more days and went to New York City to meet the families of my nieces (Sunanda, Vindhyasri and Pranavi) and nephew Sudhir (his wife Sirisha and daughter Srinika were living in a different place in the USA due to her job). They have the same love and affection for me which they have been showing since their childhood. As they knew that I would be craving for homemade food, Vindhyasri brought delicious food items with her to the airport. I ate them in the car itself. They took me to the Central Park, Grimaldi's Pizzeria, Dumbo, Brooklyn Bridge, One World Trade Center, 9/11 Memorial, Times Square, Grand Central Station, Statue of Liberty and Ellis Island.

We went to Central Park during the night time. I felt as if we were in a forest with minimal lighting. I have always loved forests since my childhood. I enjoyed that experience very much. I felt so happy to hold my nieces' and Vindhyasri's daughter Ananya's hands while going on the road. In India, I never went on the roads riding my wheelchair. I enjoyed that experience. Even my native place was once upon a time a forest area. Vindhaysri's husband Raja struggled a lot to find a place to park the car. I felt that it would be easier to travel in New York City by subway (local transport) for non-disabled people, considering the challenge in parking the car. I saw big malls in Grand Central Station with wonder (there were so many shops in the station itself).

When we went to the 9/11 Memorial, my heart became heavy remembering the unfortunate incident. We waited for a long time when we went to Grimaldi's Pizzeria. It's very famous. It was raining that day. Sudhir took me to the Brooklyn Bridge in that rain. Pranavi acted like a tour guide for us.

At One World Trade Center, it was an amazing experience to see New York and New Jersey cities from the 102nd floor. We went to the 102nd floor in just 47 seconds in the elevator. After reaching the top, for a few seconds, I felt giddiness. I was afraid for a few seconds after knowing that I was at one of the highest places. Later, I enjoyed watching the views of both the cities from there. We waited till it became dark. I played with my nieces' kids Akhil, Ananya and Nikita. Watching the view with innumerable lights in that darkness is an unforgettable memory.

Next day, Sunanda's husband Vamsi drove us to the Statue of Liberty. Watching it was one of the great moments. Travelling to Ellis Island and Statue of Liberty in a ferry was an amazing experience. At the Statue of Liberty, there was an elevator facility. But we needed to book well in advance to use it. We captured those precious moments in our mobiles. From there, we came directly to the airport. After boarding the flight, when I recollected the love and affection shown by my nieces, their families and nephew, my heart filled with joy. More than seeing all those places, their love and concern for me, their desire to show me all those places within the available short span of time, made me immensely happy.

For the first time in my life, I travelled alone from abroad to our country (though I had travelled alone within the country). Earlier, I went abroad along with our teams or with Kalyani. But this time, while coming back, I travelled alone as other participants left from other places. But with the support of the airline staff, I could manage successfully. That experience gave me more confidence.

6th National Wheelchair Basketball Championship, Our Biggest Ever

As a result of our efforts to promote the sports in new states, for the 6th nationals, we had 23 men's teams and 14 women's teams. Around 550 people were part of this event, comprising 370 players, caregivers, team managers, coaches, technical officials, classification officers and other officials. For conducting this event, we tried at many places, but after listening to the number of participants, everyone turned back saying that they didn't have accessible accommodation for that many people. While we were arranging camps in Punjab, Kalyani saw some accessible places. The government officials there were also very supportive. Hence, she started to try there. She travelled to Mohali to finalize many things. With the support of our player Latief at PRC, Mohali, she verified the accessibility part.

After putting so much effort, we finally arranged accommodation at Catering Institute, Punjab University and a few more places. Like NIEPMD in Chennai, the Catering Institute also had ramps to access all floors. It was a big surprise for us. As it was during the vacation time, we could get these two places for accommodation. A few accessible rooms were available on each floor in the Catering Institute. Punjab University accommodation for girls was also very much accessible. Actually, we thought that some of the men's teams would also get accommodation there. But at the last minute, we came to know it was not possible. We were habituated to deal with last-minute hurdles.

R. R. Donnelley volunteers had always supported us in designing all PR material and the souvenir. This time, Cognizant volunteers did virtual volunteering under the leadership of Sankara, Prithvi and Akhilesh. Getting the applications from state teams was not easy due to many challenges. Cognizant volunteers took care of it by following up with the state teams to get the applications filled and to obtain various details such as their travel information, number of wheelchair users and number of their wheelchairs (both personal and sports wheelchairs). From this data, they prepared Excel sheets for different purposes like to arrange buses (we needed wheelchairs details), to allocate accommodation (as we had limited accessible rooms, we allocated them to players with spinal cord injury and less functional abilities), etc. It was a very challenging task to utilize the limited resources to the optimum level. Apart from virtual volunteering, their volunteers from Gurgaon came to support us in receiving the players, allotting rooms to them at the stadium and on the final day to drop them at the airport/railway station. My nephew Sachin also volunteered for this event.

Volunteers formed WhatsApp groups with team managers of all the states. They used to share all the required information on these groups. When breakfast used to arrive at the accommodation places every day, volunteers sitting in various cities of India used to give information to the team managers as they were in touch with the caterer. After the event, they sent a survey link to get feedback from the participants. Taking the wheelchairs to Mohali from Chennai seemed to be very expensive if we wanted to send them by private transport options. Hence, we decided to send them by train. Volunteers from R. R. Donnelley and Cognizant helped us in booking, packing and taking them to the railway station. At Mohali, Army officials helped us in bringing the chairs to the stadium. Every task used to become a big one for us due to the funding-related challenges. We couldn't relax even after making all the arrangements. In the last minute, someone would go back from their promise and then we would struggle to fill that gap.

Inspired by the way in which IWBF had conducted the World Congress at the world championship, we decided to organize meetings with our state associations during the nationals on various topics such as accounting, anti-doping and players' fitness. Previously, when we organized the symposium solely for this purpose, we found it very expensive. We organized many sessions for our players/coaches/tech officials and state associations during the nationals. From Chennai itself, I coordinated with many people in Mohali/Chandigarh and arranged for those talks before the start of the nationals. We formed a selection committee with the coaches from all the zones under the leadership of Shanthy and our senior coach Mr Pereira. We introduced them to all the teams. Their job was to identify the best players from the national championship based on the eligibility criteria to form the national team.

We brought out souvenir with fixtures and all other details. This time, we could get the support of a team to stream the matches live and record the statistics. Government officials supported us a lot at the stadium and in arranging medical support. But it was still not an easy task to go to an entirely new place and make arrangements. The opening ceremony was graced by the Honourable Governor of Chandigarh Mr V. P. Singh Badnore and the closing ceremony by the Sports Minister of India Mr Kiren Rijiju, along with other dignitaries. We also invited the local BDHC. Officials from our partners, Cognizant and ICRC, were also present in the closing ceremony. We could give away cash prizes with the support of ICICI Bank.

I fell in love with the greenery of Chandigarh city. It is a very beautiful city. While coming back, with our treasurer Vishal and his family, Shanthy, our volunteer Subramani, my parents and Sachin, I went to Amritsar. We saw the Golden Temple from outside (as it was not accessible). We also went to the Wagha border and watched the border ceremony with rapt attention.

Another Trial to Host an International Event

We sincerely tried again to host an international event in India. We wanted to invite both men and women teams from three countries. With our Indian team, there would be four teams in each gender category. We prepared the proposal and started approaching various organizations for funding. An organization came forward to support us with 40 per cent of the estimated budget and told us to submit the confirmed promises for the remaining amount from other organizations. With that letter, we started approaching other organizations. Many people were of the view that it was a waste of time and money and suggested that it was better to rather concentrate on developing our teams. But hosting such events would help in creating more awareness and to increase the competitive skills of our players.

After seeing the performance of foreign players and their high-performance sports wheelchairs, we strongly hope that our society would realize the importance of supporting these sports. In our endeavour, I could see accessible accommodation for around 160 people in the Welcome Hotel in Chennai. I felt very happy. With a few modifications, those rooms could be made accessible. All those rooms were of deluxe and executive classes. Our efforts to get support for the rest of the funding didn't materialize. Finally, we thought of organizing the tournament only for one gender so that the budget would be reduced considerably. A few countries also showed interest in participating in the tournament.

By the time we took the decision to go with only four teams, the organization which promised 40 per cent funding informed us that the last date to execute that project was completed and they could not support any further. Our efforts to host an international tournament failed again. Both times, we spent a lot of time and energy to make it happen, but to no avail. However, one thing that we realized was that if we had funding, there was a possibility to organize an international event in an accessible environment in India. We struggled a lot and could not host even one international tournament, but our nearby country Thailand has been hosting so many international events with the support of their government and is showing a steep improvement in the performance of their players. A lot of economic activities happen due to these events in the hosting countries, which directly and indirectly generate revenue and employment for many people and create good opportunities for tourism as well. I hope a day comes when our people would realize this.

Selection Camp to Participate at Paralympics Qualifiers

Without having any confirmed support, we had taken up another Herculean task, that is, to send our men's and women's teams to participate in Paralympic Qualifiers held in Thailand. As a first step, we organized a selection camp by inviting UK coach Jaspal with the support of R. R. Donnelley. J. N. Stadium officials said that it was going to be under renovation. J. J. Stadium, due to change in its management, changed the court to a badminton court. We had to look for another indoor court. We came to know about ICF court. I went there along with our coach Prasanna and examined the place. Except for arranging a ramp at the main entrance, rest was fine. We gave a request letter to the officials and got their permission to organize the selection camp for men and women. As the accommodation at ICF was not accessible, we arranged for accommodation at a hotel. Our volunteers helped the players commuting between the hotel and the stadium. Having the court and accommodation at one place would have been good for us.

The men's camp was followed by the women's camp. On the first day of women's camp, when we were observing the session, a couple came inside, and the staff were giving them a high regard. We understood that they were some senior officials. Later, we came to know that he was the general manager of ICF. We explained our activities to them and mentioned our challenges in having accommodation at a different place. We requested him about the possibility of using the coach rooms located in the stadium as accommodation for our players. He accepted our request immediately and instructed the concerned official to support us. It was really a great support for us. Female players enjoyed that comfort. We could save a lot of time, energy and funds and were able to avoid transportation-related hassles.

Our women's team's head coach is Captain Louis (retired from Navy). One of our female players, Ishrat, selected for the camp was in J&K. The male players from J&K could not participate due to the situation there following the abolition of Article 370 of Indian Constitution. Our coach, through his Sainik School mate Colonel Isen Hover could bring Ishrat to the camp with the support of the Indian Army.

During both the camps, we took our teams to the ICF Museum and to the restaurant there, which was like a railway coach. It was a nice experience. Our players took so many photos.

It's always a great pleasure for me to be with our players, coaches and volunteers.

A player from Meghalaya, Prisca (Pris Miah), told me jovially to call her when my mood was down. She said that she could motivate me and encourage me as she was studying psychology. When we organized a camp in Meghalaya, she participated in it and later came to our 6th nationals. There, she came to know through other participants about Lovely Professional University in Jalandhar. She applied for admission there and was doing her graduation in psychology. She is a very cheerful girl and makes people around her cheerful.

Mentorship Programme

One day, while speaking to my colleagues Sunitha and Archana at the office canteen, I told them about the sessions we planned for our players by inviting experts from various fields. They suggested that I try to plan for a mentorship programme. I was already leading an initiative in my office related to women empowerment which also had a mentorship programme for our female staff. I knew its benefits. I shared this idea with our WBFI EC, and we started to work on developing that programme. Finally, we came out with a plan for this on a pilot basis for six months.

We started this initiative on 19 October 2019. The main aim of this programme was to assist our players to progress in their life and career under the guidance of experienced and knowledgeable persons from different fields. Within just 10 days, 25 mentors from renowned corporate houses in Chennai, Hyderabad and Bengaluru came forward to volunteer. Most of them were my friends or colleagues. My ex-student Aruna was also one of the mentors. The first learning for our players was the simple strategies to maintain a balanced life—eat right, sleep right, exercise daily and think right. We could see some positive output within a month from this programme, as our players were now more receptive, more confident, interacting well with the team and others and many more. Mentors were also educated on disability-related matters through their interactions with their mentees.

Mentors have also come forward to support WBFI in our activities. They are helping in our documentation, preparing CVs for our players, raising funds, bringing in more partnership, media support and many more. We now have more well-wishers and partners for WBFI through our mentors. Our mentors took sessions on topics such as prevention of sexual harassment (POSH), team building and visualization for our players. Mr Rajesh Misca from Romania was introduced by one of the mentors. He also supported us in this initiative.

After six months, we reviewed that programme and noted all our learnings for better planning in future. Present BDHC, Chennai, Mr Oliver, hosted our meeting with mentors in his office. He had worked earlier for Paralympics when it took place in London in 2012. Hence, he had a better idea about the challenges in paralympic sports. He gave us some useful suggestions.

Preparations for Paralympics Qualifiers

We tried a lot to make possible our teams' participation. For the women's team, we could get support from Barclays. But for the men's team we had to try harder. We approached many people and organizations but with no luck. After a few days, a well-wisher introduced us to the chairman of a company. He gave me an appointment. When I went to his office, he was not available. The next-level officials met me. They promised to forward my request to him. Later, they confirmed that our request for support was approved and took our details to issue the cheque. An official from their office called me and confirmed that the cheque was ready, but they were waiting for their chairman to come back from an official visit to present the cheque. After more than a week when I called, they told me that they found out that their CSR budget had already exceeded and so they could not give the cheque. I was shocked. After their approval, we were relaxed (stopped further trails in this regard) and waited for the cheque to make the payment. I called their chairman and explained our situation and sought support. He told me that there was a procedure for everything. We might have met him, explained our activities and then after getting satisfied with our performance, they were supposed to decide whether or not to support us. He asked me without even meeting how we could expect the support. He also told me that it was not right for us to pressurize him like that. I was shocked to hear his words. He was the person who gave me an appointment and did not meet me. They themselves said that they issued the cheque. After wasting 10 days of our precious time, he blamed it on us. I felt so bad listening to his words. But I didn't have much time to think about it.

Then Chandrakala from Hanon Automotive Systems came to my mind. She had helped us many times in our difficult times. Their organization was much impressed with this cause. I approached her, and they extended their support for our men's team.

Whenever my mom hears such things, she scolds me for begging people. She tells me that they didn't want to see me depending on others and that's why they tried their level best to make me independent. She gets very angry with me complaining that I was begging people for funding. But I always try to convince her saying that I am not begging, I am only reminding the people about their responsibility towards their fellow beings.

I would like to specifically mention the excellent support that has been extended by our coaches/referees/classifiers. They all are working for this cause with great passion.

We organized two camps each for the men's and women's teams simultaneously with a lot of effort as usual. For the men's team, we organized it at PRC, Mohali, and at Ramakrishna Mission Vivekananda Educational and Research Institute at Coimbatore. With the help of our mentors Sudhir and Amit, we could get support from Dow

Chemical for the women's camp held at ICF stadium, and Satyabama University helped for another camp. We did medical screening for players. Mazagaon Docks Ltd officials supported our players and presented 14 sports wheelchairs to WBFI. Our mentors helped our players in some form or the other. Many of our well-wishers visited the camps.

We invited the daughter of Honourable Vice-President of India Sri Venkaiah Naidu, Ms Deepa, to meet our female players during the camp (we met her first time when we organized an introductory camp in Nellore in Andhra Pradesh earlier). She took our team to lunch and interacted with each and every player. She conveyed her father's best wishes to the team. Our players felt very happy for their nice gesture.

We had the Deepavali festival during the women's camp held at Satyabama University. With the support of Cognizant volunteers, we took our women's team to Mahabalipuram and from there we went to a 5-star resort. This was supported by Mr Narsa Reddy. He arranged for hosting lunch for our team at the resort. Our players had a great time at the beach. They dressed in traditional wear and took many pics. We all had a great time.

I met Mr Sujith Kumar, senior HR leader at Infosys, during one of our office-related programmes. He has been extending great support through his NGO to many underprivileged students in getting higher education. I invited him to meet our female players during the camp held at ICF stadium. He is a very good motivational speaker. When he came to interact with our players, one of our players Saakshi requested for his guidance to become a motivational speaker. He guided her and later gave her an opportunity to speak in their NGO's 4th annual celebrations. He even arranged to pay her for the talk. I went for that event with Saakshi's mentor Archana. It was a great feeling to listen to our player's maiden speech in English in front of a 1,000-strong audience. Later, he continued to help her to speak in many forums.

I went to Coimbatore to see the arrangements for the men's camp held for 10 days. An organization promised us to support the camp by supplying food for the players. They were supposed to arrange for the food from the dinner on the first day itself. But at around 8:30 pm, they told us that they could not provide the same due to some problem. They promised to arrange breakfast from the next day onwards and requested us to arrange for dinner by ourselves. We thought that they might have faced some challenges due to which they could not arrange the food. Next day at 8:00 am, they called us again and told the same story that they could not send breakfast and promised that they would arrange the food from lunch onwards. I didn't like their irresponsible behaviour in supporting a very crucial item for our players. Hence, I told them that we would make our own arrangements for food during the camp and informed them not to worry about it. One can respect people who tell right away that they cannot support as it saves their time. But it's very difficult to deal with people who consistently break their promises. Last-minute arrangements at a new place are quite challenging with everything being uncertain such as the funds, availability and suitability. Fortunately, Dow Chemical helped us in arranging food for this camp.

For our trip to Thailand, based on the capacity of flights, we planned for tickets for male players from Bengaluru and for female players from Chennai. Male players needed to travel from Coimbatore to Bengaluru. We tried to get flight tickets to go to Bengaluru, but due to limited capacity, the airlines denied tickets for many players with regular and sports wheelchairs. We arranged four Innova cars with sufficient space for players with spinal cord injury to lie down on the seats. After reaching Bengaluru, they needed to wait for some time for the Thailand flight. We were thinking of ways to arrange some rest for them during the waiting time. At that time, our mentor and my colleague Jayashree came forward. Through her contacts, she arranged for their food and a place for them to rest in an Army-related institute (some of our players worked in the Army;

due to the injuries they had while they were on duty, they became wheelchair users).

It's not an easy task to make arrangements for smooth travel for persons with disabilities. But with the support of many good souls, till now we have been able to do so.

Participation at Paralympic Qualifiers

Qualifiers were held at Pattaya, Thailand. It was a 12-day event. As I had exhausted all my leaves for the year, I applied for leaves on loss of pay. Men and women teams, physios, coaches, doctors and officials—a 33-member team went to Thailand. Pattaya is a tourist place. They arranged our accommodation in a resort. The venue of the championship had four courts. Out of those four courts, two were for playing and two for training. We saw how they arranged those training courts by pasting temporary wooden sheets. That was the first time for our players to participate at that level of competition. After participating in the initial matches, their morale came down due to the high-level performance of opponents. We all tried our level best to boost their confidence. In our efforts, coaches Jess, Joe, Toufic and Brad helped a lot.

We encouraged the players and coaches to interact with other country players and coaches to learn the best practices. We prepared a questionnaire and interviewed six countries' administrators, coaches and other staff, namely Australia, Afghanistan, Cambodia, Malaysia, the Philippines and Indonesia. Some common points we observed among those countries were better support from the government and other organizations, all team members practising together for a long time, etc. So we strongly decided to put more sincere efforts to raise support for giving the opportunity to our players to practise together as a team for a longer time and also to have more international exposure. Long way to go!

Our classifier, Ambareesh, became a world-level classifier. Ashkar is a zonal-level classifier.

 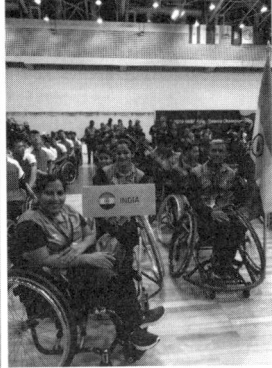

Left: With our team in Wahsington D.C. (S.V.P.) Right: Participation at AOZ paralympic qualifiers

Our accommodation was on the seashore. Our physios and coaches used to support our players to practise yoga and fitness exercises in the morning. There were many swimming pools. I used to swim daily. One day, with the support of our physios Ashkar, Ambareesh and Thayu, I swam in the sea as well. It was an amazing experience for me.

My Talks at LBSNAA

I got an opportunity to address the IAS officers who were undergoing their mid-career development programme at LBSNAA, Mussoorie, Uttarakhand. First talk was in July 2019. The topic was 'Unheard Voices: Expectations from the Policymakers'. It was really a great opportunity to meet more than 100 policymakers from across India. I went to Mussoorie with dad. I got the opportunity to meet Amudha Madam (who supported us through the PVP). She was the chief coordinator for that training programme. She took very good care of me. I tried my level best to convey the challenges we, persons with disabilities, face in general and with sports in particular, giving examples from my experiences and sharing our expectations. As I was accommodated in their guest house in the same complex, I took my stool along with me for the talk. I told how my stool was helping me within the country and outside the country. After my talk, some officials touched my father's feet out of great respect for him. It showed their regard for my dad for bringing me up with great confidence and positive attitude. They also included dad for the group pic. It was a great emotional moment.

After my talk, LBSNAA officials took me around their institute with a request to provide my suggestions to make their institute more inclusive. They noted down my suggestions. They had a beautiful pool. I swam there. Since my childhood, I kept a long-lasting desire to see the Himalayas. LBSNAA is on the lower range of the Himalayas. From my room, I could see the Himalayas. It was an amazing scenic beauty. Colours of the sky used to change very frequently. Due to fog, mountains would suddenly disappear and then reappear. Although my stay was for a very short duration, I enjoyed those few hours very much.

The Mussoorie trip gave me immense happiness in two regards—One in creating more awareness about our challenges and expectations among the most influential officials and the other for getting the opportunity to sit in the lap of beautiful nature.

I got another opportunity to address another batch of officials in December 2019. I went there with my sister Anantham. I would like to share a few experiences I had during this flight journey. Air hostesses used to speak to my sister if they wanted to ask anything related to me. They might have thought that I was a patient and could not respond to their queries or I might not appear competent enough to respond to their queries. And while taking me to the restroom, my helper received a call. He was telling the other person on the call that he was taking a wheelchair to the restroom and after finishing he would take the wheelchair to the gate. Airlines provided a helper and a good wheelchair with straps for my safety. And the helper duly accepted all my requests. Everything was fine except the fact that he was considering their customer as a wheelchair (and not a human being). Of course, such experiences were not specific to this journey but a general tendency. I shared these experiences in my talk at LBSNAA. I felt that it helped me to bring out the importance of the human element in our day-to-day interactions and the need for the intervention of the top management to make their staff at every level understand their inclusive policies for their better implementation.

When I went for the second time, I visited the holy river Ganga for the first and only time in my life so far. As I told earlier, I have great respect for the river Ganga. It has a major role in Hindu mythology and is a vital source for many people in the country. Many people have it as their only wish in life to take a dip in the river at Kashi (Varanasi) before they die. I always wondered and wanted to visit it as I got more curious to see and experience its holiness.

Inspired by my talk, some of the officials came forward to support our initiatives. We planned our first camp in March 2020 in Surat with the support of Surat Municipal Corporation Commissioner Mr Banchhanidhi Pani, Mr Supreet Gulati (another senior official in Gujarat government) and other senior leaders. Both these officials attended my talk at LBSNAA. Our women's team head coach Captain Louis went there from Mumbai (as it was nearer to him) three to four times to see the facilities with Gujarat players.

Pain in Elbows

The year 2019 became very hectic for me. I started getting pain in both my elbows. I didn't have time to take care of it with my hectic schedule. By the end of December 2019, I found it difficult to use my hands. Initially, we thought it was the golfer's elbow and tried to give it a rest. But there was no relief from pain. Later, Anand found out that it was due to weakness in the elbow joint capsule. I tried to give some rest to my body and used elbow braces while driving and working in the office. It took a few months for me to come out from that severe pain. All these health issues may be part of PPS. I realized the importance of listening to our body. Our body would definitely give signs for us to take rest. If we don't pay attention to it, one day it would get back at us with the consequences.

Little did I realize that I wouldn't have to drive to work or travel and strain my elbows further in the coming months due to the pandemic. And also, that all of our lifestyles were about to change drastically taking away access to many basic things that we took for granted so far, depriving us from sunlight, fresh air, open land to walk or jog and a social life, let alone swimming pools or fancy gym equipment.

35

Year 2020: Adapting to the New Normal

COVID-19

We finalized everything with the support of the Government of Gujarat officials from Surat to invite our national men' and women's teams players for the camp at Surat, Gujarat, in March 2020. At that time, I also got another opportunity to give a talk at LBSNAA. We started hearing about COVID-19, which is contagious through human contact. All my family members strongly suggested that I drop the idea of travelling to Mussoorie due to the prevalence of COVID-19. Although I was keen to go, seeing their anxiety I dropped the idea.

At that time, we didn't know that soon we were going to be locked down at homes. We had to cancel all the programmes we had planned for our players.

For the first time in my life, I started to work from home. From 19 March 2020 till February 2021, I did not step out, following the precautions as per the government advisory. My boss Renuka made all the arrangements for me to work from home without causing any inconvenience to me. Work from home has some advantages such as avoiding driving in heavy traffic, having the flexibility to work in convenient positions and spending more time with my parents. But, at the same time, I miss the fun we have with our colleagues in the office.

Now, the entire world is under lockdown. We are not stepping out even from our flat. I miss my swimming which is an essential requirement for me to maintain my day-to-day activities. Right now, I am religiously doing exercises, yoga, laughing yoga, meditation, etc., to maintain my health. But all these together are also not equivalent to swimming in my case. As all the pools are closed in the city as per government instructions, I don't have any other option but to resort to exercises and yoga.

We have adapted to this new situation fast. During this time, my niece Padmasri has helped us a lot in buying essential items online. We have started managing household work without external domestic help. I have begun finding ways to support my parents (both nearly 80 years of age) in doing household work and especially in cooking, as I could not see them struggling with all the daily chores. We are complementing each other and somehow managing things. This situation has developed an interest in me to experiment with cooking different items with the support of my parents. Earlier, my mother used to prepare pickles and other eatables and send them to my siblings. Now due to her health condition, my sisters and sister-in-law have started sending them to us.

While adjusting ourselves at home to the new situation, we started thinking on how best we can support our players in these challenging times. We started many initiatives for our players. During lockdown in the country, many people are facing financial challenges in getting essentials such as food, groceries and medicines. Apart from these challenges, issues related to mental health, lack of guidance for keeping themselves fit, etc., are also there. We prepared a questionnaire and with the support of my colleagues called all the players who were reachable and found out their requirements. Many of our well-wishers came forward to support the players by either crediting the amount into their accounts or providing the required items. With the support of our partner ICRC, we extended financial support to 224 players who lost income or were facing livelihood challenges due to the pandemic.

We also started organizing webinars for our players on various topics. We planned for soft skills sessions for our players in their regional languages with the support of Cognizant. We organized many programmes for their physical, mental and economic well-being with the support of our partners and other well-wishers. We finally conducted a virtual national challenge (we named it Virtually Unstoppable!!!) for our players instead of our on-the-court national championship with the intention that our players should not miss the opportunity to participate, compete, have fun and entertainment, get appreciation and recognition, etc.

Our programme manager Aakash and volunteer Aditya helped us a lot in conducting all the virtual events including the virtual national challenge. Our players enjoyed it a lot. The virtual national challenge comprised four categories: sports skills challenge, fitness challenge, art-related challenge and online challenge. We conducted this at two levels, namely zonal and national. As some of the players don't have good Internet connectivity, for three categories, we allowed the players to take part in the competition by having participants work offline and upload videos. Our referees, classifiers and artist friends acted as judges. Coaches from India and abroad trained the players for online quizzes. Our well-wisher Dr Sumanth C. Raman conducted the online quiz in a professional way. With the support of CPC Diagnostics and Swarna Bharat Trust, we could even give away cash prizes for the winners. Our players told us how these programmes helped them in meeting their essential needs, learning theory part of the sport, connecting with players from across the country and the recognition they got due to the participation in the virtual national challenge. It was an amazing experience for all of us. And, yes, we are really unstoppable!

I continued to give talks through online meetings. Through some of my virtual talks, we could get support for our WBFI. One such talk was at Dive In 2020 (the festival for D&I in insurance). Dive In is a global movement in the insurance sector to support the development of inclusive workplace cultures. I gave a talk on 24 September 2020 in this programme. In my talk, I explained the challenges faced by our WBFI in getting insurance coverage for our players and events due to the sceptical nature of the insurance industry towards the persons with disabilities in general and adaptive sports in particular. After my talk, Mr Shankar, Head of Lloyds India Operations, promised to support us in this matter. As promised, he connected me with Global Insurance Brokers who were able to find a few insurance companies who showed interest to work with WBFI.

I gave another virtual talk at a gated community 'NEST' in Chennai under their initiative 'Thought Streaming'. Ex-Cognizant head Ramkumar took the initiative to invite me. This was my first talk for the residents of an apartment colony. I was very much excited to know about this initiative. They were inviting guests from various fields to talk on different topics of interest for all the age groups of their residents. Along with me, they had invited our coach Thayu and player Ramesh at my request. I thought that it would give them an overall idea about this sport and its benefits. It was also a great opportunity for us, as we could address very senior people in various organizations at one place, along with their families. They all appreciated our efforts very much and promised to extend possible support. With every talk, I could make new friends, and they are also joining hands with us for the cause we have been working for so many years.

A recent incident touched my heart. This was about how WBFI, the state association and my network collectively worked to save the life of one of our athletes. I received a call from one of our state associations, informing me that one of our athletes had fractured her leg. It turned out that immediate surgery was essential. We had to be quick to find support for her. Suddenly, I remembered Mr Ravi Jha, IAS, who had coordinated my first talk at LBSNAA, Mussoorie. I messaged him on a Friday night. He immediately connected me with Mr Abhinav Bharadwaj, IRS, from Delhi, who instantly worked to have the IRS Officers Association also to support the athlete. Ms Nitika, many IRS officials and an IPS officer personally contributed to her surgery. Mr Shakeel (from J&K) and other officials spoke to the doctor, who, without waiting for the payment of fees, did the surgery successfully on Sunday evening. I was truly overwhelmed by the miracle that had happened almost overnight. The kind hearts and helping hands of a few friends and many strangers had united for the well-being of an athlete. May God bless them all with good health and happiness. Today, the player is well and healthy.

I got the opportunity to interact with Dr Mohanraj, a consultant psychiatrist, while inviting him to address our players. Later, I attended many of his virtual sessions meant for non-psychiatrists on various topics like understanding procrastination, sleep, emotions, etc. He explains very complex topics in a lucid way. My general empathy towards people around me improved after listening to his sessions, as I tried to think from their perspective even more.

Conclusion

Earlier in my life, I didn't care much about fitness or maintenance of health. As a child, I very well remember how reluctant I was to do exercises. But today I am a big advocate of the fitness and exercise regime. Life is unpredictable.

Now I know that sport is a powerful tool to motivate people to be active in all phases of their lives. Rather than insisting people do something, I love to find ways to motivate them. If we support them in developing a passion towards these activities, they will never leave them.

I am seeing many posts on social media by our players about their motivational talks, the recognition they are getting in their local societies, their collective efforts to start their own businesses with the confidence they gained through sports and so on. Whenever I see such posts, my heart fills with bliss.

After starting all these social activities, I got a wonderful opportunity to meet many good souls. Whenever I meet such people, my heart fills with great joy, something that I can't express in words. It is because of them that this world, despite having so many challenges, will continue moving forward successfully.

Yes, there will also be some people who will criticize. But rather than judging them, we need to analyse and find the valid points in their criticism. We should make changes accordingly in our style of working/attitude. But we should never get discouraged listening to such comments and stop the good things we do. It's not easy to practise though. But it's very important to move forward bravely in life as per the values we strongly believe in. No one is 100 per cent knowledgeable in everything. Over a period of time, with experience, we can learn many things. If our intentions are good, even if we are not in a powerful position or rich, God would show us some good souls with whom we can work together for the cause to which we are committed to.

If not for the support of such thoughtful and compassionate people, how would it be possible for us to plan and organize these many programmes for the betterment of our players without having any basic facilities such as proper office and staff. I believe that with all our efforts and support from our well-wishers, we could lay the foundation for the federation and it would strengthen more in the years to come with the impact it has created so far in the lives of our players.

This year, we had elections for our federation. I worked as the president for two consecutive terms after launching the WBFI. I strongly felt that it was high time for new leadership to come in. Hence,

Me and my parents

I decided not to contest in the elections this time. Now a new leadership team has taken the charge. I am confident that under this new leadership, development and well-being of players will be taken care of in all aspects. WBFI is like a darling child for all our founding members. I wish and hope that our child will grow and reach greater heights. I will always be available for WBFI to contribute in any manner possible for me at my personal capacity as a volunteer.

Until my last breath, I will contribute to the 'Yes, We Too Can!!!' movement, which I started to empower my fellow beings with disabilities. I know that together, with the help of so many great people, we will change the world and make it a more open, welcoming place for all of us.

About the Author

Madhavi Latha Prathigudupu is an Associate Vice-President in an MNC bank group. She is a former national para swimming champion, the founder general secretary of the Paralympic Swimming Association of Tamil Nadu and the founder president of WBFI. She founded the 'Yes, We Too Can!!!' movement to encourage persons with disabilities to participate in sports.

She is a TEDx speaker. She is also a toastmaster and has worked as the president for the Toastmasters Club in her organization. She led a 15-member team of Indian wheelchair basketball administrators and coaches to the USA on a sports visitor programme.

She has spoken at various prestigious platforms such as LBSNAA, Mussoorie, Indian Red Cross Society, National Association for the Blind, Times of India Global Sports Business Show 2017, IIT Madras, IIM Indore, Tedx events and several corporate events. She has served as a panellist for events organized by the British Deputy High Commission, Madras Chamber of Commerce Women's Day celebrations, India CSR Summit, Australian Consulute-General for South India, Disability Inclusive Roundtable, etc. Her efforts and achievements have been covered widely by the print and electronic media.

She was also a part of the Rajiv Gandhi Khel Ratna and Arjuna Award selection committee in 2017.

The proceeds of royalty on this book would be utilized for the activities of her YWTC Charitable Trust (YWTC stands for Yes, We Too Can!!!).

www.pmlatha.com
www.ywtc.org

Stay INFORMED
Stay INSPIRED

Read up on the most contentious and compelling topics in history and the contemporary world.

For special offers on these books and more, visit **stealadeal.sagepub.in** **Steal A Deal** YOUR ONE-STOP-SHOP FOR LOWEST PRICE

www.sagepub.in